McCOOK

Giants of America

★ ★ ★ ★

The Founding Fathers

James Monroe

★ ★ ★ ★ ★ ★

JAMES
MONROE

The Home of James Monroe

DANIEL C. GILMAN

ARLINGTON HOUSE *New Rochelle, N.Y.*

Library of Congress Catalog Card Number 72-111227
SBN 87000–089–6
MANUFACTURED IN THE UNITED STATES OF AMERICA

PREFACE TO REVISED EDITION

AT the time of the original preparation of
this memoir the Monroe manuscripts, mentioned in my preface thereto as being in the
Department of State and in the possession of
Mrs. Gouverneur, had not been calendared or
arranged, and it was difficult to examine them
with thoroughness. Since then the Department
has published a calendar of the correspondence
of James Monroe, which greatly enhances the
value of the collection, and the present Libra-
rian, S. M. Hamilton, has begun the publication
of the writings of Monroe, which are to appear
in several octavo volumes during the course of
the next few months. By his courtesy and that
of the publishers, Messrs. G. P. Putnam's Sons,
I have been favored with advanced sheets of
the first volume, with the aid of which I have
revised the earlier chapters of this memoir; and
I am very sorry that this edition must go to the
press without my having an opportunity to see
the complete collection of the writings. When
they have appeared, a study of Monroe's two

administrations, like that of the administrations of Jefferson and Madison by Henry Adams, will be called for. I wish that he would undertake such a continuation of his "History of the United States."

I desire to renew the expression, made in my earlier preface, of my obligations to Professor Jameson, now of Brown University, and then of Johns Hopkins University. In view of the importance of the Monroe Doctrine in current political debates, the bibliography, prepared by him and made a part of this volume, is of great utility. It has been revised and enlarged for this edition.

DANIEL C. GILMAN.

July 19, 1898.

CONTENTS

ILLUSTRATIONS

ANNALS OF MONROE'S LIFE

BOYHOOD AND MILITARY SERVICE.

BEGINNING OF CIVIL SERVICE. — U. S. SENATOR.

ANNALS OF MONROE'S LIFE

FIRST DIPLOMATIC EXPERIENCE. — GOVERNOR.

SECOND DIPLOMATIC EXPERIENCE. — GOVERNOR.

ANNALS OF MONROE'S LIFE

IN THE CABINET OF MADISON.

PRESIDENT.

OLD AGE.

JAMES MONROE

CHAPTER I

THE name of James Monroe, fifth president
of the United States, is associated with the chief
political events in the history of this country
during a period of somewhat more than fifty
years. He served with gallantry in the army
of the Revolution and was high in office during
the progress of the second contest with Great
Britain, and during the Seminole war; he was
a delegate and a senator in Congress; he was
called to the chief legislative and executive stations in Virginia; he represented the United
States in France, Spain, and England; he was
a prominent agent in the purchase of Louisiana
and Florida; he was a member of Madison's
cabinet, and directed (for a while simultaneously) the departments of State and War; he
was twice chosen president, the second time
by an almost unanimous vote of the electoral

college; his name is given to a political doctrine
of fundamental importance; his administration
is known as "the era of good feeling:" yet no
adequate memoir of his life has been written,
and while the papers of Washington, Adams,
Jefferson, and Madison — his four predecessors
in the office of president — have been collected
and printed in a convenient form, the student
of Monroe's career must search for the data in
numerous public documents, and in the unas-
sorted files of unpublished correspondence.

Monroe is not alone among the illustrious
Virginians whose memory it is well to revive.
Many years ago, St. George Tucker wrote to
William Wirt, in a half-playful, half-earnest
tone, that Socrates himself would pass unnoticed
and forgotten in Virginia, if he were not a public
character and some of his speeches preserved in
a newspaper. "Who knows anything," he asks,
"of Peyton Randolph, once the most popular
man in Virginia? Who remembers Thompson
Mason, esteemed the first lawyer at the bar; or
his brother George Mason, of whom I have heard
Mr. Madison say that he possessed the greatest
talents for debate of any man he had ever heard
speak? What is known of Dabney Carr but
that he made the motion for appointing committees of correspondence in 1773? Virginia
has produced few men of finer talents, as I

have repeatedly heard. I might name a number of others," continues Tucker, "highly respected and influential men, . . . yet how little is known of one half of them at the present day?" Certainly in this second "era of good feeling" the impartial study of such lives is a most inviting field of biographical research, and may especially be commended to advanced students in our universities, who can, by careful delineations, each of some one career, contribute to the general stock of historical knowledge, and acquire, at the same time, a vivid personal interest in the progress of past events.

I shall not attempt to give in detail the personal and domestic history of Monroe, nor can I, in the space at command, do justice to his voluminous writings; but I shall endeavor to show what he was in public, how he bore himself in the legislative, diplomatic, and administrative positions to which he was called, and what influence he exerted upon the progress of this country. It will be necessary for the completeness of the study to inquire into the early training which gave an impulse to his life, and to examine, in conclusion, the opinions pronounced upon his conduct by those who knew him and by those who came after him. Another hand will doubtless draw a more elaborate portrait; I shall only try to give a faithful sketch of an

honest and patriotic citizen as he discharged the
duties of exalted stations. The materials for a
complete memoir will soon be at command, when
the publication of the writings of James Monroe,
edited by S. M. Hamilton, shall be completed.[1]

James Monroe, according to the family tradition recorded by his son-in-law, came from a
family of Scotch cavaliers, descendants of Hector Monroe, an officer of Charles I.[2] His parentage on both sides was Virginian. The father
of James was Spence Monroe, and his mother
was Eliza Jones, of King George County, a
sister of Joseph Jones, who was twice sent as a
delegate from Virginia to the Continental Congress, and afterwards, in 1789, was appointed
judge of the district court in the same State.
Westmoreland County, where the future president was born, lies on the right bank of the
Potomac, between that river and the Rappahan-
nock. It is famous for the fertility of its soil,
and for the eminent men who have been among
its inhabitants. Near the head of Monroe's
Creek, which empties into the Potomac, James
Monroe was born, April 28, 1758. Not far
away, nearer the Potomac, was the birthplace
of George Washington. In the same vicinity

[1] New York: G. P. Putnam's Sons, 6 vols. 8vo.   1898.
[2] See Appendix.

dwelt Richard Henry Lee and his noted brothers, and also their famous cousin, Henry Lee, known as "Light Horse Harry," whose still more famous son, Robert E. Lee, led the Confederate army in the recent war. Here also was the early home of Bushrod Washington. The birthplace of James Madison was in the same peninsula, though not in the same county. It is not strange that the enthusiastic antiquaries, half a century ago, — Martin, Barber, and the rest, — should speak of this region as the Athens of Virginia, an expression which may not be regarded as exact by classical scholars, but cannot be called unpatriotic. The ascendency of this region is not without its parallel.[1]

During Monroe's boyhood, his neighbors and friends were greatly excited by the passage of the Stamp Act. In 1766, several of them, in-

[1] A recent writer (Hon. F. J. Kingsbury) on old Connecticut makes the following remark: "From the earliest settlement of Connecticut down to the end of the first quarter of the present century, agriculture was the important branch of our industry, and land was the source as well as the representative of most of our wealth. For two hundred years it is safe to say that the good land governed the State. Everywhere it was only necessary to know the soil in order to know also the character of the people. The best soil bore everywhere the best men and women, and that seed which had been winnowed out of the granaries of the old world to plant in the new, did not take unkindly to the strong uplands and rich bottoms of the great river and its tributaries."

cluding Richard Henry Lee, Spence Monroe,
and John Monroe, joined in a remonstrance
against the execution of the act, and in many
other ways showed their hostility to the arbitrary rule of the British government. Lee had
received an academic training about ten years
before at an academy in Wakefield, Yorkshire,
and was a correspondent of men of station in
London. He suggested to his neighbors, in
1767, that they should subscribe for a portrait
of Camden, then Lord High Chancellor, as a
token of their admiration for his opposition to
the Stamp Act. The amount which they raised,
£76 8s., was sent to Mr. Edmund Jennings, Lin-
coln's Inn, London, with a request that he would
take the requisite steps to procure the portrait.
Sir Joshua Reynolds was " the limner " selected
by the Virginians, but Lee did not hesitate to
give his personal opinion that " Mr. West, being
an American, ought to be preferred in this matter." Lord Camden, wrote Jennings, "having
appointed several different times for Mr. West's
attending on him, hath at length, it seems, totally forgot his promise. . . . Draw for the
money, and should his lordship at any time
recollect his engagement, and be worthy of
your approbation and honoring, I shall beg the
gentlemen [of Westmoreland] to accept from
me his portrait." The Virginians were also

eager to have a portrait of Lord Chatham, and their correspondent, Mr. Jennings, had a fine likeness copied and sent to the old Dominion. Lee wrote from Chantilly, in 1769, that the gentlemen of Westmoreland returned their thanks "for the very genteel present of Lord Chatham's picture. It arrived in fine order, and is very much admired. They propose to place it in the courthouse, thinking the Assembly may furnish themselves with his lordship's picture." He adds that his brother, Dr. Lee, can show Mr. Jennings "the proceedings of our last Assembly, by which you may judge how bright the flame of liberty burns here, and may surely convince a tyrannous administration that honesty and equity alone can secure the cordiality and affection of Virginia." Under influences like these the young Monroe was trained in the love of civil liberty. Indeed, Bishop Meade declares that Virginia had been fighting the battles of the Revolution for one hundred and fifty years before the Declaration.[1]

The College of William and Mary had been in existence, with varying fortunes, not far from one hundred and fifteen years, when James Monroe entered it as a student, a short time before the beginning of the war. Its historian claims that it was then the richest college in

[1] *Old Churches, etc., of Virginia*, i. 15.

North America, having an annual income of
£4,000. A scholar cannot read the early accounts of that venerable foundation, next in age
to Harvard, and examine the list of those who
have been trained for their country's service
within its walls, without deep regret that the
fire and the sword have so often interfered with
its prosperity, or without rejoicing that its name
and usefulness are still honorably perpetuated.

When Monroe began his college studies, Williamsburg, the strategic point of the peninsula
between the James and the York, was the seat
both of the colonial government and of the college. Bishop Meade, with conscious exaggera-
tion, speaks of the capital as a miniature copy
of the Court of St. James, " while the old church
and its grave-yard, and the college chapel were
— *si licet cum magnis componere parva* — the
Westminster Abbey and the St. Paul's of London, where the great ones were interred."

At the signal of rebellion against the British
authority, three of the professors and between
twenty-five and thirty students are said to have
joined their comrades from Harvard, Yale, and
Princeton in the· military ranks. Among the
volunteers John Marshall and James Monroe
were found. In allusion to these young patriots,
Hon. H. B. Grigsby, in his historical discourse
on the Virginia Convention of 1776, spoke as
follows : —

" I see that generous band of students who at the beginning of the Revolution hurriedly cast aside the gown and sallied forth to fight the battles of the United Colonies ; . . . and when the struggle was past I see two tall and gallant youths, who had been classmates in early youth, and whose valor had shone on many a field, enter their names on your lists and, after an abode beneath your roof, depart once more to serve their country in the Senate and in the most celebrated courts of Europe, crowning their past career by filling, one the chief magistracy of the Union, the other the highest of the federal judiciary."

It is also worthy of incidental mention that the Phi Beta Kappa Society, still flourishing in American colleges, the earliest of " Greek-letter fraternities," was formed at William and Mary, December 5, 1776. The first meeting, we are told, was held in the Apollo Hall of the old Raleigh tavern, a room in which the burning words of Patrick Henry had been heard. In the printed list of original members the names of John Marshall and Bushrod Washington appear, but I do not find James Monroe's.

The public career of James Monroe began in 1776 with his joining the Continental army at the headquarters of Washington near New York, as a lieutenant in the third Virginian regiment under Colonel Hugh Mercer. He was with the troops at Harlem (September 16), and at

White Plains (October 28), and at Trenton, where he received an honorable wound (December 26). His part in the last mentioned engagement is described by General Wilkinson in his printed memoirs, and with slightly different language in a manuscript preserved in the Gouverneur papers. From this statement it appears that, as the British were forming in the main street of Trenton, the advanced guard of the American left was led by Captain William Washington and Lieutenant James Monroe. The British were driven back and two pieces of artillery were captured. Captain Washington was wounded through the wrist, and Lieutenant Monroe through the shoulder. " These particular acts of gallantry," says the narrative, " have never been noticed, yet they cannot be too highly appreciated, since to them may, in a great measure, be ascribed the facility of our success."

During the campaigns of 1777–78 Monroe served as a volunteer aid, and with the rank of major, on the staff of the Earl of Stirling, and took part in the battles of Brandywine (September 11), Germantown (October 4), and Monmouth (June 28).[1] His temporary promotion appears to have been an obstacle to his

[1] He is said to have been with Lafayette when the latter was wounded.

permanent preferment, for by it he lost his
place in the Continental line. Strong influences
were brought to bear in Virginia to secure for
him some suitable position in the forces of that
State. Lord Stirling gave him testimonials,
and the commander-in-chief wrote a long letter, — addressed to Colonel Archibald Cary, and
doubtless intended for other eyes, — rehearsing
in terms of careful commendation the merits of
young Monroe. These are the words of Washington : —

" The zeal he discovered by entering the service at
an early period, the character he supported in his
regiment, and the manner in which he distinguished
himself at Trenton, when he received a wound, in-
duced me to appoint him to a captaincy in one of the
additional regiments. This regiment failing, from the
difficulty of recruiting, he entered into Lord Stirling's
family and has served two campaigns as a volunteer
aid to his lordship. He has in every instance maintained the reputation of a brave, active, and sensible
officer. As we cannot introduce him into the Continental line, it were to be wished that the State could
do something for him. If an event of this kind could
take place, it would give me particular pleasure ; as
the esteem I have for him, and a regard to his merit,
conspire to make me earnestly wish to see him provided for in some handsome way."

But even the possession of a good record,

and the encouragement of Washington, with the indorsements of Lord Stirling and the patronage of Jefferson, could not effect everything. Mr. Adams says the exhausted state of the country prevented the raising of a new regiment, and the active military services of Monroe were afterwards restricted to occasional duties as a volunteer in defense of the State against the distressing invasions with which it was visited. Once, after the fall of Charleston, S. C., in 1780, according to the same writer, he re-appeared, by request of Governor Jefferson, as a military commissioner to collect and report information with regard to the condition and prospects of the Southern army, — a trust which he discharged to the satisfaction of the authorities.[1] He thus attained to the rank of lieutenant-colonel, and here his military services were interrupted.

It is not surprising to discover that the young officer, who had quickly attained distinction, was paralyzed by inactivity. " Till lately," he writes to Lord Stirling in September, 1782, apologizing for a long epistolary silence, " I have been a recluse. Chagrined with my disappointment in not attaining the rank and command I sought, chagrined with some disappointments in a private line, I retired from society

[1] Eulogy by J. Q. Adams.

with almost a resolution never to return to it again."

In this state of mind he thought of going abroad, to spend some time in the south of France, probably at Montpellier, with perhaps a year at the Temple in London. Jefferson wrote a letter introducing him to Franklin, then resident in Paris, but "a series of disappointments respecting the vessels he had expected to sail in" prevented his departure; and he continued, under Jefferson's guidance, the reading of law. There is an interesting letter addressed to Monroe, in the time of his despondency, by Judge Jones, whose name has already been mentioned. It combines the shrewd remarks upon political affairs of a man in public life, with confidential suggestions to a nephew whom he was watching with almost paternal affection. Monroe had consulted his uncle as to whether it would be best for him to follow the lectures on law to be given by Mr. Wythe, in the college at Williamsburg, or to follow the fortunes of Mr. Jefferson, then governor, at Richmond. He received the following reply: —

JOSEPH JONES TO JAMES MONROE, MARCH 7, 1780.

"This post will bring you a letter from me, accounting for your not hearing sooner what had been done in your affairs. If your overseer sends up before next post-day you shall hear the particulars.

Charles Lewis, going down to the college, gives me
an opportunity of answering, by him, your inquiry
respecting your removal with the governor, or attending Mr. Wythe's lectures. If Mr. Wythe means
to pursue Mr. Blackstone's method I should think
you ought to attend him from the commencement of
his course, if at all, and to judge of this, for want of
proper information, is difficult; indeed I incline to
think Mr. Wythe, under the present state of our
laws, will be much embarrassed to deliver lectures
with that perspicuity and precision which might be
expected from him under a more established and settled state of them. The undertaking is arduous and
the subject intricate at the best, but is rendered much
more so from the circumstances of the country and
the imperfect system now in use, inconsistent in some
instances with the principles of the Constitution of the
national government. Should the revision be passed
the next session, it would, I think, lighten his labors
and render them more useful to the student; otherwise he will be obliged to pursue the science under
the old form, pointing out in his course the inconsist-
ency with the present established government and
the proposed alterations. Whichever method he may
like, or whatever plan he may lay down to govern
him, I doubt not it will be executed with credit to
himself and satisfaction and benefit to his auditors.
The governor need not fear the favor of the community as to his future appointment, while he continues
to make the common good his study. I have no intimate acquaintance with Mr. Jefferson, but from the

knowledge I have of him, he is in my opinion as proper a man as can be put into the office, having the requisites of ability, firmness, and diligence. You do well to cultivate his friendship, and cannot fail to entertain a grateful sense of the favors he has conferred upon you, and while you continue to deserve his esteem he will not withdraw his countenance. If, therefore, upon conferring with him upon the subject he wishes or shows a desire that you go with him, I would gratify him. Should you remain to attend Mr. Wythe, I would do it with his approbation, and under the expectation that when you come to Richmond you shall hope for the continuance of his friendship and assistance. There is likelihood the campaign will this year be to the South, and in the course of it events may require the exertions of the militia of this State; in which case, should a considerable body be called for, I hope Mr. Jefferson will head them himself; and you no doubt will be ready cheerfully to give him your company and assistance, as well to make some return of civility to him as to satisfy your own feelings for the common good."

No one will be surprised to find that under such circumstances, and with such advice, the young aspirant attached himself to the governor. He writes to Lord Stirling, in the letter already quoted, "I submitted the direction of my time and plan to my friend Mr. Jefferson, one of our wisest and most virtuous republicans, and aided by his advice I have hitherto, of late, lived." In September, 1780, he writes to Jefferson a warm expression of gratitude.

A variety of disappointments, he says, had perplexed his plan of life and exposed him to inconveniences which had nearly destroyed him. " In this situation you [Mr. Jefferson] became acquainted with me, and undertook the direction of my studies ; and, believe me, I feel that whatever I am at present in the opinion of others, or whatever I may be in future, has greatly arisen from your friendship. My plan of life is now fixed."

It is clear that his intimacy with Jefferson, the early stages of which are here described, was the key to Monroe's political career. On many subsequent occasions the support and counsel of the older statesman had a marked influence upon the life of the younger. Their friendship continued till it was broken by Jefferson's death. Fifty years after the incidents here narrated the teacher and the pupil, having both served in the office of president, were associated with a third ex-president, the life-long friend of both, in the control of the University of Virginia, and repeatedly met in council at Charlottesville.

CHAPTER II

LEGISLATOR AND GOVERNOR OF VIRGINIA

MONROE was called into service as a legislator at a very early period of his life. If his public career had been restricted to the service of his native State, he would have been conspicuous among the statesmen of Virginia. He was first a delegate to the Assembly from King George County, and a member of the executive council; he went to the fourth, fifth, and sixth Congresses of the Confederation; he was one of the commissioners appointed to revise the laws of Virginia; for a second time he was returned to the Assembly; he was a member of the convention in Virginia which adopted the United States Constitution; he was a senator of the United States before his diplomatic service began; and after long interruptions, and the attainment of national eminence, his presence gave dignity to the convention which adopted the Constitution of 1830, though age and infirmities precluded an active participation in the proceedings. Eleven years of his early life were nearly all devoted to legislative work, but so far as this

related to the affairs of Virginia I do not discover any traces of noteworthy influence. A
letter of his to Jefferson, in 1782, when the
latter in an aggrieved mood was absenting himself from the House of Delegates, has been
printed, and the reply which it drew forth.[1]
The plainness of Monroe's words and the frankness of the reply which he received, indicate a
continuance of the intimacy already referred to.
It was likewise to Monroe that Jefferson wrote,
three years later, from Paris, explaining why he
did not publish his printed notes on Virginia :
" I fear the terms in which I speak of slavery
and of our Constitution will do more harm than
good ; " and again, " I sincerely wish you may
find it convenient to come here ; the pleasure of
the trip will be less than you expect, but the
utility greater. It will make you adore your
own country, its soil, its climate, its equality,
liberty, laws, people, and manners."

On the other hand, as a delegate in Congress
Monroe was conspicuous, and the record of his
service is closely involved with those important
discussions which revealed the imperfection of
the Confederation. His term of service extended from 1783 to 1786, and he attended the
sessions which were held in Annapolis, — where
he saw Washington resign his commission, —

[1] Jefferson's *Works*, i. 316. Randall's *Jefferson*, i. 413.

Trenton, and New York. During this period he corresponded intimately, sometimes using a cipher, with Joseph Jones, Richard Henry Lee, Madison, and Jefferson; and a large part of his letters are still extant, with many of the answers.

An interesting letter from Monroe to Lee states succinctly the problems which perplexed the national legislature, now that peace was secured. "There are before us," he writes, "some questions of the utmost consequence that can arise in the councils of any nation," and he enumerates the peace establishment; the regulation of commerce; the maintenance of troops for the protection of the frontiers; the regulation of settlements in the country westward; and the counteraction of the narrow commercial policy of European powers. The determination of a site "for the residence of Congress" likewise demanded serious consideration, and Monroe served upon a committee which visited George-town in May, 1784, and decided to report in favor of the Maryland side of the Potomac, the present site of the capital.

As the powers of the Confederation were quite inadequate for the proper regulation of commerce, Congress, and thoughtful men who were not in Congress, were seriously engaged in searching for the remedy. Monroe took a

prominent part in the discussions, and the noteworthy motion which he made upon the subject
was referred to a special committee, who reported a recommendation, that the ninth of the
articles of confederation be so altered as to
secure to Congress the power to regulate commerce, with the assent of nine States in Congress assembled.[1]

He favored a regulation that all imposts
should be collected under the authority and
accrue to the use of the State in which the
same might be payable. The report embodying
this proviso was read in Congress March 28,
1785, and the copy of it preserved in the public archives has a few corrections in Monroe's
handwriting. Many interesting papers are extant which bear upon this question, — among
them a letter from James McHenry to Washington, and the latter's reply. The Virginia
Assembly also engaged in the discussion of a
series of propositions which tended in the same
direction. Monroe's views can readily be traced
in his letters to Jefferson and Madison during
the session of Congress in the winter of 1784–85.
On April 12 Monroe wrote to Jefferson, sending

---

[1] This subject has been carefully studied by Mr. Bancroft,
and presented in his new volumes with so much fullness that
I can only follow his guidance. See his *Hist. of the U. S.
Const.* i. 192–196. Cf. Sparks, *Washington*, ix. 503–507.

him the committee's report, and saying that he
thinks it best to postpone action on it for a
time. "It hath been brought so far," he adds,
"without a prejudice against it. If carried
farther here, prejudices will take place." He
thinks it better that the States should act sepa-
rately upon the measure. A few weeks later he
wrote again to Jefferson as follows: "The report upon the ninth article hath not been taken
up; the importance of the subject and the deep
and radical change it will create in the bond of
the Union, together with the conviction that
something must be done, seems to create an
aversion or rather a fear of acting on it." Then,
as if he foresaw the coming concentration of
powers in the general government, he expresses
a belief that the proposed change, if adopted,
will certainly form "the most permanent and
powerful principle in the Confederation." [1] A
month later (July 15) Jefferson was again told
how the debate went forward. "In my opinion,"
says Monroe, "the reasons in favor of changing
the ninth article are conclusive, but the opposition is respectable in point of numbers as well
as talents. What will be done is uncertain."
To Madison he afterwards writes, summing up

[1] Bancroft, *Hist. of the U. S. Const.* i. 450–455. See the
entire letter dated June 16, 1785, given with many others in
The Writings of James Monroe, vol. i. New York, 1898.

quite carefully the arguments on both sides.
December came and Congress did not act.
"The advocates for the measure will scarcely
succeed," said Randolph to Washington, "so
strong are the apprehensions in some minds of
an abuse of the power." At the end of the
month, Monroe, still sure of the necessity of
committing to the United States the power of
regulating trade, wrote once more to Madison.
In February the prospect was no better. In
May there was a gleam of light. The plan of
a convention at Annapolis, which in March
Monroe himself had not favored, had taken
the subject from before Congress. "As it ori-
ginated with our State," he writes, "we think
it our duty to promote its object by all the
means in our power. Of its success I must
confess I have some hope. . . . Truth and
sound state policy in every instance will urge
the commission of the power to the United
States." Thus it was that Congress by its
own lack of power was led to the convention
which formed the Constitution, and, in a far
wiser manner than that originally suggested,
provided for the regulation of trade. But in
August Monroe was despondent. "Our affairs,"
he writes, "are daily falling into a worse situation;" there is a party, he says, ready to dis-
member the confederacy and throw the States

eastward of the Hudson into one government. He urges Madison to use his utmost exertions in the convention to obtain good as well as to prevent mischief, and adds to his appeal this pregnant postscript : " I have always considered the regulation of trade in the hands of the United States as necessary to preserve the Union ; without it, it will infallibly tumble to pieces ; but I earnestly wish the admission of a few additional States into the confederacy in the Southern scale." The question, it is well known, was finally settled in the convention at Philadelphia, when Delaware and South Carolina voted with the North against Maryland, Virginia, North Carolina, and Georgia.[1]

In March, 1784, Monroe, with Jefferson, Hardy, and A. Lee, delivered to Congress a deed which ceded to the United States Virginia's claims to the Northwest Territory, and thenceforward the government of that region continued to be one of the subjects in which he took most interest. During the summer recess of Congress he made an extended tour of observation. To Jefferson, July 20, he wrote as follows : " The day after to-morrow I set out upon the route through the western country. I have changed the direction and shall commence for the westward upon the North River by Albany. I shall

[1] Bancroft, ii. 162.

pass through the lakes, visit the posts, and come down to the Ohio and thence home." Thus he hopes " to acquire a better knowledge of the posts which we should occupy, the cause of the delay of the evacuation by British troops, the temper of the Indians toward us, — as well as of the soil, waters, and in general the natural view of the country." Upon his return he wrote to Governor Harrison, October 30, respecting unfriendly, if not hostile, manifestations which had been made in Canada; and to Madison, November 15, on the importance of garrisoning the western forts, about to be given up by the British. To Jefferson a confidential letter was sent especially bearing upon the relation of Canada to the United States.[1] It was intended to throw light upon the provisions of a commercial treaty with England.

Some months later, when a conference was to be held at the mouth of the Great Miami with the Shawnees, Monroe again went beyond the Alleghanies, as far as Fort Pitt, and began the descent of the Ohio, but abandoned the expedition on account of the low state of the water, and returned to Richmond. These two journeys had a marked influence upon his action in Congress, as the careful narrative of Bancroft, already repeatedly cited, shows most clearly.

[1] See *The Writings of James Monroe*, vol. i. p. 41.

On the motion of Monroe a grand committee
was appointed by Congress to consider the division of the western territory, and their report
was presented March 24. A little later, another
committee, of which Monroe was chairman, was
appointed to consider and report a form of temporary government for the Western States.
His report, which said nothing of slavery, failed
of adoption. A year later a new committee
prepared a new ordinance, which embodied the
best parts of the work of their predecessors. I
will give the rest of the story in Bancroft's
language: —

" The ordinance contained no allusion to slavery;
and in that form it received its first reading and was
ordered to be printed. Grayson, then presiding officer of Congress, had always opposed slavery. Two
years before he had wished success to the attempt of
King for its restriction; and everything points to
him as the immediate cause of the tranquil spirit of
disinterested statesmanship which took possession of
every Southern man in the assembly. Of the members of Virginia, Richard Henry Lee had stood
against Jefferson on this very question; but now he
acted with Grayson, and from the States of which no
man had yielded before, every one chose the part
which was to bring on their memory the benedictions
of all coming ages. Obeying an intimation from the
South, Nathan Dane copied from Jefferson the prohibition of involuntary servitude in the territory, and

quieted alarm by adding from the report of King
a clause for the delivering up of the fugitive slave.
This, at the second reading of the ordinance, he
moved as a sixth article of compact, and on the
thirteenth day of July, 1787, the great statute for-
bidding slavery to cross the river Ohio was passed
by the vote of Georgia, South Carolina, North Carolina, Virginia, Delaware, New Jersey, New York,
and Massachusetts, all the States that were then present in Congress. Pennsylvania and three States of
New England were absent; Maryland only of the
South."

At the next Assembly in Virginia, a committee, of which Monroe was a member, " brought
forward the bill by which Virginia confirmed
the ordinance for the colonization of all the territory then in the possession of the United
States by freemen alone."

Among other subjects in which Monroe took
a deep interest while a delegate in Congress,
the navigation of the Mississippi was prominent.
The treaty with Great Britain had stipulated
that this river from its source to its mouth
should be open to the subjects of Great Britain
and the citizens of the United States. Spain
objected. Some parties were ready to surrender this right, but among those who persistently
refused to do so were the Virginia delegates,
including Monroe, who wrote a memoir in 1786

to prove the right of the inhabitants of the western country to a free navigation of the Mississippi. Positive action was postponed until the new government was about to be organized, and Congress then declared its opinion in clear and bold terms. It was due to the foresight and firmness of a few strong men that the claims of Spain were not acknowledged, and that the acquisition of the territory involved was finally completed after Monroe became president.

Near the end of the year 1784, Monroe was selected as one of nine judges to decide the boundary dispute in which Massachusetts and New York were involved, and after some deliberation he accepted the position, and was on the way to Williamsburg, when he received advices that the session of the court had been deferred; the case being thus postponed, he resigned and another commissioner was chosen. There is the authority of Mr. Adams for saying that Monroe had been conspicuous above all others in proceedings which concerned the navigation of the Mississippi, and had taken the lead in opposition to Jay, who proposed a compromise with Spain; and that it was in the heat of temper kindled by this discord that Monroe resigned his commission.[1]

[1] J. Q. Adams, *Eulogy*, pp. 225–232.

Of the convention which formed the Constitution of the United States, Monroe was not a member. Virginia was represented by Washington, Madison, Patrick Henry, George Mason, George Wythe, and John Blair. The organization of the convention was made May 25, 1787, with Washington president, and the adjournment took place September 17, 1787. Monroe was a doubtful observer of the progress of events. " My anxiety for the general welfare," he writes, "hath not been diminished. The affairs of the federal government are, I believe, in the utmost confusion. The convention . . . will either recover us from our present embarrassments, or complete our ruin; for I do suspect that if what they recommend should be rejected, this would be the case." This was written to Jefferson, July 27, 1787. He suspects the hostility toward himself of Edmund Randolph and Madison, members of the convention; nevertheless, he thinks that he shall be " strongly impressed in favor of and inclined to vote for whatever they will recommend."

In the Virginia convention of 1788, the party favoring the United States Constitution was led by Madison, Marshall, and Edmund Randolph. The leader of the opposition was Patrick Henry, and James Monroe stood by his

side in company with William Grayson and
George Mason. Two of his speeches as reported in the Debates are worthy of mention
here.[1] In the first of them, delivered June 10,
he made an elaborate historical argument in
which the experience of the Amphictyonic council, the Achæan league, the Germanic system,
the Swiss cantons and the New England confederacy were successively referred to, — a
theme which seems to have been the germ of
a posthumous publication, to which reference
will hereafter be made. He assumes the value
of the Union, to which " the people from New
Hampshire to Georgia, Rhode Island excepted,
have uniformly shown attachment." Examining the proposed Constitution, he claims that
there are no adequate checks upon the exercise
of power; he foresees conflict between the national and State authorities. As for the President, he foresees that " when he is once elected
he may be elected forever."

In closing the speech he says that he regards
the proposed government as dangerous, and cal-
culated to secure neither the interests nor the
rights of our countrymen. " Under such an
one I shall be averse to embark the best hopes
of a free people. We have struggled long to

[1] *Debates of the Convention of Virginia*, 1788, reported by
David Robertson, p. 154.

bring about this revolution by which we enjoy our present freedom and security. Why then this haste, this wild precipitation?"

At a later stage Monroe explained the Congressional disputes about the free navigation of the Mississippi, the purport of which was to show that the western country would be less secure under the Constitution than it was under the Confederation. He finally assented to a ratification of the Constitution by Virginia upon the condition that her amendments should be accepted. His chief objections were these: the power of direct taxation; the absence of a bill of rights; the lack of legislative and executive responsibility and the reëligibility of the President.

Many years later he thus, in a letter to Andrew Jackson, gave his recollections of the monarchical tendencies which were shown by his contemporaries before and after the adoption of the Constitution. He writes as follows:—

December, 1816. "We have heretofore been divided into two great parties. That some of the leaders of the Federal party entertained principles unfriendly to our system of government, I have been thoroughly convinced; and that they meant to work a change in it by taking advantage of favorable circumstances, I am equally satisfied. It happened that

I was a member of Congress under the Confederation, just before the change made by the adoption
of the present Constitution, and afterwards of the
Senate, beginning shortly after its adoption.   In the
former I served three years, and in the latter rather
a longer term.   In these stations I saw indications
of the kind suggested.   It was an epoch at which the
views of men were most likely to unfold themselves,
as, if anything favorable to a higher toned government was to be obtained, that was the time.   The
movement in France tended also then to test the
opinions and principles of men, which was disclosed
in a manner to leave no doubt on my mind of what
I have suggested.   No daring attempt was ever
made, because there was no opportunity for it.   I
thought that Washington was opposed to their
schemes, and not being able to take him with them,
that they were forced to work, in regard to him,
under-handed, using his name and standing with the
nation, as far as circumstances permitted, to serve
their purposes.   The opposition, which was carried
on with great firmness, checked the career of this
party, and kept it within moderate limits.   Many of
the circumstances, on which my opinion is founded,
took place in debate and in society, and therefore
find no place in any public document.   I am satisfied, however, that sufficient proof exists, founded
on facts and opinions of distinguished individuals,
which became public, to justify that [opinion] which
I had formed. . . .

   " My candid opinion is that the dangerous purposes

I have adverted to were never adopted, if they were
known, especially in their full extent, by any large
portion of the Federal party, but were confined to
certain leaders, and they principally to the eastward.
The manly and patriotic conduct of a great propor-
tion of that party in the other States, I might perhaps say all who had an opportunity of displaying it,
is a convincing proof of this fact."

Jefferson, referring to the same period, spoke
as follows in the introduction to his " Ana : "
" The contests of that day were contests of principle between the advocates of republican and
those of kingly government."

A familiar letter to Jefferson written July 12,
1788, gives an inside view of the discussions in
the Virginia convention.   Before it met, Monroe
endeavored to maintain a non-committal attitude.   He prepared, however, a few days before
the convention, a communication to his constituents ; but the printing of this letter was delayed so long and was so incorrectly made and
" the whole performance was so loosely drawn,"
that the author thought best to suppress it.   He
inclosed a copy to Jefferson.   What appears to
be Monroe's own copy has lately been discovered
in the archives of the State Department, and
given to the press.[1]   Its significance is however
less important than that of the " Observations

[1] *Writings of James Monroe*, vol. i. pp. 307, 349.

on the Federal Government," attributed to Monroe. A copy of this pamphlet (excessively rare, if not unique, and hitherto unnoticed by any bibliographer) has been found among the Madison papers in the Department of State, and reprinted in the first volume of Monroe's writings.

Notwithstanding Monroe's opposition to the adoption of the new Constitution, he was among the earliest to take office under it. The first choice of Virginia for senators fell on Richard Henry Lee and William Grayson. The latter died soon after his appointment, and Monroe was selected by the legislature to fill the vacant place, instead of John Walker, who had been named by the Executive of the State. He took his seat in the Senate December 6, 1790, and held the position until May, 1794. Jefferson was in Philadelphia, as secretary of state, during the early part of Monroe's senatorial career, so that letters to him are wanting, but in 1793–94 Monroe again writes him confidentially on the progress of affairs, and particularly on the strained relations of the United States with England and France. It does not appear that he was conspicuous as a debater; but he made himself felt in other ways, and was regarded as among the most decided opponents of Washington's administration. He was particularly hostile to Hamilton, and on one occasion, when the latter was talked about as likely to be sent to England, transgressed the limits of senatorial courtesy by addressing a letter to the President with intimations of what he could say if an opportunity were afforded him. He was opposed to the measures which were carried for establishing on a sound basis the national finances. He proposed a suspension of the fourth article of the definitive treaty with Great Britain until that power complied with her stipulations. He strongly objected to the selection of Morris and Jay as ministers respectively to France and England. Indeed, during all this period he appears in the part of an obstructionist, who doubted the wisdom of the dominant views in respect to the new order of government, and who did not hesitate to put obstacles in the way of those who were endeavoring to give dignity and force to the new United States. He was therefore surprised, and so were many others, that he was selected, while still a senator, to be the successor of Gouverneur Morris as minister to France. He had objected to Jay's appointment partly on the ground that such an office should not be given to one of the federal judiciary, and the wiseacres were not slow to taunt him for accepting, in place of his senatorial rank, the dignity of a diplomatic station. The rest of this story will be told in the following chapter.

Although it is not next in order, it is convenient to place here the little which is to be said of the executive station to which Monroe, on his return from diplomatic services, was twice called in his native State. He was first chosen governor of Virginia in 1799, after his recall from France, and served for a period of three years. He was again chosen in 1811, held the office for part of a year, and gave it up in order to enter the cabinet of Madison. His first election was opposed by John Breckenridge, who received 66 votes, while Monroe received 101. The Richmond " Federalist " of December 7 declared the day before to be " a day of mourning." Virginia's " misfortunes may be comprised in one short sentence : Monroe is elected governor ! "

During his first administration a conspiracy among the slaves was brought to light, and was suppressed by his power as governor. The incident has recently been called to mind by a widely read novel, in which there is a graphic picture of a servile insurrection and its timely discovery.[1] Howison's story is as follows.[2] Not far from Richmond dwelt Thomas Prosser, who

[1] *Homoselle,* by Mrs. Tiernan.
[2] Howison, *History of Virginia,* p. 390.

owned a number of slaves, among them one who
became known as "General Gabriel," a man
"distinguished for his intelligence and his influence with his class." Near by lived another
slave called "Jack Bowler." By their agency
nearly a thousand slaves, it was supposed, were
secretly enlisted in a plot to attack Richmond
by night and there begin a war of extermination
against the whites. Just before the proposed
assault a slave named "Pharaoh" escaped from
the conspirators during a storm and revealed
the project to the people of Richmond. The
tidings were carried to Governor Monroe, the
alarm was given, the militia called out, and
preparations were made to meet the assailants.
The streams were so swollen by the fall of rain
that the movements of the insurgents were delayed, and they soon perceived that their secret
had been discovered. The ringleaders were subsequently found and punished; and so many
others were inculpated that a reaction took
place in public feeling, and a merciful arrest of
justice occurred before all the guilty had been
reached.

For several years, after 1806, John Randolph
was a frequent correspondent of Monroe. He
urges him to come back from England; he
guards him against compromitment to men in
whom he cannot wholly confide; he gives him a

dark hint of "the stage effect" he will be made
to produce; he flatters him with expectations of
the next nomination to the presidency; he dis-
parages Madison; he says that Monroe will
hardly know the country when he arrives; "intrigue has arrived at a pitch which I hardly supposed it would have reached in five centuries;"
"life has afforded me few enjoyments which
I value in comparison with your friendship."
These flattering words, tempered with insinuations against Madison, were addressed to Monroe in the belief and wish that he could be
brought forward as a candidate for the presidency at the close of Jefferson's term. Randolph's purpose failed, Madison became president and Monroe governor, after brief service
in the Assembly. A little later Randolph
quarreled with Monroe, because, as he thought,
the latter was inclined to repudiate the views he
had held on his return from England. He
charged him with tergiversation in order to become chief magistrate of the Commonwealth.
The climax of their disagreement was reached
when Monroe was called to the cabinet of Madison.

Many years later, in 1814, Randolph, still
quarrelsome, attacked Monroe's conscription project by pointing out the course of the latter in
respect to federal usurpation when he was gover-

nor, charging upon him the fact that the grand armory at Richmond was built to enable Virginia to resist encroachment upon her indisputable rights.[1]

[1] For all this story, in detail, and many original letters, see the *Life of John Randolph* by Henry Adams, in a volume of this Series.

CHAPTER III

MONROE'S career as a diplomatist exhibits first
the misfortune and then the good fortune which
may attend ministerial action in a foreign land,
when long periods must elapse before letters can
be interchanged with the government at home.
In critical junctures responsibility must be assumed by the representative of a nation, who
runs the risk that his words and actions, however
wise and necessary they appear to him, will not
be approved by those who sent him abroad. In
quiet days a foreign embassy is an enviable position, but Monroe was neither the first envoy
nor the last who has found in troublesome times
that it is difficult to act with a near-sighted view
of the field so as to keep the support of those
who are far-sighted. His first mission to France
began brilliantly, but ended with an irritation
of his spirit which he carried with him, like the
bullet received at Trenton, to the very end of
his life ; his second mission to France, undertaken with some distrust, led to a fortunate

negotiation which brightened all his subsequent
days.

While a senator in Congress, Monroe was selected, as we have seen, to represent the United
States in Paris, after it became necessary for
Gouverneur Morris to give way. Washington's
first choice for the position was Thomas Pinckney, whom he would have transferred from England to France, if Jay would consent to remain
as minister in England after concluding a treaty.
As this arrangement could not be effected, the
appointment was offered to Robert R. Livingston, who did not accept it. Madison had already
declined. Aaron Burr was a competitor. A
few weeks later, on May 28, 1794, Monroe was
commissioned. The appointment took him by
surprise, as he told Mr. Randolph, the secretary
of state : " I really thought I was among the
last men to whom the proposition would be
made," were his words. Randolph replied that
the President was resolved to send a Republican
to France ; that Livingston and Madison had
refused, and that Burr would not be appointed.
If Monroe declined, the post would probably be
offered to Governor Price of Maryland, or to
some person not yet thought of. Monroe's attitude toward the administration was of course
perfectly well known, but it was thought that his
admiration for the French and his sympathy

with the Revolution might secure for him a
favorable reception. Washington's position was
one of extreme responsibility. There was danger
that the United States, scarcely beginning to recover from the Revolutionary struggle, and with
the experiment of the Constitution not yet five
years old, would be involved in war with France
or England in consequence of their unjustifiable
reprisals and their attitude in respect to the commerce of neutrals. It was most important for
the safety of the Union as well as for the prosperity of the people that hostilities should be
avoided, and much appeared to depend upon the
envoys. So Jay was sent to England and Monroe to France, each of whom was supposed to be
acceptable to the country to which he was appointed.

Looking back on these appointments, nearly
forty years afterwards, John Quincy Adams declared them to be among the most memorable
events in the history of this Union. To understand this in our day, we must remember the
bitter relations, "tinged with infusions of the
wormwood and the gall," which then divided
France and England ; and the partisan feelings
which already separated Republicans from Federalists.

The state of feeling in Congress prior to Monroe's mission is familiar enough to all historical

readers; but I have before me a long file of letters which have never been made public, exhibiting in the intimacy of fraternal correspondence the current of opinion in Congress; — and I make from them the following extracts to give a fresh and original record of a tale which has often been told: [1] —

January, 1794. " I think we are in no danger of being drawn into the European war, unless the French should be mad enough to declare war against everybody that will not fraternize with them."

January, 1794. " It may, I believe, fairly be presumed that we shall not get into a wrangle with the French nation."

January 25, 1794. " We have announced to us in a letter from the President this day, that he has from the French Court assurances that M. Genet's conduct here has met with unequivocal disapprobation, and that his recall will be expected as soon as possible. I give it you nearly in the words of his letter. Why he has not before made the communication, as it arrived by the Dispatch (a sloop of about thirty tons) last week; whether he has letters from the French ministry or only from Mr. Morris, — I am without information."

January 31, 1794. " A strange portion [*sic*] of French frenzy is working in this country. We see

[1] These extracts are from letters by Joshua Coit of New London, Conn., a representative in Congress, to his brother, Daniel L. Coit.

much of it in Congress, principally among the Southern members. It enters, as you will see, into the debates on Mr. Madison's propositions. I have mentioned it to you, I believe, in a former letter. One would have expected from these owners of slaves and men of large fortunes a different complexion; but our rankest democratical principle is all from the South, and they consider us New England men as aristocrats. I feel more apprehension of the general government being too weak than that it will gather a strength dangerous to the liberties of the people. I would hope, however, that no more of party is mixed in our composition than may be wholesome. Mr. M.'s resolutions have now been under discussion for about a fortnight. Gentlemen take an amazing latitude in their discussions, and from the debates one would be led to suppose we were forming commercial treaties that were to embrace all the interests of the United States. The first resolution is a mighty vague, general thing, and will apply to any alteration of our revenue system almost; perhaps this may be carried, but I think the others, or anything like them, cannot; they have engrossed all the time of Congress for this fortnight past."

February 15, 1794. "The fact is, I think, every day more and more evinced, that some of our Southern gentlemen, Virginians especially, have a most unconquerable aversion for the British nation, and partiality for France. The debts due from that country to G. B. may have their effect in fomenting and keeping up their animosity, and they seem to wish to fix some immovable obstructions to a friendly intercourse between the two countries, and there is but too much reason to fear that the measures they pursue are in good degree influenced by their dissatisfaction at some steps that have been taken since the establishment of the present government, — the funding system and bank especially. They profess peace — that energetic measures are those only by which it can be preserved. Britain is to be so afflicted with our non-importation agreement that, to persuade us to give it up, she is to do everything which we may demand of her ; and if, on the contrary, she is disposed to fight, she is exhausted and weakened by the war in which she is now engaged, and with the help of France we shall give her the worst of it. I still hope peace ; but if this measure is carried through, I shall then despair."

March 7, 1794. " The measures you mention are regarded as very extraordinary ; equally so is that of the French detaining our ships in their ports. 'T is perhaps fortunate for us that we are ill-treated by both the belligerent powers ; experiencing no favor from either, we shall be less an object of jealousy from either, and probably less in danger of rushing into the war than if we were ill-treated by one only. I believe we had better suffer almost anything than get into the war. Time and patience will, I hope, cure all."

March 13, 1794. " It seems to me the British nation must contemplate some inconvenience in the loss of our trade in case of a rupture, and that the fair and honorable neutrality we have preferred should command their respect. But they apprehend we feel a partiality for the French, and nations at war very readily regard as enemies those who are not their friends, and they very naturally contemplate the going to war with another nation with much less reluctance than changing from peace to war. No measures will be taken hastily on the subject by us, I believe. The infancy of our government, and our revenue depending almost altogether on foreign commerce, which would by a war be greatly deranged if not cut off, make the evils to be apprehended by us in this event peculiarly serious. But if they will fight with us, we must do the best we can."

March 24, 1794. "The minds of people are so much agitated, and resentments are so warm, that there is reason to fear that we shall be hurried into the torrent that is ravaging Europe."

March 25, 1794. "If the embargo gets through, I shall be almost inclined to think the Rubicon is passed and that war is inevitable. Not so much that the British will regard it as a hostile measure, but that it will tend to sharpen the minds of people, and precipitate us, from the heat of our passions, into the war."

March 27, 1794. "If we must enter into a war, I should feel very unhappy to enter it under the auspices of an act which would appear to me a complication of villainy and bad policy."

March 28, 1794. "We have a mad proposition before the House, brought in yesterday, for seques-

tering British debts to form a fund for compensation
to the sufferers by British spoliations. I feared it
would pass, but the fever of the mind seems to be
cooling a little, and I begin to hope for better things."

April 8, 1794. " I am still persuaded that the
threatening appearances will blow over and leave us
at peace, in spite of the unaccountable proceedings
of the British in the West Indies. I do not believe
they mean to go to war with us."

April 13, 1794. " A minister to the Court of
London is still talked of, but this is not determined
on, and these people appear to be very anxious to
have something done which, as they say, shall give
weight to negotiation; but their views and professions
are apprehended to be widely different, and that instead of wishing to give effect, they would prefer
doing something that should impede the negotiation.
The President, with whom alone lies the power, is
very cautious; perhaps fortunately so for the country,
as well as for his own reputation, but unluckily, (as it
is more with the Legislature to lay the grounds by
which negotiation might be facilitated or impeded,
and to determine the popularity of the measure,) I
suspect he hesitates and waits to see how the discussion in our House will issue. Had he already sent a
negotiator, it would have furnished an argument for
our leaving things as they were when the negotiator
left the country."

April 16, 1794. " Mr. Jay is nominated. There
is not perhaps a man in the United States whose
character as a negotiator stands on higher ground.

The appointment marks a disposition in the President to come forward before mischief is done, and to try the ground of negotiation fairly with G. Britain, before any obstruction is thrown in the way by our confiscating British debts, or passing a non-importation act."

April 19, 1794. " The embargo is again on, to last till the 25th of May in the same way as before ; passed House of Representatives day before yesterday, and in Senate yesterday. I had not expected it."

April 22, 1794. " It is a doubt with many whether our present form of government continue many years. The jealousies which exist in the Southern States respecting the funding system and most of the measures of consequence which have been adopted, added to some strange and fantastical notions about liberty which they entertain, approaching nearly to French extravagance of liberty and equality absolute, render the continuance of our Union for many years, even of peace, doubtful. But should a war take place, I think we have scarcely ground to hope a continuance of the Union."

April 24, 1794. " We have perhaps as much to fear from the fever of French politics taking too strong a hold of the minds of the people of this country as from any other source."

There is an interruption in the file of letters from which these extracts are taken, and I find in them no mention of the envoy to France, whose commission came a month later.

Monroe's instructions, as given to him by Randolph, were very minute, and contained the following pregnant sentences as the conclusion:

"To conclude. You go, sir, to France, to strengthen our friendship with that country; and you are well acquainted with the line of freedom and ease to which you may advance without betraying the dignity of the United States. You will show our confidence in the French Republic without betraying the most remote mark of undue complaisance. *You will let it be seen that, in case of war with any nation on earth, we shall consider France as our first and natural ally.* You may dwell *upon the sense which we entertain of past services*, and for the more recent interposition in our behalf with the Dey of Algiers. Among the great events with which the world is now teeming, there may be an opening for *France to become instrumental in securing to us the free navigation of the Mississippi.* Spain may, perhaps, *negotiate a peace, separate from Great Britain, with France.* If she does, the *Mississippi may be acquired through this channel*, especially if you contrive to have our mediation in any manner solicited."

Monroe arrived in Paris just after the fall of Robespierre. Notwithstanding his outspoken good will for the popular cause, the Committee of Public Safety hesitated to receive him. His proceedings in consequence were full of romance. Not another civilized nation upon earth, says Mr. Adams, had a recognized representative in

France at that time. " I waited," says Monroe,
" eight or ten days without progressing an iota,
and as I had heard that a minister from Geneva
had been here about six weeks before me, and
had not been received, I was fearful I might remain as long, and, perhaps, much longer, in the
same situation." He therefore addressed a letter to the president of the Convention, " not
knowing the competent department nor the
forms established by law for my reception."
A decree was passed at once that the minister
of the United States " be introduced into the
bosom of the Convention to-morrow at two
P. M." Accordingly he appeared before the
Convention, August 15, 1794, and presented an
address in English, with a translation of it into
French, which latter was read by a secretary,
together with two letters from Edmund Randolph, secretary of state, acknowledging the
letter received by Congress from the Committee
of Public Safety.

Monroe's address was as follows : —

" *Citizens, President, and Representatives of the
French People*, — My admission into this assembly,
in presence of the French nation (for all the citizens
of France are represented here) to be recognized
as the representative of the American Republic,
impresses me with a degree of sensibility which I
cannot express. I consider it a new proof of that

friendship and regard which the French nation has always shown to their ally, the United States of America.

"Republics should approach near to each other. In many respects they have all the same interest; but this is more especially the case with the American and French republics. Their governments are similar; they both cherish the same principles, and rest on the same basis, the equal and unalienable rights of man. The recollection, too, of common dangers and difficulties will increase their harmony and cement their union. America had her day of oppression, difficulty, and war; but her sons were virtuous and brave, and the storm which long clouded her political horizon has passed, and left them in the enjoyment of peace, liberty, and independence. France, our ally and our friend, and who aided in the contest, has now embarked in the same noble career; and I am happy to add, that whilst the fortitude, magnanimity, and heroic valor of her troops command the admiration and applause of the astonished world, the wisdom and firmness of her councils unite equally in securing the happiest result.

"America is not an unfeeling spectator of your affairs at the present crisis. I lay before you, in the declarations of every department of our government, — declarations which are founded in the affections of the citizens at large, — the most decided proof of her sincere attachment to the liberty, prosperity, and happiness of the French Republic. Each branch of the Congress, according to the course of proceeding there, has requested the President to make this known to you in its behalf ; and, in fulfilling the desires of those branches, I am instructed to declare to you that he has expressed his own.

" In discharging the duties of the office which I am now called to execute, I promise myself the highest satisfaction, because I well know that, whilst I pursue the dictates of my own heart in wishing the liberty and happiness of the French nation, and which I most sincerely do, I speak the sentiments of my own country ; and that, by doing everything in my power to preserve and perpetuate the harmony so happily subsisting between the two republics, I shall promote the interest of both. To this great object, therefore, all my efforts will be directed. If I can be so fortunate as to succeed in such manner as to merit the approbation of both republics, I shall deem it the happiest event of my life, and retire hereafter with a consolation which those who mean well, and have served the cause of liberty, alone can feel."

A comparison of this speech with Randolph's injunctions, already quoted, will show how far Monroe was carried by the enthusiasm of his youth and the unparalleled circumstances in which he was placed. That speech of ten minutes, received with applause and afterwards printed by order of " the Convention, in the two languages, French and American," was the occasion of many a pang to the orator, in his after life.

The account of Monroe's reception may readily be found in the American State Papers,[1]
but a document, hitherto hidden, was lately
brought to light by Mr. Washburne, the American minister, who looked up, in the national
archives of France, the *procès verbal* on the
day referred to, August 15, 1794. Here is the
interesting extract which he sent to Mr. Fish
"to fill the gap" in the diplomatic records of
that period.[2]

*Extract from the "procès verbal" of the National Con-
vention of August 15, 1794. — Translation.*

The Citizen James Monroe, Minister Plenipotentiary of the United States of America near the
French Republic, is admitted in the hall of the sit-
ting of the National Convention. He takes his place
in the midst of the representatives of the people,
and remits to the President with his letters of credence, a translation of a discourse addressed to the
National Convention ; it is read by one of the secretaries. The expressions of fraternity, of union between the two people, and the interest which the
people of the United States take in the success of the
French Republic, are heard with the liveliest sensibility and covered with applause.

Reading is also given to the letters of credence of

[1] Vol. i. p. 672.
[2] *Foreign Relations of the U. S.* 1876. Mr. Washburne to
Mr. Fish, Paris, October 23, 1876.

Citizen Monroe, as well as to those written by the American Congress and by its President, to the National Convention and to the Committee of Public Safety.

In witness of the fraternity which unites the two peoples, French and American, the President [1] gives the *accolade* (fraternal embrace) to Citizen Monroe.

Afterward, upon the proposition of many members, the National Convention passes with unanimity the following decree : —

ARTICLE I. The reading and verification being had of the powers of Citizen James Monroe, he is recognized and proclaimed minister plenipotentiary of the United States of America near the French Republic.

ARTICLE II. The letters of credence of Citizen James Monroe, minister plenipotentiary of the United States of America, those which he has remitted on the part of the American Congress and its President, addressed to the National Convention and to the Committee of Public Safety, the discourse of Citizen Monroe, the response of the President of the Convention, shall be printed in the two languages, French and American, and inserted in the bulletin of correspondence.

ARTICLE III. The flags of the United States of America shall be joined to those of France, and displayed in the hall of the sittings of the Convention, in sign of the union and eternal fraternity of the two people.

Mr. Washburne calls attention to the phrase, " the two languages, French and American," as illustrating the hatred of the English ; and he

[1] Merlin de Douai.

gives to Secretary Fish the following amusing interpretation of the *accolade*, based upon his own experience in the new republic.

" For many days," he says, " after I had, by your instructions, recognized the republic, which was proclaimed on the 4th of September, 1870, regiment after regiment of the national guard marched to the legation to make known to our government, through me, their profound appreciation of its prompt action in recognizing the government of the national defense. Forming on the corner of the rue de Chaillot and the avenue Josephine, they would send up cheers and cries of 'Vive la République,' till I would appear on the balcony to make my acknowledgments. Then some officers of the regiment would be deputed to call upon me in the chambers of the legation, to tender me their personal thanks for my agency in the matter of recognition of their new government, and to give me the fraternal embrace ('*accolade*'), which was carried out in letter and spirit, and sometimes much to the amusement of the numerous visitors who were present on the occasion."

A short time after his reception Monroe presented an American flag to the Convention, intrusting its carriage to Captain, afterwards Commodore, Barney, an officer of the United States Navy, with whom Monroe had crossed the Atlantic. Captain Barney made a brief speech on the occasion in the presence of the Convention, received an *accolade* from the Presi-

dent, and was complimented with a proposal to
enter the naval service of France. When the
body of Rousseau was deposited in the Pantheon, this flag, borne by young Barney and
a nephew of Monroe, preceded the column of
Americans. The American minister and his
suite, we are told, were the only persons permitted to enter the Pantheon with the National
Convention to witness the conclusion of the
ceremony.

Several months later, March 6, 1795, Monroe
makes this casual mention of the flag in his
dispatch : —

" I had forgotten to notify you officially the present
I had made to the Convention of our flag. It was
done in consequence of the order of that body for its
suspension in its hall, and an intimation from the
President himself that they had none, and were igno-
rant of the model."

Near the close of his life Monroe said that
when he first arrived in France his situation
was the most difficult and painful he had ever
experienced. War with the United States was
seriously menaced. He tells us that he could
make no impression on the Committee of Public
Safety, and so he determined to appeal to the
real government, the People, through the nom-
inal one, the Convention, and thus fairly bring

the cause before the nation. He knew that their object was liberty, and that many French citizens had brought home from America the spirit of our struggle and infused it among their countrymen. At the head of our government stood one who was rightly held in the highest veneration by the French people; and he felt sure that if he brought before them convincing proofs of Washington's good wishes for their success, supported by that of the other branches of our government, the hostile spirit of the French government would be subdued and his official recognition would follow. On this principle he spoke to the Convention with the desired effect. As this address was the subject of severe animadversions at home, and as he was charged with going beyond his instructions, the following extract from a long letter to Judge Jones, April 4, 1794,[1] may be taken as evidence that the envoy acted according to his understanding of the instructions he had received.

"I inclose you a copy of my address, etc., to the Convention upon my introduction, and of the President's reply. I thought it my duty to lay those papers before the Convention as the basis of my mission, containing the declaration of every department in favor of the French revolution, or implying it strongly. My address, you will observe, goes no farther than the declarations of both houses."

[1] Gouverneur MSS.

Flattered by his reception in the Convention, Monroe was destined to a profound disappointment when he received a dispatch from home, written by Randolph " in the frankness of friendship," criticising severely the course he had pursued.

" When you left us," said the secretary of state, " we all supposed that your reception as the minister of the United States would take place in the private chamber of some committee. Your letter of credence contained the degree of profession which the government was desirous of making ; and though the language of it would not have been cooled, even if its subsquent publicity had been foreseen, still it was natural to expect that the remarks with which you might accompany its delivery would be merely oral, and therefore not exposed to the rancorous criticism of nations at war with France.

" It seems that, upon your arrival, the downfall of Robespierre and the suspension of the usual routine of business, combined, perhaps, with an anxiety to demonstrate an affection for the United States, had shut up for a time the diplomatic cabinet, and rendered the hall of the National Convention the theatre of diplomatic civilities. We should have supposed that an introduction there would have brought to mind these ideas : ' The United States are neutral ; the allied Powers jealous ; with England we are now in treaty ; by England we have been impeached for breaches of faith in favor of France ; our citizens are

notoriously Gallican in their hearts; it will be wise
to hazard as little as possible on the score of good
humor; and, therefore, in the disclosure of my feelings, something is due to the possibility of fostering
new suspicions.'   Under the influence of these sentiments, we should have hoped that your address to
the National Convention would have been so framed
as to leave heart-burning nowhere.   If private affection and opinions had been the only points to be
consulted, it would have been immaterial where or
how they were delivered.   But the range of a public
minister's mind will go to all the relations of our
country with the whole world.   We do not perceive
that your instructions have imposed upon you the
extreme glow of some parts of your address; and
my letter in behalf of the House of Representatives, which has been considered by some gentlemen as too strong, was not to be viewed in any other
light than as executing the task assigned by that
body.

"After these remarks, which are never to be interpreted into any dereliction of the French cause, I
must observe to you that they are made principally
to recommend caution, lest we should be obliged at
some time or other to explain away or disavow an
excess of fervor, so as to reduce it down to the cool
system of neutrality.   You have it still in charge to
cultivate the French Republic with zeal, but without
any unnecessary *éclat;* because the dictates of sin-
cerity do not demand that we should render notorious
all our feelings in favor of that nation."

A little later Randolph took a more conciliatory tone, and Monroe believed that he would never have spoken so severely if all the dispatches had reached him in due order.

Early in his residence the American minister was involved in a discussion with respect to Mr. Morris's passports, of so delicate a character that the story was privately communicated by Monroe to Washington.[1] This letter illustrates the delays of correspondence, for it is dated November 18, and acknowledges Washington's of June 25, "which would have been answered sooner if any safe opportunity had offered for Bordeaux, from whence vessels most frequently sail for America." Such delays had a significant bearing upon the continuous misunderstandings between the administration and its distant representative.[2] Monroe was also engaged in a complex correspondence with reference to the release of Lafayette from imprisonment at Olmütz, and concerning pecuniary assistance to Madame Lafayette, in whose release he was instrumental. In the "Household Life of the Lafayettes," by Edith Sichel,

[1] Gouverneur MSS.

[2] On February 15, 1795, the secretary of state acknowledges Monroe's last date, September 15, 1794, which had been received November 27. Monroe's dispatches of August 11 and 25 were received between December 2 and 5.

the particulars respecting the imprisonment of
these noble people are given.   Many of our vessels had been seized and condemned with their
cargoes, and hundreds of our citizens were then
in Paris and the seaports of France, many of
them imprisoned, and all treated like enemies.
This involved the American minister in weighty
responsibilities, and employed his utmost energy.
His effort to secure the release of Thomas Paine
from imprisonment was another noteworthy transaction, to which frequent reference was made
in subsequent days, both by friends and opponents.   " Mr. Paine," he wrote, September 15,
1795, " has lived in my house for about ten
months past.   He was, upon my arrival, confined
in the Luxembourg, and released on my application ; after which, being sick, he has remained with me. . . . The symptoms have become worse, and the prospect now is that he
will not be able to hold out more than a month
or two at the farthest.   I shall certainly pay
the utmost attention to this gentleman, as he is
one of those whose merits in our Revolution
were most distinguished."

It was not long before Monroe became entangled in a much more serious complication.   A
treaty with Great Britain had been negotiated
by Jay ; so much as this was positively known
in Paris near the close of 1794, and more was

inferred in respect to it. Citizen Merlin de Douai, the one who gave Monroe the *accolade* a few months before, and four of his associates in the Committee of Public Safety demanded a copy of the treaty. This was their letter, December 27, 1794 : —

" We are informed, Citizen, that there was lately concluded at London a treaty of alliance and commerce between the British government and Citizen Jay, Envoy Extraordinary of the United States.

" A vague report spreads itself abroad that in this treaty the Citizen Jay has forgotten those things which our treaties with the American people, and the sacrifices which the French people made to render them free, gave us a right to expect, on the part of a minister of a nation which we have so many motives to consider as friendly.

" It is important that we know positively in what light we are to hold this affair. There ought not to subsist between two free peoples the dissimulation which belongs to courts ; and it gives us pleasure to declare that we consider you as much opposed, personally, to that kind of policy as we are ourselves.

" We invite you, then, to communicate to us as soon as possible the treaty whereof there is question. It is the only means whereby you can enable the French nation justly to appreciate those reports so injurious to the American government, and to which that treaty gave birth."

In reply to this and other demands for exact

information Monroe pleaded ignorance, and he refused to receive from Jay confidential and informal statements in respect to the treaty. He contented himself with general expressions in reference to the purport of the English mission, and with strenuous efforts to allay the French excitement. When the treaty reached him he wrote to Judge Jones: " Jay's treaty surpasses all that I feared, great as my fears were of his mission. Indeed, it is the most shameful transaction I have ever known of the kind." [1]

The language in which he reported to the authorities at home, a few months before, the condition of affairs, is this, January 13, 1795: —

" After my late communications to the Committee of Public Safety, in which were exposed freely the object of Mr. Jay's mission to England, and the real situation of the United States with Britain and Spain, I had reason to believe that all apprehension on those points was done away, and that the utmost cordiality had now likewise taken place in that body towards us. I considered the report above recited, and upon which the decree was founded, as the unequivocal proof of that change of sentiment, and flattered myself that, in every respect, we had now the best prospect of the most perfect and permanent harmony between the two republics. I am very sorry, however, to add, that latterly this prospect has been somewhat clouded by accounts from England, that

[1] Gouverneur MSS.

Mr. Jay had not only adjusted the points in controversy, but concluded a treaty of commerce with that government. Some of those accounts state that he had also concluded a treaty of alliance, offensive and defensive. As I knew the baneful effect which these reports would produce, I deemed it my duty, by repeating what I had said before of his powers, to use my utmost endeavors, informally, to discredit them. This, however, did not arrest the progress of the report, nor remove the disquietude it had created, for I was finally applied to, directly, by the committee, in a letter, which stated what had been heard, and requested information of what I knew in regard to it. As I had just before received one from Mr. Jay, announcing that he had concluded a treaty, and which contained a declaration that our previous treaties should not be affected by it, I thought fit to make this letter the basis of my reply. And as it is necessary that you should be apprised of whatever has passed here on this subject, I now transmit to you copies of these several papers, and which comprise a full statement thereof, up to the present time.

" I cannot admit, for a moment, that Mr. Jay has exceeded his powers, or that anything has been done which will give just cause of complaint to this republic. I lament, however, that he has not thought himself at liberty to give me correct information on that subject ; for until it is known that their interest has not been wounded, the report will certainly keep alive suspicion, and which always weakens the bonds of friendship. I trust, therefore, you will deem it expedient to advise me on this head as soon as possible."

The irritation of the French, when at length they discovered the actual purport of Jay's treaty, was very great. In February, 1796, it appeared that the Directory considered the alliance between France and the United States as ceasing to exist from the moment the treaty was ratified, and intended to send a special envoy to the United States in order to express their extreme dissatisfaction. Monroe succeeded in changing their purpose, and elicited from M. de la Croix, the foreign minister, a summary, in three headings, of the French complaints, to which he sent an elaborate reply. The two countries had come to the very verge of war. But the administration at home was angry with the envoy for not having endeavored more strenuously to allay the apprehensions of France, and for failing to avert the impending danger.

During the progress of these events, the portfolio of foreign affairs had been given up by Randolph, and taken up by Pickering, who began his correspondence September 12, 1795, by acknowledging a series of letters, of which the first was written ten months before. Monroe gained nothing by this change in the councils at home. Randolph's censures were mild in com-

parison with those which his successor bestowed
on the unfortunate envoy. One of the severest
of his letters is that of June 13, 1796, in which
he complains that Monroe failed to make a suitable vindication of the United States government at a time when the justice, the faith, and
the honor of our country were questioned, and
the most important interests were at stake. This
is followed a short time afterwards by a notifica-
tion that he is superseded by C. C. Pinckney.

On his arrival in Paris, Pinckney was presented by Monroe to the minister of foreign
affairs, but was refused recognition by the Directory, and was not permitted to remain in
Paris. Mr. Ticknor has recorded a conversation
with Baron Pichon to this effect: — that Paine
lived in Monroe's house at Paris, and had a
great deal too much influence over him; that
Monroe's insinuations, and representations of
General Pinckney's character as an aristocrat,
prevented his reception as minister by the Directory; and that, in general, Monroe, with whose
negotiations and affairs Pichon was specially
charged, acted as a party Democrat against the
interests of General Washington's administration, and against what Pichon considered the
interests of the United States.[1] On the other
hand, we have Pinckney's assertion, that during

[1] *Life of George Ticknor*, ii. 113.

his brief residence he saw Monroe frequently, and found him open and candid, and disposed to make every communication which would be of service to our country. It should also be said that Monroe was treated with coolness by the French government some time before his recall, though the civilities to him were renewed when his return to America was evidently at hand.

The ceremony of flag presentation was repeated in this country. A French flag, sent across the water, was received by Congress near New Year's Day in 1796.

" A mighty foolish ceremony it was," writes the Federalist already quoted.[1] " It may, however, have the good effect of quieting the minds of some people who are afraid that the French are very angry about our treaty with Great Britain ; that nation is said to have been long famed for their address in meddling with the politics of foreign nations, and they have supported well the character in this country, but I hope we shall keep clear of their influence. The administrators of our government have no British attachment, but wish to keep clear of all foreign politics, and but for the madness of party I think the people of the United States would universally see and approve the policy. The treaty with Great Britain was necessary to settle existing disputes, in its most important articles ; the commercial part of it is ex-

[1] Joshua Coit, January 5, 1796.

perimental, and throws no restraint on our commerce
with other nations, has no tendency to form political
connections, and I believe secures important advantages to us."

Monroe's recall was dated August 22. Men-
tioning this fact to Joseph Jones, he intimated
that the letter was probably kept back to prevent his arrival before the elections. " I shall
decline a winter passage," he added, " and therefore most probably shall not embark till April
or May." [1] He reached home full of wrath,
but the opposition party gave him a cordial
greeting, and he was entertained in Philadelphia at a public dinner where Jefferson, the
Vice-President, Dayton, the Speaker, Chief Justice McKean, and other conspicuous men were
present. Monroe's failure, it is clear, was not
personal, it was a party failure. His hand
was soon turned against the administration of
Adams. He demanded of Pickering the reasons of his recall, and drew from the secretary,
who was not at all afraid of saying what he
thought, a very explicit response. Washington,
in a note to Pickering (Mt. Vernon, August
29, 1797), mentioned that Colonel Monroe had
passed through Alexandria, but did not honor
him with a call.

The envoy's neglect did not mean silence.

[1] Gouverneur MSS.

He soon published a pamphlet of five hundred pages, entitled, " A View of the Conduct of the Executive," in which he printed his instructions, correspondence with the French and United States governments, speeches, and letters received from Americans resident in Paris. It remains to this day a most extraordinary volume, full of entertaining and instructive lessons to young diplomatists. Washington, retired from public life, appears to have kept quiet under strong provocation; but he sent a letter upon the subject to John Nicholas, and in his copy of the " View " he wrote his animadversions, paragraph by paragraph. These notes, long suppressed, were at length given to the world by Sparks.[1]

Monroe enumerates the following points, which, taken collectively, are to show his diplomatic position and the attitude of the administration toward him. He mentions : —

1. The appointment of Gouverneur Morris, a known enemy of the French Revolution.

2. His continuance in office till troubles came.

3. His removal at the demand of the French government.

4. The subsequent appointment of Monroe, an opponent of the administration, especially in its foreign policy.

---

[1] *Washington's Writings*, vol. x. pp. 226, 504.

5. The instructions given to Monroe as to the explanation he should give the French in respect to Jay's mission, which concealed the power given him to form a commercial treaty.

6. The strong expressions of attachment to France and the principles of the French Revolution given to Monroe.

7. The resentment of the administration when these documents were made public.

8. The approval of Monroe's endeavor to secure a repeal of the obnoxious decrees, and the silence which followed their repeal.

9. Jay's power to form a commercial treaty with England, without corresponding advances to France.

10. The withholding from Monroe of the contents of the treaty, an evidence of unfair dealing.

11. The submission of this treaty to M. Adet, after the advice of the Senate, and before its ratification by the President.

12. The character of Jay's treaty, which departs from the modern rule of contraband, and yields the principle, " Free ships shall make free goods."

13. The irritable bearing of the administration toward France, after the ratification, in contrast with its bearing toward England, when it was proposed to decline the ratification.

14. Monroe's recall, just when he had succeeded in quieting the French government for the time, and was likely to do so effectually.

I have not been able to trace Washington's copy of the " View " which, according to Sparks, was given to a distinguished jurist; but in the library of Cornell University Sparks's transcript of Washington's notes is preserved. In this are the notes of Washington, hitherto not printed, on Monroe's appendix. By the permission of the authorities, I am able to print upon a subsequent page these fresh annotations.[1] Here three examples only will be given. Monroe, in a dispatch, February 12, 1795, having spoken of the danger of war with France, inquires: What course then was I to pursue? The note of Washington is this: " As nothing but justice and the fulfillment of a contract was asked, it dictated firmness conducted with temperance in the pursuit of it." Monroe: " The doors of the Committee [of Public Safety] were closed against me." Washington: " This appears nowhere but in his own conjectures." Again, incidentally, Washington writes: " The truth is, Mr. Monroe was cajoled, flattered, and made to believe strange things. In return he did, or was disposed to do, whatever was pleasing to that nation, reluctantly urging the rights of his own."

[1] See Appendix.

A war of pamphlets and newspaper articles followed the publication of the " View," in which Federalists and Republicans damaged each other's reputations as much as they could.

Party feeling was ablaze before Monroe published his book, but the flames rose fiercely when it appeared. Oliver Wolcott wrote to Washington that it was a wicked misrepresentation of facts; that the author's conduct was detested by all *good* men, though he was sorry to say that many applauded it. As to Washington's character and administration, he was sure that the " View" would make no impression beyond the circle of Tom Paine's admirers. John Adams wrote that he was hurt at the levity of the Americans in Paris. Fisher Ames's satirical touch is seen in a letter to Christopher Gore, written after the election of Jefferson, where he says, " Monroe will, if he likes, return to France to embrace liberty again."

From another section of the Federalists this opinion comes. Harper of South Carolina, in a speech on the Foreign Intercourse Bill, speaking of the " View," remarks : —

" In this book is to be found the most complete justification of the Executive for his recall, in every respect except that it was so long delayed ; for the book contains the most singular display of incapacity, unfaithfulness, and presumption, of neglect of orders, forgetfulness of the dignity, rights, and interests of his own country, and servile devotedness to the government of the country to which he was sent, that can be found in the history of diplomacy."

He even intimates that Monroe was influenced by bribery. But this was going quite too far. The historian Hildreth, who is not less severe than the most severe critic yet quoted, in his estimate of Monroe repudiates the insinuation of Harper. "These gross insinuations," he says, "were totally baseless. The time had not yet come when American statesmen were to be purchased for money. How perfectly sincere Monroe was in his opinions is manifest throughout the whole correspondence, which no purchased tool of France, none but a man blinded by enthusiastic passion, could ever have written, and still less would have published. Nor were such views at all confined to Monroe. They were shared by most of the leaders and by the great mass of the opposition party." These are the words of the Federalist historian, half a century after the "View" appeared.[1]

Some extracts should also be given from the writings of Monroe's friends. For example, Edward Church wrote from Lisbon, December 24, 1796, "My ideas of the importance of observing inviolate our friendship and alliance with

Hildreth's *United States, Second Series*, ii. 101.

the French nation go far beyond yours, as I conceive the connection essentially necessary to our preservation as independent states, it being evidently our best, if not our only security against the danger of becoming once more the poor, pitiful, servile, dependent slaves of Britain." [1]

The wrath of another of Monroe's correspondents, in Paris, found expression in these terms : —

"Were I able to draw the contrast, which the subject so richly deserves, between this extraordinary man's military exit and that of the late idolized statute [*sic*] of the people of my country, I would so paint Mr. Washington on his milk-white steed, receiving the incense of all the little girls on Trenton Bridge, and then I would march him about in the streets of Boston, so like a roasted ox that I once saw carried a whole day in triumph by the people of that famous town, that the automaton chief should groan and sweat under the weight of those laurels, which are momently dropping from his brows into the sink and dirt of his puny and anti-republican administration." [2]

There is a significant paragraph in Thiers's " History of the French Revolution," which may be regarded, I think, as showing the impression

[1] Gouverneur MSS.
[2] Gouverneur MSS.   May 15, 1797.

which Monroe made upon the people to whom
he was accredited : —

" In the French government there were persons in
favor of a rupture with the United States.   Monroe,
who was ambassador to Paris, gave the Directory
the most prudent advice on this occasion.   War with
France, said he, will force the American government
to throw itself into the arms of England and to sub-
mit to her influence ; aristocracy will gain supreme
control in the United States, and liberty will be com-
promised.   By patiently enduring, on the contrary,
the wrongs of the present President, you will leave
him without excuse, you will enlighten the Americans,
and decide a contrary choice at the next election.
All the wrongs of which France may have to complain will then be repaired.   This wise and provident
advice had its effect upon the Directory.   Rewbell,
Barras, and Laréveillère had caused it to be adopted
in opposition to the opinion of the systematic Carnot,
who, though in general favorably disposed to peace,
insisted on the cession of Louisiana, with a view to
attempt the establishment of a republic there."

In addition to this diplomatic controversy,
Monroe was involved in another more personal
collision with Hamilton, occasioned by the Callender publication,[1] — but into the details of
this disagreeable story I see no reason for entering now.

[1] " An undigested and garrulous collection of libels."   *Hildreth, Second Series*, ii. 104.

Monroe was much displeased by the publication of that part of his dispatches which related to the Jacobins, and thus wrote to Judge Jones, June 20, 1795 : —

"The publication of extracts from my letters respecting the Jacobins was an unbecoming and uncandid thing, as they were the only parts of my correspondence that were published. I stated the truth, and therefore am not dissatisfied with the publication in that respect. But to me it appears strange that the fortunes of that misguided club should be the only subject treated in my correspondence upon which it was necessary to convey the information it could to our countrymen. Certainly, in relation to the honor and welfare of my country, it was the least important of all the subjects upon which I treated. Besides, that club was as unlike the patriotic societies in America as light is to darkness, the former being a society that had absolutely annihilated all other government in France, and whose denunciations carried immediately any of the deputies to the scaffold, whereas the latter are societies of enlightened men, who discuss measures and principles, and of course whose opinions have no other weight than as they are well founded and have reason on their side, to extirpate which is to extirpate liberty itself."

During all his exciting residence in Paris, it is interesting to trace the minute interest maintained by Monroe in whatever pertained to his domestic affairs. There are long letters in the

Gouverneur collection devoted to his financial business, to the welfare of his brothers, Andrew and Joseph, and of his sister, to his land bought near Monticello, his servants, fruit-trees, etc., besides many a passage in regard to his nephew Joseph, who was at school at St. Germain, and young Rutledge, likewise placed under the envoy's paternal care. His interest in the progress of these American boys in their French school betrays an unvarying kindness of heart in the midst of pressing anxieties and cares.

Times change. Five years after Monroe's recall, Jefferson writes: [1] " We have ever looked to France as our natural friend, one with whom we could never have an occasion of difference; but there is one spot on the globe, the possessor of which is our natural enemy. That spot is New Orleans. France placing herself in that door assumes to us the attitude of defiance. . . . From that moment we must marry ourselves to the British fleet and nation."

[1] To Livingston, April 18, 1802.

CHAPTER IV

ENVOY IN FRANCE, SPAIN, AND ENGLAND

JEFFERSON, never wanting in interest when Monroe's affairs required counsel, and trusting him implicitly, wrote to the despondent and angry envoy that he ought to come forward again into public life. " Come to Congress," was his advice, as if coming to Congress was an act of the will, — " reappear on the public theatre ; Cabel has said he would give way to you." [1] But instead of entering at once into national affairs, Monroe became governor of Virginia, and held the office three years. Jefferson, meanwhile, had become President, and soon had an opportunity to return Monroe to the legation in France. The story of this second embassy includes the purchase of Louisiana, and has therefore been examined over and over again by those who are interested in the growth of our national territory.

In addition to the usual publication of the correspondence of the times, much reliance is

[1] Letter to Monroe, May 21, 1798. *Jefferson*, iv. 241–243.

placed on the volume by Barbé Marbois, in
which he reports his interviews with Bonaparte.
The English translation of this work is attributed to William Beach Lawrence;[1] its
appendix omits some statements which are
given in the original French. Among the
manuscripts of Monroe I have met with this
remark: — "The work of Marbois is written in a
spirit of great candor, and with friendly feeling
for me, but he is mistaken in some facts which
I have documents to show."[2]

The importance of the outlet of the Mississippi to the inhabitants of the great valley of
the West was always obvious. As early as
1784 Monroe had written in regard to it, and
in his first mission to France, as we have seen,
he had been instructed to press the claims of
the United States.

In the spring of 1801 intelligence reached
this country that Spain had ceded her rights in
Louisiana to France, and the next year the
Spanish intendant gave notice that New Orleans would no longer be a "place of deposit."[3]
Jefferson communicated this highly significant
information to Congress when it assembled
in December. There was great excitement
through the country, especially in the West,

[1] C. F. Hart, in *Penn Monthly*.   [2] May 29, 1829.
[3] October 16, 1802.

and one newspaper, at least, raised the cry of disunion.

The conclusion was quickly reached, to purchase from France, if possible, the outlet to the Gulf of Mexico. Congress appropriated the sum of two million dollars for this object; and Jefferson selected Monroe to go as a special minister and act with Livingston, our resident representative at Paris, in an endeavor to secure the coveted domain. Almost simultaneously Lewis and Clarke were recommended for the exploration of the upper Mississippi. Monroe accordingly went upon his embassy, and within a month after his arrival was able, with his colleague, to report the purchase of Louisiana. The treaty was ratified by Bonaparte in May, 1803, and by the Senate of the United States in the next October.

It is not always that the interior history of a great international bargain is so fully revealed to the public as it is in the present case, and Monroe's relation to it must now be more carefully considered.

The interests of four nations were closely involved in this transaction: Spain, who had promised to yield her rights in Louisiana, but retained her control of the Floridas, and had not, according to Talleyrand's statements, quite perfected the transfer; England, in a hostile

attitude toward France, and not unlikely at any
time to make a descent upon a portion of her
territory; France, in anxious expectation of an
outbreak of hostilities, in want of money, and
predisposed to build up in America a power
which should rival England; and the United
States, eager to secure the maritime outlet of
its great river system, and almost inclined to
seize it by force.

Six individuals were conspicuous in the negotiation. On the American side were Jefferson,
once minister to France, now sixty years old
and half way through his first presidential term,
whose sagacity recognized the importance of
securing Louisiana, and initiated the purchase;
R. R. Livingston, two years younger, who had
been for two years resident as the American
minister in France, who had been pressing
the American claim to be indemnified for the
French spoliations, and had brought the government to consider the possibility of ceding
the desired territory; and Monroe, forty-five
years old, whose former residence in Paris was
not forgotten, and who entered upon his second
diplomatic mission fresh from the instructions
of Jefferson and Madison, and from the inspira-
tion of popular enthusiasm with respect to the
acquisition which he was sent to secure. On
the French side stood Bonaparte, the youngest

of the group, thirty-five years old, then First
Consul, and in the flush of his military and
civil power; Talleyrand, a man of forty-nine
years, holding the portfolio of foreign affairs,
not wholly trusted by the Consul, but well qual-
ified by his skill in diplomacy and by his acquaintance with the United States to take a
part in the business; and Marbois, about the
age of Livingston, who had held a diplomatic
position in America, and who was now the minister of the treasury, enjoying the confidence of
Bonaparte, and called by him to be leader in
this negotiation. In his history of this transaction, Marbois attributes its rapid and feli-
citous progress to the fact that the plenipotentiaries had been long acquainted, and were
disposed to treat one another with mutual confidence.

Livingston, as soon as he heard of Monroe's
arrival in Havre, sent him the following letter
of welcome, written in a tone of despondency:—

"10th April, 1803.

"I congratulate you on your safe arrival. We
have long and anxiously waited for you. God grant
that your mission may answer your and the public
expectation. War may do something for us; nothing
else would. I have paved the way for you, and if
you could add to my memoirs an assurance that we
were now in possession of New Orleans, we should

do well; but I detain Mr. Bentalou, who is impatient to fly to the arms of his wife. I have apprised the minister of your arrival, and told him you would be here on Tuesday or Wednesday."

It so happened that on this very day, April 10, after the solemnities of Easter Sunday, Bonaparte discussed with Talleyrand and Marbois the Louisiana question. They were divided in counsel; the conference was prolonged into the night, and the ministers remained at St. Cloud. At daybreak Bonaparte, having already received alarming dispatches from England, summoned Marbois, who had advised the cession, and said to him in substance : " I renounce Louisiana. Negotiate for its cession. Don't wait for Monroe. I want fifty million francs; for less I will not treat. Acquaint me day by day, hour by hour, with your progress. Keep Talleyrand informed." Armed with these instructions, Marbois sought Livingston. Before they met, Talleyrand had been unsuccessfully endeavoring to reach some point of agreement. He had asked Livingston if the United States wished for the whole of Louisiana. The answer had been No; but that it would be politic in France to give it up. The price to be paid was the matter in question.

At this juncture Monroe reached Paris. He heard with surprise from Livingston of the readiness of the French to sell the territory, and the two envoys proceeded to discuss the price which they could venture to promise. While Monroe was taking his first dinner with Livingston, in company with other American gentlemen, Marbois appeared in the garden and presently joined the party. Before leaving he led Livingston into a free conference upon the cession, and invited him to continue the talk at a later hour after the company had dispersed. Livingston went to the house of Marbois, and stayed there till midnight. The whole country of Louisiana was then offered to the United States for one hundred million francs, and the claims. Livingston pronounced it an exorbitant price, and Marbois did not deny that it was. No conclusion could be reached without consulting Monroe; but Livingston, without waiting to do so, sat up until three o'clock and wrote a midnight dispatch to Madison, narrating the interview with Marbois, and saying that he was sure the purchase was wise. He also made a suggestion, which in these days is astounding, that if the price is too high, the outlay may be reimbursed by the " sale of the territory west of the Mississippi, with the right of sovereignty, to some Power in Europe, whose vicinity we should not fear." [1] This is not precisely in

[1] *State Papers*, ii. 554.

accordance with what was afterwards known as the Monroe doctrine.

From this time on, Talleyrand was not conspicuous in the scenes, though it is more than possible that behind them his hand was at work, perhaps obstructively. At any rate, for one reason or another, he delayed the presentation of Monroe to Bonaparte until May 1, and even then failed to be personally present, leaving to Livingston the ceremonious duty of naming his colleague. Probably he was annoyed that the First Consul agreed with Marbois, and had given to him the authority to proceed with the Louisiana negotiation.

Livingston and Monroe, after reviewing the situation, made up their minds that they could give fifty millions, and, in the bargaining spirit which governed both sides, offered forty millions, one half to be returned to American claimants. Marbois expressed his regret that they could not give more, and proposed to consult the Consul. He came back from St. Cloud, saying that the business might be considered as no longer in his hands, so coolly had Bonaparte received their proposition. He advised that some pressure be brought to bear upon Talleyrand in order to secure the early presentation of Monroe. Later in the day Marbois came in to a dinner which Cambacérès was giving, and told the American envoys that if the Consul did not reopen the question they might consider the plan relinquished. They quickly proceeded to offer fifty millions. Marbois doubted whether this would be accepted. Here came a significant pause lasting for several days. "We were resting on our oars," says one of the negotiators.

On April 17 Bonaparte made an official announcement to the Pope and others that, in consequence of England's violation of the Peace of Amiens, France was involved in war with her. It is easy to see the bearing of this on the American negotiations. Ten days later Marbois laid before Livingston and Monroe the draft of a treaty given him by the government,[1] and another which was his own. In the latter he proposed as the price eighty million francs, which was to include the sum requisite for the American claimants. Our envoys offered fifty millions, with twenty more for the claimants, but at last acceded to the figures of Marbois.

This concluded the business. Marbois tells us that when Bonaparte heard what sum had been agreed upon, he received the intelligence

[1] In the *Correspondance de Napoléon*, vol. viii., the *projet* of a secret convention between France and the United States is printed (without signature), dated April 23, 1803, from the *Archives de France.*

with opposition. He had forgotten, or he
feigned to forget, his original willingness to sell
for fifty millions, and he objected to the allowance of twenty millions to the American suitors;
but he soon grew calmer and acquiesced in the
cession. " I have given to England," he said
exultingly, " a maritime rival which will sooner
or later humble her pride." Some details were
worked out in respect to the mode of payment;
Monroe's presentation to the Consul soon followed; and at length, May 2, the plenipotentiaries signed the French copy of the treaty,
and two or three days later the copy in English.
On the thirteenth of the month a ratified copy
was transmitted to Madison. Two conventions
proceeded from the treaty of cession, the first in
respect to the mode of payment for the cession ;
the second in respect to American claims.

As soon as they had signed the treaty the
plenipotentiaries rose and shook hands, when
Livingston said, expressing the general satisfaction, " We have lived long, but this is the
noblest work of our whole lives." [1] This har-

---

[1] His speech as reported by Marbois, p. 310, is full of interest. The Mémoires of Lucien Bonaparte contain many
interesting particulars of the negotiation. The whole story of
the Louisiana purchase and the discussions to which it led is
told with admirable vivacity and with ample details in the
*History of the United States under the First Administration of
Jefferson*, by Henry Adams, vol. ii.

monious conclusion was not reached without
some personal rivalry — if jealousy is too harsh
a term to be employed — between the American
representatives; and there is a long letter still
extant in which Monroe recounts the embarrassments of the situation arising from the conduct
of his colleague. But their personal feelings
were fortunately kept in the background until
the business was concluded, although they may
be incidentally traced in their public and official
correspondence.[1]

On May 21 Marbois received the following
letter of acknowledgment:[2] —

"Sur les 240,000 francs, Citoyen Ministre, que
doivent les six banquiers du trésor public, 48,000
francs seront donnés en gratification, conformément
à ma lettre de ce jour; 192,000 francs seront à
votre disposition pour suppléer à l'insuffisance de
votre traitement, ayant l'intention que vous voyiez
dans cette disposition le désir que j'ai de vous té-
moigner ma satisfaction de vos travaux importants et
du bon ordre que vous avez mis dans votre ministère,
qui ont valu à la République un grand nombre de
millions.   BONAPARTE."

Monroe took leave of Bonaparte June 24,
having been presented to him for this purpose

[1] Monroe MSS.
[2] *Correspondance de Napoléon Ier*, An XI. (1803).

by Talleyrand at St. Cloud. The First Consul asked if he were about going to London, and Monroe replied that he had lately received the orders of the President, in case our affairs here were amicably adjusted, to repair to London; that the resignation of our minister there, and the want of a *chargé*, made it necessary to go at once. He then gave a formal expression of American good-will; to which Bonaparte replied that "no one wished more than himself the preservation of a good understanding; that the cession he had made was not so much on account of the price given as from motives of policy; and that he wished for friendship between the republics."[1]

In the progress of this affair the French had promised the Americans to exert their good influences with Spain to induce her to yield the Floridas, — the limit separating these possessions from Louisiana being then in dispute. Monroe, as soon as the Louisiana purchase was completed, determined to go to Madrid and treat for the Floridas, but Cambacérès, who heard him say this one day at dinner, almost forbade him, for reasons which were not quite easy to be discovered. He accordingly called on the Spanish minister, and there to his surprise he found that Livingston had already begun that

[1] Monroe MSS.

negotiation with Spain which Monroe had been especially charged to undertake. This led to serious explanations between the two American envoys. Monroe postponed his visit to Spain and went to London. He had left the United States accredited to France, Spain and England, — the commission to the Court of St. James having been an afterthought, and dated three months later.

As a sequel to this narrative, the following letter to Marbois from Monroe will be read with interest:[1] —

"LONDON, *February* 14, 1804.

"My last letter from the secretary of state (of December 26) mentioned that Louisiana was surrendered to the Prefect of France the latter end of November, who was to transfer it to the commissioners of the United States on their arrival at New Orleans, which was expected in a day or two from that date. Mr. Madison adds that he considers all difficulties on that subject as happily terminated. Mr. B. is expected here daily with everything belonging to a complete execution of this transaction. In the mean time I am persuaded that the house in Holland will consider it as concluded and act accordingly.

"It gives me pleasure to observe that the prompt and unconditional exchange of ratifications by your *chargé d'affaires* at Washington, and his correct conduct in promoting the transfer of the territory of the

United States, in obedience to the orders of his government, are unequivocal proofs of the good faith with which the treaties were formed. The manner in which the President expressed himself in his message to Congress of the enlarged liberty and friendly policy which governed the First Consul in the transaction, shows in strong terms the sense which he entertains of it. May it seal forever the friendship of the two nations. To have been in any degree instrumental to that important result is one of the circumstances of my life which will always give me the highest satisfaction. In society with my respectable colleague, to have met an old friend on the other side, who had experienced, as well as myself, some vicissitudes in the extraordinary movements of the epoch in which we live, is an incident which adds not a little to the gratification which I derive from the event.

"You have doubtless heard that Jerome Bonaparte is married to Miss Patterson of Baltimore. Her father is one of the most respectable citizens of that town or rather of the State of Maryland. Her mother is a sister of General Smith, a member of the Senate of the United States, the officer who defended Mud Island below Philadelphia in our Revolution. The connection is every way as respectable as he could have formed in the United States. The young lady is amiable, very handsome, and perfectly innocent. The bearer of this is her brother, who goes to Paris from this place, to carry a letter from Jerome to the First Consul, which was transmitted

to me by her father. As he has also written to Mr.
Livingston, I inclose to him the letter to the First
Consul, as he might expect that the communication
should be made through him. Nevertheless, I have
taken the liberty to present to you the young man,
and apprise you of the above facts, in confidence that
you will make such friendly representations of the
affair as you may find necessary."

The letter concludes with messages of private
friendship.

Livingston was never quite at his ease in respect to Monroe. He naturally felt some cha-
grin in not being allowed to conclude, without
the support of a fresh colleague, the negotiation
he had undertaken, and he was careful not to
yield any of his own prerogatives or to conceal
his own services. The apprehensions under
which he opened his correspondence with Monroe, on the latter's arrival in Havre, he subsequently explained as due to the dissimulations
of Talleyrand. These were his explanations to
Madison : [1] —

"I have in my former letter informed you of M.
Talleyrand's calling upon me, previous to the arrival
of Mr. Monroe, for a proposition for the whole of
Louisiana ; of his afterwards trifling with me, and
telling me *that what he said was unauthorize l*.
This circumstance, for which I have accounted to

[1] November 15, 1803.

you in one of my letters, led me to think, though it
afterwards appeared without reason, that some change
had taken place in the determination which I knew
the Consul had before taken to sell. I had just then
received a line from Mr. Monroe, informing me of
his arrival. I wrote to him a hasty answer, under
the influence of ideas excited by these prevarications
of the minister, expressing the hope that he had
brought information that New Orleans was in our
possession; that I hoped our negotiation might be
successful; but that, while I feared nothing but war
would avail us anything, I had paved the way for
him. This letter is very imprudently shown and
spoken of by Mr. Monroe's particular friends as a
proof that he had been the principal agent in the
negotiation. So far, indeed, as it may tend to this
object, it is of little moment, because facts and dates
are too well known to be contradicted. For instance,
it is known to everybody here that the Consul had
taken his resolution to sell previous to Mr. Monroe's
arrival. It is a fact well known that M. Marbois
was authorized, informally, by the First Consul, to
treat with me, before Mr. Monroe reached Paris;
that he actually made me the very proposition we
ultimately agreed to, before Mr. Monroe had seen a
minister, except M. Marbois, for a moment, at my
house, where he came to make the proposition, Mr.
Monroe not having been presented to M. Talleyrand,
to whom I introduced him the afternoon of the next
day. All, then, that remained to negotiate, after his
arrival, was a diminution of the price, and in this

our joint mission was unfortunate; for we came up, as soon as Mr. Monroe's illness would suffer him to do business, after a few days delay, to the minister's offers. There is no doubt that Mr. Monroe's talents and address would have enabled him, had he been placed in my circumstances, to have effected what I have done. But he, unfortunately, came too late to do more than assent to the propositions that were made us, and to aid in reducing them to form. I think he has too much candor not to be displeased that his friends should publicly endeavor to depreciate me by speaking of a private letter, hastily written, under circumstances of irritation with which Mr. Monroe is fully acquainted; a letter, too, which may contribute in two ways to advance the views of the enemies of the administration. It is in this light only that it gives me pain."

In looking over this extraordinary chapter in history, which records probably the largest transaction in real estate which the world has ever known, it is interesting to trace the concurrence of so many factors. The ambition of Napoleon, the sagacity of Jefferson, the diplomacy of Talleyrand and Marbois, the caution of Livingston, the enthusiasm of Monroe, were all manifested in the sale of a part of the North American continent, the boundaries of which were uncertain, the title insecure, and the price incapable of being determined by any market standard nearer than " the cost of Etruria,"

which was the price of the cession of Louisiana
by Spain. Yet back of these personal influences were great ideas controlling the action of
vigorous nations; there was the English determination to put down the rising dominion of
Napoleon; there was the willingness of Spain
to give up New Orleans; there was the American resolution to secure, by diplomacy or by
force, the Mississippi outlet; there was the readiness of France to prevent the seizure of New
Orleans by the English, and to build up in the
new world a powerful rival to Great Britain.
France was enough involved with financial difficulties to need money; the United States, by a
wise financial policy, was in good credit at Am-
sterdam; and so, when the price had been fixed,
there was no trouble about payment, and no
delay in the transfer.

Nobody could foretell the momentous consequences which would proceed from this sale.
Bonaparte thought that two or three hundred
years later American influence might be over-
powering, a contingency so remote that even his
aspirations were not affected by it; and Jefferson was far-seeing enough to devise an explor-
ing expedition which should proceed to the extreme Northwest and report with as much
precision as the science of the day would permit
in respect to the sources of the great rivers.

But this was all.   Beyond the Mississippi was a land unknown.   The Americans did not ask for it, and Livingston comforted himself with the thought that perhaps a part of it could be resold ; France pressed its purchase on those who were only asking for New Orleans and the Floridas.   By this marvelous combination of circumstances Louisiana, including the far Northwest, became ours.

The subsequent history of the United States has been closely connected with this famous acquisition.   The Missouri compromise, the annexation of Texas, the northwestern boundary disputes, the acquisition of California and of the northern provinces of Mexico, the discovery of gold and silver, the Nebraska bill, the Mormon difficulty, the Indian policy, the Alaska purchase, the Pacific railroads, the isthmus canal question, the Chinese immigration, — who can say that any one of these controversies and events would ever have come to the front if Spain, or France, or Great Britain had remained in control of that half of our domain which lies beyond the Mississippi?

Among the concurrent circumstances there is none so extraordinary to us who are accustomed to constitutional limitations, as the arbitrary power then held in France by one who was still a young man, and who, a few years previous, — at the beginning, let us say, of Monroe's first mission, — was comparatively unknown, and without the slightest prescience of his coming authority. The memoirs of Marbois, Livingston and Monroe, and the correspondence of Napoleon, do not give any indication that the First Consul, in this far-reaching exercise of his authority, was guided by the opinion of a cabinet or council, or restricted by any fundamental law. He speaks to Marbois in the singular number, like the owner of a house or farm, as if he were, indeed, the personification of France. He does, it is true, consult two ministers of state, but he turns abruptly away from the advice of one of them, and to the other he gives directions as positive and arbitrary as if he were directing a broker to sell a cargo. The mighty deeds of Napoleon's sword have been undone, but the stroke of his pen wrought a change which now, after fourscore years have passed, is no more liable to counterchange than the Mississippi is to flow into the lakes.

Soon after Monroe's arrival in England he received from Madison, the secretary of state, the plan of a convention to be proposed to the British government, with particular reference to our maritime rights. We had suffered so much from impressment of seamen, blockade, and the search of our vessels, that it was quite time to insist on the national claims. Early in April, 1804, the subject was brought to the attention of Lord Hawkesbury; but before any response was received Addington had yielded the leadership to Pitt, and Lord Harrowby had taken the foreign office. He received Monroe in a manner which was fitted to wound and irritate; not a friendly sentiment toward the United States escaped him; and the American minister considered these concerns as postponed indefinitely. Before autumn the foreign minister grew more conciliatory, but no conclusions were reached at the beginning of October, when, by mutual consent, the negotiations were postponed, and Monroe left London on an absence of several months.

Looking forward to a release from the public service, Monroe wrote to Judge Jones from London, May 16, 1804, saying that he should gather a collection of law books and bring them home with a view to continuing the practice of the law. He hoped that thus, with the aid of a farm, he might gain enough to support a family without the aid of other resources. He indicated his strong preference for Richmond and directed the sale of his land above Charlottesville, as it brought no income. He said he could live better on two thousand dollars per year in Richmond than on two thousand pounds

in London. He had thought seriously of accepting the appointment in Louisiana which Madison was willing to give him, though the administration seemed to prefer that he should remain
in London. Jefferson intimated that he might
be sent to Spain. The whole tenor of the letter
is that of one who is longing for repose at home,
suffering from fatigue and poor health abroad,
and in want of sufficient means to maintain
agreeably his diplomatic station.[1]

It will be remembered that he went from the
United States commissioned to Spain as well as
France, but did not continue his journey to
Madrid. In the autumn of 1804 he resumed
the proposed negotiations with Spain, and, as he
went through Paris, solicited from Talleyrand
the French support in his endeavor to secure
from the Spaniards the cession of their possessions to the east of the mouths of the Mississippi. The exact eastern boundary of the
Louisiana Territory already acquired by the
United States was undetermined, and Florida
was wanted. Months previous Napoleon had
pledged his good offices in the promotion of the
plans of the United States; but when they were
now solicited he failed to make the expected
response, although cautiously warned that there
was danger of an immediate rupture between

[1] Gouverneur MSS.

Spain and the United States, which would, indirectly at least, be harmful to France. Monroe and Pinckney accordingly prosecuted their mission as best they could without the French coöperation. From January to May they were in constant negotiation with the Spanish minister, Don Pedro Cevallos, — but it all resulted in nothing and Monroe returned to his residence in London.

Lord Mulgrave was now in the foreign office. New seizures of American vessels by the British gave renewed emphasis to the American complaints, which were met with dilatory and provoking responses. The death of Pitt brought about another change of ministry early in 1806, and the whole story of our demands was presented to the more friendly consideration of Fox, who promised to give his immediate attention to the business and pursue it without delay until it was concluded. But he again encountered obstacles among his colleagues. Meanwhile, as Monroe had been sent to reinforce other ministers, William Pinkney was sent to reinforce Monroe. He had previously been resident in London for a long time, and had pressed to a successful issue the claims of the State of Maryland to some stock in the Bank of England. He had held the office of commissioner under the treaty of 1794. The joint

commission of the two envoys was dated May
17, 1806, and covered a larger field of negotiation and convention than that which had been
intrusted to Monroe alone. Their early communications to Madison contained the same old
story of delay. Fox was now ill beyond the
hope of recovery, and the good offices of his
nephew, Lord Holland, were solicited to secure
an official recognition from the king. Lord
Grenville now assumed the direction of affairs,
and he soon informed the Americans that Lord
Auckland and Lord Holland were appointed as
a special commission to discuss all matters pend-
ing between the two governments. Toward the
end of August, 1806, serious negotiations began
in Downing Street, and as the last day of the
year was reached, these wearisome and complex
deliberations were concluded by a treaty. This
was forwarded to Washington at once by the
hand of Mr. Purviance, but it did not reach Mr.
Jefferson until March 15. Twelve days before,
on March 3, just before the adjournment of
Congress, the President saw a copy of the treaty
which Mr. Erskine, the British minister, had
received.[1]

Long as the negotiations had been, and voluminous as were the results, the treaty failed
in two fundamental points. It made no provi-

[1] J. Q. Adams's *Diary*, i. 466.

sion against the impressment of our seamen;
and it secured no indemnity for losses which
Americans had incurred in the seizure of their
goods and vessels.   Jefferson " pigeon-holed "
it.   He took the responsibility, without sum-
moning the Senate, to withhold his ratification.
When it became evident that this would be the
result, the secretary of state wrote to the commissioners that the President thought it better,
if no satisfactory or formal stipulation on the
subject of impressment were attainable, that the
negotiation should terminate without any formal
compact whatever.   A fresh draft of the American expectations was then drawn up, upon
which the two envoys might renew their negotiations.

In his memoirs of the Whig party Lord
Holland has given a graphic picture of the
American commissioners, and of the attitude of
the English government, which may here be
quoted : —

" Without notice or explanation, an order for detaining all neutrals engaged in such a commerce was
suddenly issued ; and a prodigious number of Americans were brought into our ports by his majesty's
cruisers in the summer and autumn of 1805.   The
principle of these seizures was not likely to be very
readily admitted by any independent power whose
subjects had suffered by the application of it.   The

sudden and peremptory manner of enforcing it was
yet more offensive, and aggravated that hostile feeling which long mismanagement on our part, and
some folly on theirs, had created in the leading party
in North America. Mr. Monroe and Mr. Pinkney
were instructed to insist on an explanation upon this
important point, on some regulation of the impressment of British seamen found in American merchant
vessels, on the right and practice of searching for
them at sea, and on many other inferior but difficult
subjects. When, however, the death of Mr. Pitt
was known, the spirit, though not the substance, of
their instructions was softened, and the mission was
authorized to assume a more conciliatory tone than
their original instructions seemed to breathe. The
two gentlemen were empowered to negotiate and
conclude a treaty of commerce, which should regulate
all disputed points, and place the two countries per-
manently on a more amicable footing. We found
the two American commissioners fair, explicit, frank
and intelligent. Mr. Monroe (afterwards President)
was a sincere Republican, who during the Revolution
in France had imbibed a strong predilection for that
country, and no slight aversion to this. But he had
candor and principle. A nearer view of the consu-
lar and imperial government of France, and of our
constitution in England, converted him from both
these opinions. 'I find,' said he to me, 'your monarchy more republican than monarchical, and the
French republic infinitely more monarchical than
your monarchy.' He was plain in his manners and

somewhat slow in his apprehension; but he was a diligent, earnest, sensible, and even profound man. His colleague, who had been partly educated in England and was a lawyer by profession, had more of the forms and readiness of business, and greater knowledge and cultivation of mind; but perhaps his opinions were neither so firmly rooted nor so deeply considered as those of Mr. Monroe. Throughout our negotiation they were conciliatory, both in form and in substance. They exceeded their instructions by signing a treaty which left the article of impressment unsettled. My colleague and I took credit to ourselves for having convinced them of the extreme difficulty of the subject, arising from the impossibility of our allowing seamen to withdraw themselves from our service during war, and from the inefficacy of all the regulations which they had been enabled to propose for preventing their entering into American ships. They, on the other hand, persuaded us that they were themselves sincere in wishing to prevent it; and we saw no reason for suspecting that the government of the United States was less so. But though they professed, and I believe felt, a strong wish to enforce such a provision, they did not convince us that they had the power or means of enforcing it. There was, consequently, no article in the treaty upon the subject. Upon this omission and upon other more frivolous pretexts, but with the real purpose and effect of defeating Mr. Monroe's views on the presidentship, Mr. Jefferson refused to ratify a treaty which would have secured his countrymen from all further vexations, and prevented a war between two nations, whose habits, language, and interests should unite them in perpetual alliance and good-fellowship.

"I had an opportunity during this negotiation of observing the influence of situation over men's opinions. The atmosphere of the admiralty made those who breathed it shudder at anything like concessions to the Americans; while the anxiety to avoid war and to enlarge our resources by commerce, so natural in the treasury, softened natures otherwise less yielding, and led them to listen with favor to every conciliatory expedient."

Events were driving the two nations into a collision which might have been averted by diplomacy, but which soon developed into war. On July 24 the American commissioners, in accordance with their instructions, had reopened a correspondence with Mr. Canning, now foreign secretary in the Portland ministry, and on the very next day intelligence was received in London that the British ship Leopard, asserting the right to search for deserters, had attacked the American frigate Chesapeake, off the Chesapeake capes.[1] Of course this brought still more delay. After the settlement of this aggression had been transferred from London to Washington, the treaty was again brought up for recon-

[1] June 23, 1807.

sideration by the British minister in October.
Before much progress could be made, the famous
" orders in council," full of menace to American commerce, were passed, and remonstrances
against them were presented by Pinkney, who
now assumed the entire responsibility of the
legation.

Monroe returned to America near the close of
1807, and soon drew up an elaborate defense of
his diplomatic conduct in England in a letter
to Madison, which covers ten folio pages of the
State Papers.[1] The enthusiasm with which he
might have been received immediately after the
Louisiana purchase was dampened by his failure
in the English negotiations. Politicians were
already discussing the presidential succession,
the Republican party being divided in their
preferences for Madison and Monroe. Jefferson endeavored to remain neutral; Wirt was in
favor of Madison ; at length the legislature of
Virginia settled the choice by pronouncing in
favor of the latter. Monroe's friends acquiesced. Soon afterwards Madison was placed in
the chair of the President, and Monroe, after a
brief interval, was reëlected to the post of governor. It was a mark of the confidence of those
who knew him best that thus a second time, on
his return from a foreign land, more or less dis-

[1] February 28, 1808.

appointed, if not under a cloud, he should be called to the highest office in the gift of the people of the State.

I cannot discover that the failure of Monroe to accomplish the purpose of his mission to Spain and England indicates any want of intelligence, assiduity, or fidelity on his part. Although there is a curious gap in the published papers just before his departure for England, I do not see any evidence that the administration lost their confidence in him. He failed because the times were not propitious for success. Spain was not ready to give up the Floridas. England was determined not to yield the right of search; not even after a disastrous war would she acknowledge the wrongs against which the United States protested. During Monroe's short mission to London he was obliged to be absent from that city several months, and he was actually brought into negotiations with six successive foreign secretaries, besides the two special commissioners; and these secretaries were involved in the perplexities which arose from prolonged hostilities with a most vigorous foe. The delays which were thus occasioned may have been inevitable, but they were very costly. War followed in their train.

CHAPTER V

MADISON became president in 1809. Monroe, who had been a rival aspirant for the office, was called to the post of secretary of state in 1811, as the successor of Robert Smith of Maryland. His associates in the cabinet at that time were Gallatin, Eustis, Paul Hamilton, and, a little later, William Pinkney. The war, which for several years had seemed inevitable, was now imminent. Congress indicated a desire for positive measures, and although the President still favored peace, bills were passed for augmenting the army and navy, for enlisting volunteers, and for organizing the militia. The administration was floated onward by the current of public opinion. The British " orders in council " were the immediate occasion of this spirit of resistance, but the troubles had begun long before. After hearing Mr. Perceval's public declaration in February, 1812, that England could not listen to the pretensions of neutral nations, the American minister in London, Mr. Russell, wrote home that war could not honorably be avoided.

This expectation soon became a fact, and war was declared on June 18, 1812. It was a curious coincidence that the act of declaration was drawn by William Pinkney, and communicated to England by James Monroe, the two commissioners in London whose efforts to maintain peace by a reasonable treaty had been unsuccessful a few years before.

Then followed a long period of tumult, disaster, and victory, the story of which has been so often told that it will here be referred to only in illustration of the life of Monroe. Moreover this part of his history is so well known that I cannot shed any new light upon it. As secretary of state his duties were not at the beginning more complex than the ordinary, but he was afterwards charged with the additional responsibilities of the war department, and thus his position became doubly powerful and difficult. Monroe — who was commonly designated by his military title, Colonel Monroe, and who had the renown of brave service in the Revolution — seriously deliberated whether he should take the field in person, as a volunteer, if not to command ; but he restrained his military ardor.

During the summer and autumn of 1811 the secretary of state was engaged in a brisk correspondence with Mr. Foster, the British minister in Washington. His most extended dispatch was that of July 23, in which he vigorously defends the rights of neutrals. His concluding sentences have an eloquent ring. " It is the interest of belligerents," he argues, " to mitigate the calamities of war, and neutral powers possess ample means to promote that object, provided they sustain, with impartiality and firmness, the dignity of their station. If belligerents expect advantage from neutrals, they should leave them in the full enjoyment of their rights. The present war has been oppressive beyond example by its duration, and by the desolation it has spread throughout Europe. It is highly important that it should assume at least a milder character. By the revocation of the French edicts, so far as they respected the neutral commerce of the United States, some advance is made towards that most desirable and consoling result. Let Great Britain follow the example. The ground thus gained will soon be enlarged by the concurring and pressing interests of all parties ; and whatever is gained will accrue to the advantage of afflicted humanity." [1] Six months later, January 14, 1812, he writes again to Mr. Foster, complaining that in the conduct of the British government it is impossible to see anything

[1] *State Papers*, iii.

short of a determined hostility to the rights and interests of the United States.

The relations of the United States with France also required careful attention from the secretary, though they were less critical than those with England. Joel Barlow was commissioned as minister to the Emperor of the French, and the secretary, July 26, 1811, gave him extended instructions with reference to the claims of the United States. France, he assumes, has changed her policy towards the United States, as the revocation of her decrees indicates, but much is yet to be done by her to satisfy American claims. " If she wishes to profit by neutral commerce she must become the advocate of neutral rights, as well by her practice as by her theory." Such was the message sent to the emperor, and it had some influence upon his subsequent action. A treaty of commerce was proposed; but as delay was expected in negotiating it, Barlow endeavored to secure an official memorandum of the agreement of the two powers, but was obliged to be content with general assurances from the emperor, that the principles contended for were adopted and would be put in operation.[1]

The inauspicious opening of the war is a familiar story. Much of the blame for the dis-

[1] *State Papers*, iii. 516.

asters which occurred was thrown upon the
secretary of war, Dr. Eustis, a surgeon in the
Revolutionary army, who at length gave way.
Monroe acted *ad interim* until the appointment
of General John Armstrong, who had held the
rank of major in the Revolutionary army, and
had since then been called to many conspicuous
public stations, among them that of minister to
France.   The war did not go much better after
the change in the secretary's office.   Monroe
looked with great suspicion on his colleague's
conduct of affairs, and at length addressed the
President as follows, after a short conversation
the evening previous : [1] —

JAMES MONROE TO PRESIDENT MADISON.

July 25, 1813.

You intimated that you had understood that General Armstrong intended to repair to the northern
frontiers and to direct the operations of the campaign ; and it was afterwards suggested to me that
he would, as secretary at war, perform the duties of
lieutenant-general.   It merits consideration how far
the exercise of such a power is strictly constitutional
and correct in itself ; and secondly, how far it may
affect the character of your administration and of
those acting in it ; and thirdly, whether it is not
otherwise liable to objection on the ground of policy.
I shall be able to present to your consideration a

[1] Monroe MSS.

few hints only on each of these propositions. The departments of the government, being recognized by the Constitution, have appropriate duties under it as organs of the executive will; they contain records of its transactions, and are in that sense checks on the Executive. If the secretary of war leaves the seat of government (the chief magistrate remaining there) and performs the duties of a general, the powers of the chief magistrate, of the secretary at war, and general are all united in the latter. There ceases to be a check on executive power as to military operations; indeed, the executive power as known to the Constitution is destroyed; the whole is transferred from the Executive to the general at the head of the army. It is completely absorbed in hands where it is most dangerous.

It may be said that the President is commander-in-chief; that the secretary at war is his organ as to military operations, and that he may allow him to go to the army, as being well informed in military affairs, and act for himself. I am inclined to think that the President, unless he takes the command of the army in person, acts, in directing its movements, more as the executive power than as commander-in-chief. What would become of the secretary at war if the President took command of the army, I do not know. I rather suppose, however, that although some of his powers would be transferred to the military staff about the President, he would, nevertheless, retain his appropriate constitutional character in all other respects. The adjutant-general would become the

organ of the Executive as to military operations, but
the secretary of war would be *that* for every other
measure, indeed for all except movements in the
field. The Department at War would therefore still
form some check on the Executive at the head of the
army, but there would be none on the secretary,
when he was general.

On the second head, the effect it might have on
the credit of your administration, there can be little
doubt. If there is cause to suspect the measure on
constitutional grounds, that circumstance alone would
wound its credit deeply. But a total yielding of the
power, as would be inferred, and might and probably would be assumed, (for any act which would be
performed or order given without the sanction of the
chief magistrate would, in a degree, operate in that
way), would affect it in another sense not less in-
juriously. It is impossible for the secretary at war
to go to the frontier, and perform the offices contemplated, without exercising all those of the military
commander, *especially*. He would carry with him,
of course, those of the War Department, for by the
powers of that department would he act as general,
and control all military and other operations, and
being forced to act by circumstances and take his
measures by the day, he could have no order or
sanction from the chief magistrate. This would be
seen by the public and imperil greatly the credit of
the administration. If General Armstrong is the
person most fit to command the armies, let him be
appointed such ; there will then be a check on him in

the chief magistrate and in the War Department.
Does he possess in a prominent degree the public
confidence for that trust? Do we not know the fact
to be otherwise, that it was with difficulty he was
appointed a brigadier-general, and still greater difficulty that he was appointed secretary at war?

On the ground of policy I have already made some
remarks; but there are other objections to it on that
ground. If he withdraws from the seat of government, and takes his station with the northern troops,
what will become of every other army, — that under
Harrison, Pinckney, and Wilkinson, and of those
stationed in other quarters, especially along the coast?
Who will direct the general movement, supervise their
supplies, etc. ?

I cannot close these remarks without adding something in relation to myself. Stimulated by a deep
sense of the misfortunes of our country, as well as its
disgrace by the surrender of Hull, the misconduct of
Van Rensselaer and Smyth, and by the total want
of character in the northern campaign, and dreading
its effects on your administration, on the Republican
party and cause, I have repeatedly offered my service
in a military station, not that I wished to take it by
preference to my present one, which to all others I
prefer, but from a dread of the consequences above-
mentioned.

I was willing to take the Department of War per-
manently, if, in leaving my present station, it was
thought I might be more useful there than in a military command. I thought otherwise. What passed

on this subject proves that I considered the Department of War as a very different trust from that of the military commander.

You appeared to think I might be more useful with the army, as did Mr. Gallatin, with whom I conferred on the subject. I was convinced that the duties of secretary of war and military commander were not only incompatible under our government, but that they could not be exercised by the same person. I was equally satisfied that the secretary at war could not perform, in his character as secretary, the duties of general of the army. The movement of the army must be regulated daily by events which occur daily, and the movement of all its parts, to be combined and simultaneous, must be under the control of the general in the field, not of the War Department. That this is the opinion of General Armstrong also, is evident from his disposition to join the army. He knows that *here* he cannot direct the movements of the armies. He knows also that he could not be appointed the lieutenant-general, and that it is only in his present character as secretary at war that he can expect to exercise his functions of general.

As soon as General Armstrong took charge of the Department at War I thought I saw his plan, that is, after he had held it a few days. I saw distinctly that he intended to have no grade in the army which should be competent to a general control of military operations; that he meant to keep the whole in his own hands; that each operation should be distinct and separate, with distinct and separate objects, and, of course, to be directed by himself, not simply in the outline but detail. I anticipated mischief from this, because I knew that the movement could not be directed from this place; I did not then anticipate the remedy which he had in view.

I was animated by much zeal (in offering my services in a military station) in favor of your administration and the cause of free government, which I have long considered intimately connected together. I flattered myself that by my long services, and what the country knew of me, that I should give some impulse to the recruiting business, and otherwise aid the cause. The misfortunes and dangers attending the cause produced so much excitement that my zeal may have exposed me to the appearance of repulse and disappointment in the course things have taken. But, as I well know that you have justly appreciated my motives, and that the public cannot fail to do it, should any imputation of the kind alluded to be made, these are considerations which have no effect on my mind.

Having seen into these things, from my little knowledge of military affairs and the management of the War Department for some weeks (which gave me a knowledge of the state of things there), and foreseeing some danger to your administration as well as to the public interest, from the causes above stated, I have felt it a duty which I owe to you, as well as to the public, to communicate to you my sentiments on them. I have written them in much truth and without reserve. You will, I am satisfied, bestow on them the consideration which they deserve.

I am, dear sir, sincerely and respectfully your friend,   JAMES MONROE.

I will add that I cease to have any desire of a military station, having never wished one with a view to myself, and always under a conviction that I should incur risks and make sacrifices by it; it is in consequence of feeling it strongly my duty that I entirely relinquish the idea. These hints are intended to bring to your consideration the other circumstances to which they allude.

Six months later he sent to the President the following remonstrance against Armstrong's plan of a conscription, with an urgent plea for his removal: —

WASHINGTON, *December* 27, 1813.

The following communication from the secretary of the navy is the cause of this letter.

Just before I left the office he came into it and informed me that General Armstrong had adopted the idea of a conscription, and was engaged in communications with members of Congress, in which he endeavored to reconcile them to it, stating that the militia could not be relied on, and regular troops could not be enlisted. Mr. Jones was fearful, should such an idea get into circulation, that it would go far, with other circumstances, to ruin the administration. He told me that he had his information from General Jacock, and he authorized me to communicate it to you.

I suspect that many other members have already been sounded on it, as Mr. Roberts remarked to me yesterday that General Armstrong had returned and had many projects prepared for them.

Other circumstances which have come to my knowledge ought to be known to you. Mr. Dawson called on me yesterday week and informed me that Mr. Fisk of New York intended to move on the next day a resolution calling on you to state by what authority General Armstrong had commanded the northern army during the late campaign; who had discharged the duties of his office in his absence; and for other information relating particularly to his issuing communications and exercising all the duties of secretary of war on the frontiers. I satisfied Mr. Dawson that an attack on the secretary on those grounds would be an attack on you, and that we must all support him against it, to support you. He assured me that he should represent it in that light to Mr. Fisk and endeavor to prevail on him to decline the measure. I presume he did so.

General M., whom I have seen, informed me that this gentleman was engaged in the seduction of the officers of the army, particularly the young men of talents, promising to one the rank of brigadier, to another that of major-general, as he presumed without your knowledge; teaching them to look to him, and not you, for preferment, and exciting their resentment against you if it did not take effect. He says that the most corrupting system is carried on throughout the State of New York, by placing in office, parti-

cularly in the quartermaster's department, his tools
and the sons of influential men under them as clerks,
etc. I did not go into detail. Other remarks of his
I will take another opportunity of communicating to
you. It is painful to me to make this communication
to you, nor should I do it if I did not most conscien-
tiously believe that this man, if continued in office,
will ruin not you and the administration only, but
the whole Republican party and cause. He has already gone far to do it, and it is my opinion, if he is
not promptly removed, he will soon accomplish it.

The letter continues in confidential terms to
exhibit the writer's estimate of Armstrong.

Armstrong retained his portfolio, notwithstanding this remonstrance from his colleague.
The battle of Bladensburg, however, effected a
change which no peaceful protest could bring
about. It revealed the utter inadequacy of the
national defense, and quickened the administration to wiser methods of carrying on the war.
During the approach of the British to Washington, says General Cullum, —

" all in our army was confusion, and though Winder
was called the commander of this motley mass, there
was more than one volunteer generalissimo from the
President's mounted cabinet, one of whom, the secretary of state, without Winder's knowledge, changed
his order of battle, and another, the secretary of

war, had a few hours before been invested by the
President with the supreme command, though, fortunately, his order was suspended before the battle
began."

From the various narratives, it appears that
Monroe went out from Washington, on August
20, with a slender escort of twenty-five or thirty
dragoons, to reconnoitre the enemy's position,
and he continued to watch their movements until
after the battle of Bladensburg.   On the 22d
he informed the President that imminent danger
threatened the capital, advised the removal of
the government records, and suggested that materials be in readiness for the destruction of the
bridges.   Then came the panic and the exodus
of the inhabitants on the eve of an action.   On
the 24th, Monroe was with the President at
General Winder's headquarters, when it was
discovered that the enemy were marching to
Bladensburg, and he repaired without loss of
time to General Stansbury's position, in order
to inform him of this movement.   The accounts
of what he did on the field are confused.   Colonel Williams says there are discrepancies in the
statements of various participants in the action
which it is impossible to reconcile, the more
singular because the statements were prepared
for the information of Congress but a few weeks
after the battle.   Forty years later the recollec-

tions of Richard Rush were drawn out in a letter, which gives a brief and vivid narrative of the sequence of events in that stirring week, and indicates the relation of the President and his cabinet to the various movements. It is not possible for us to read this chapter in the national history with composure, and it is not easy on the field of Bladensburg to gather laurels for any one; on the other hand, I shall not attempt to distribute the responsibilities of the disaster. The immediate result of it was that Ross and Cockburn lost no time in entering Washington, and soon the public buildings were in flames; the ultimate result was popular determination to secure a more vigorous conduct of the war, in which Monroe became a prominent actor.[1]

Among contemporary narratives of these events two drafts have been preserved of a narrative written or inspired by Monroe, one of which will here be given. It belongs to the class of *mémoires pour servir*, or semi-official memoranda, and will serve to give prominence to the secretary's proceedings at this time, as he would like to have them remembered. The date is September, 1814, a few weeks at most (and possibly but a few days) after the battle of

[1] On this subject see G. W. Cullum, *Campaigns of 1812*, pp. 285–288; J. S. Williams, *Capture of Washington*, p. 209; especially the letter of R. Rush on p. 274.

Bladensburg and the burning of the capital, —
dire events which are referred to euphuistically
as " the affair of the twenty-fourth." The circumstances which placed Monroe in charge of
the War Department are here fully indicated.

" The President, secretary of state, and attorney-
general returned to the city of Washington on Satur-
day, the 27th of August, at which time the enemy's
squadron were battering the fort below Alexandria,
whose unprotected inhabitants were in consternation,
as were those of the city and of Georgetown, and indeed of all the neighboring country. After the affair
of the 24th, General Winder rallied the principal part
of the militia engaged in it at Montgomery Court-
House, where he remained on the 25th and part of
the 26th, preparing for a new movement, the necessity of which he anticipated. The secretary of state
joined him ; a portion of the forces from Baltimore
at Montgomery Court-House on the 25th had returned
to that city. About midday on the 26th the general
having received intelligence that the enemy were in
motion towards Bladensburg, probably with intention
to visit Baltimore, formed his troops without delay,
and commenced his march towards Ellicott's Mills,
with intention to hang on the enemy's left flank in
case Baltimore was their object, and of meeting them
at the mills if they took that route. Late in the evening of that day he resolved to proceed in person to
Baltimore, to prepare that city for the attack with
which it was menaced. As commander of the mili-

tary district, it was his duty to look to every part and
to make the necessary preparation for its defense,
and none appeared then to be in greater danger or to
have a stronger claim to his attention than the city
of Baltimore. He announced this, his resolution, to
Generals Stansbury and Smith, instructing them to
watch the movements of the enemy, and to act with
the force under their command as circumstances
might require, and departed about 7 P. M. The
secretary of state remained with Generals Stansbury
and Smith.

" The President [had] crossed the Potomac on the
evening of the 24th, accompanied by the attorney-
general and General Mason, and remained on the
south side of the river a few miles above the lower
falls, on the 25th. On the 26th he recrossed the
Potomac, and went to Brookville, in the neighborhood of Montgomery Court-House, with intention to
join General Winder.

" On the 27th the secretary of state, having heard
that the enemy had evacuated the city, notified it, by
express, to the President, and advised immediate return to the city for the purpose of reëstablishing the
government there. He joined the President on the
same day at Brookville, and he, accompanied by the
secretary of state and attorney-general, set out immediately for Washington, where they arrived at five
in the afternoon. The enemy's squadron was then
battering Fort Washington, which was evacuated and
blown up by the commander, on that evening, without
the least resistance. The unprotected inhabitants of

Alexandria in consternation capitulated, and those
of Georgetown and the city were preparing to follow
the example.   Such was the state of affairs when the
President entered the city on the evening of the 27th.
There was no force organized for its defense.   The
secretary of war was at Fredericktown, and General
Winder at Baltimore.   The effect of the late disaster
on the whole Union and the world was anticipated.
Prompt measures were indispensable.   Under these
circumstances, the President requested Mr. Monroe
to take charge of the Department of War, and command of the District *ad interim*, with which he immediately complied.   On the 28th in the morning, the
President, with Mr. Monroe and the attorney-general,
visited the navy yard, the arsenal at Greenleaf's
Point, and passing along the shore of the Potomac,
up towards Georgetown, Mr. Monroe, as secretary
of war and military commander, adopted measures,
under sanction of the President, for the defense of
the city and of Georgetown.   As they passed near
the capital he was informed that the citizens of
Washington were preparing to send a deputation to
the British commander for the purpose of capitu-
lating.

"He forbade the measure.   It was then remarked
that the situation of the inhabitants was deplorable;
there being no force prepared for their defense, their
houses might be burnt down.   Mr. Monroe then observed that he had been charged by the President
with authority to take measures for the defense of
the city, and that it should be defended; that if any

deputation moved towards the enemy it should be repelled by the bayonet. He took immediate measures for mounting a battery at Greenleaf's Point, another near the bridge, a third at the windmill point, and sent an order to Colonel Winder, who was in charge of some cannon, on the opposite shore above the ferry landing, to move three of the pieces to the lower end of Mason's Island, and the others some distance below that point on the Virginia shore, to coöperate with the batteries on the Maryland side. Colonel Winder refused to obey the order, on which Mr. Monroe passed the river, and riding to the colonel gave the order in person. The colonel replied that he did not know Mr. Monroe as secretary of war or commanding general. Mr. Monroe then stated that he acted under the authority of the President, and that he must either obey the order or leave the field. The colonel preferred the latter." [1]

The following letter from William Robinson, a political opponent of Monroe, was written in 1823, to counteract certain disparaging reports which were abroad in reference to the defense at Washington : [2] —

"I have it in perfect recollection that on the morning of the 27th August I met with Colonel Monroe at Snell's bridge on the route to Baltimore. The army was in march from Montgomery Court House, where it had reassembled after the battle of Bladensburg; much confusion prevailed in consequence of

[1] Monroe MSS.   [2] Gouverneur MSS.

the recent defeat, and the disorganization and dispersion of the officers of the government. Colonel Monroe expressed great anxiety for the immediate return of the President and high officers of government to Washington city, with a view to the restoration of order and effective resistance of the enemy. He was pleased to intrust me with an open letter, or billet, to that effect, ordering my utmost dispatch in search of the President, whom I found at the village of Brookville, where he was soon found by the colonel, and both proceeded to Washington. I then proceeded to Montgomery Court House, where I found Jones, the secretary of the navy, and delivered a summons for an immediate attendance at Washington. General Armstrong had gone to Fredericktown in Maryland, and not considering my orders reached so far, I returned to Georgetown in the evening. The sentiment common in the army was so decidedly inimical to General Armstrong, that I feel assured that his person would have been endangered had he attempted to join us."

Whatever may have been Monroe's course on the battle-field at Bladensburg, there can be no doubt that, when he assumed the duties of secretary of war, vigor was at once infused into all the military operations. Washington was defended ; Baltimore was rescued, and the national banner continued to wave over Fort McHenry; the dispatches sent to Jackson in the southwest had the ring of determination and authority.

Monroe appears at this time in his best aspect, enthusiastic, determined, confident of the popular support, daring. "Hasten your militia to New Orleans," he wrote in rousing dispatches to the governors near the seat of war in Louisiana; "do not wait for this government to arm them; put all the arms you can find into their hands; let every man bring his rifle with him; we shall see you paid." [1]

Having thus indicated Monroe's relations to the war, it does not seem necessary to dwell on the innumerable details which pertain to that period.

[1] Schouler comes to the defense of Monroe. See his note, *Hist. of U. S.* ii. pp. 409, and the text, p. 414, 459.

CHAPTER VI

MONROE held the office of president of the United States during two full terms, from 1817 to 1825. It has already been stated that eight years previous to his first election he was seriously considered as a candidate, when Madison received the nomination. He was nearly fifty-nine years old when first called to the presidency, about the age at which Jefferson and Madison attained the same position; Washington became President a little younger, at fifty-seven, and John Adams a little older, at sixty-one.

At his first election, Monroe received 183 votes in the electoral college against 34 which were given for Rufus King, the candidate of the Federalists; at his second election, but one electoral vote was given against him, and that was cast for John Quincy Adams. No one but Washington was ever reëlected to the highest office in the land with so near an approach to unanimity.

Daniel D. Tompkins was Vice-President during both presidential terms.

Let us now ask on whose counsel the new President could rely and whose opposition he must expect. Jefferson and Madison had never failed to be his friends, whatever slight estrangement may have arisen, and they were now in the mood of cordial coöperation. The old Federalists, no longer bound by party allegiance, had not forgotten their former animosities. The coldness of John Adams was not likely to be seriously modified, even though his son came into the cabinet. Jackson, already extremely popular, was ready to volunteer suggestions on the conduct of civil affairs. Henry Clay was a leader in the House of Representatives, where for several years (with an interruption) he had been the speaker. Richard Rush was conspicuous. Benton was soon to be prominent, but he was not yet a man of national mark, and his thirty years' reminiscences begin with 1820. Webster had been for two terms a member of the House, but was now determined to pursue a professional life, and was about to come forward as a constitutional lawyer in the Dartmouth College case.

The cabinet, as finally made up after various delays, included four men who remained in it during both presidential terms, — J. Q. Adams, J. C. Calhoun, W. H. Crawford, and W. Wirt, — respectively appointed secretary of state, secretary of war, secretary of the treasury, and attorney-general. The Post Office was first directed by R. J. Meigs, and then by J. McLean. The Navy Department remained for a time under Mr. Madison's secretary, Benjamin W. Crowninshield, but he was soon succeeded by Smith Thompson.[1] In all political affairs, as distinguished from administrative duties, the four first named were undoubtedly the strong men. They were younger than Monroe : Adams at that time being fifty years old; Crawford, forty-four; Calhoun, thirty-five; and Wirt, forty-five ; and they represented different ideas of public policy, as well as competing claims to the presidential succession. Their personal rivalries were not concealed. Adams, when he became secretary of state, was, perhaps, the most distinguished American then actively engaged in public life. He took this office thoroughly trained for its responsibilities. He had been favored with a liberal academic education, and had participated to an unusual extent in the conduct of affairs. At the age of eleven he went with his father to Paris, when the latter was envoy to France. At fourteen, this " mature youngster " (as Mr. Morse has called him) accompanied Mr. Dana to St. Petersburg, in the post of private secretary. Later on he was

[1] Thompson was followed by S. L. Southard.

successively minister to Holland, Prussia, Russia, and England. He secured a treaty of amity between Prussia and the United States, was one of the commissioners who negotiated the treaty of Ghent, and was afterwards one of those who signed the commercial treaty with England. He was thus a participant in the diplomatic questions evolved by two wars, — the Revolution and the war of 1812. Inheriting strong intellectual qualities which have been conspicuous in his descendants, governed by absolute independence in the formation of his opinions, and sustained in the popular good-will by his unquestioned integrity and patriotism, he was the man of all who could be thought of to give wisdom, weight, and dignity to the cabinet of which he became the head. The most serious questions of Monroe's administration arose in the State Department, and it was fortunate that its affairs were guided by a statesman of such varied information and experience. The wonderful diary, which Adams, when a child, began at the instance of his father, is rich in its memoranda of this period, and the eulogy which he delivered on the death of Monroe remains to this day the best history of his political standing.

Calhoun's career had been very different from that of Adams. He was called to the cabinet while comparatively a young man, fifteen years

the junior of the secretary of state. His political experience had been restricted to that of a
representative in Congress. From the time of
his election to the House, he was felt to be a
power. Important positions were assigned to
him, and his words bore the weight of authority.
But although the public lives of these two men
were so different, and although they ultimately
became representatives of bitter antagonisms,
they were not unlike in some marked peculiarities. In early days both were surrounded by
strong religious influences. Calhoun was born
and bred under the rigid orthodoxy characteristic of the Irish Presbyterians, to whose faith both
his father and his mother and their parents adhered. Adams, as his latest biographer tells
us, remained through life " a complete and thorough Puritan, wonderfully little modified by
times and circumstances." Both were graduated
in New England colleges, one at Harvard, and
the other at Yale. Both were independent
thinkers, and true to their convictions, however
unpopular. One became a leading opponent of
the encroachments of slavery, the other a leader
in nullification ; but during the administration
of Monroe, and long afterwards, Calhoun was
quite as outspoken as Adams in his love for the
Union. Both were loyal admirers of the President into whose council they were called, and

they remained on terms of intimacy with him as long as he lived. Both were honest, fearless, powerful, independent statesmen. After Monroe's retirement, one became President, the other Vice-President. Both remained in public service to the very close of life, Calhoun dying while senator, and Adams while a representative. Both are credited by their biographers with that sagacity which points out in advance the dangers covered up by a political measure. Calhoun, says Von Holst, "reads the future as if the book of fate were lying wide open before him." Adams, says Morse, "discerned in passing events 'the title-page to a great tragic volume,'" and "few men at that day read the future so clearly."

Unlike the two ministers already named, Crawford was what has been termed "a self-made man." He was continued in charge of the Treasury Department, to which, after his return from the embassy to France and after a brief service as secretary of war, he had been called by Madison. In the congressional caucus which nominated Monroe, Crawford was the chief opposing candidate; and a shrewd observer, who was a member of that body, has recorded his opinion that when Congress first assembled a majority of Republican members were for Crawford. But the nomination was postponed from time to time, and at length, through the influence of Madison or other causes, sixty-five votes were cast for Monroe and fifty-four for his opponent.[1] Crawford, however, continued to be regarded as in the line of succession to the presidency, and received a part of the electoral vote in 1824.

William Wirt was the choice of the President for the office of attorney-general. His biographer, John P. Kennedy, in the vivid portrait with which he begins the memoir, dwells on the Teutonic aspect of Wirt, not unlike to Goethe's. Born in Maryland, he was of German origin, his father having migrated to this country from Switzerland many years before the Revolution, and his mother being a German. Previously a prominent advocate in the courts of Virginia, he won a national reputation by the part he took in the prosecution of Aaron Burr. Having a limited education and a very moderate library to begin with, he had risen by his talents to a conspicuous rank as a lawyer and as a writer. He had recently completed his memoir of Patrick Henry. He came into office as the personal friend of Monroe, after it was decided that Richard Rush should go to England, and he was attracted to the attorney-gen-

[1] Many other details in respect to the nomination are given in Hammond's *Political History*.

eralship not so much on account of the political preferment as because of the professional standing which it gave him. Unlike Adams, Calhoun, and Crawford, he did not aspire to the presidency. To William Pope's suggestions he replied, "I am already higher than I had any reason to expect, and I should be light-headed indeed, because I have been placed on this knoll, where I feel safe, to aspire at the mountain's pinnacle in order to be blown to atoms. Therefore let this matter rest." And so it rested. Wirt remained in office twelve years, and although he did not confine his professional labors to the service of the government, he exalted the station which he held by an assiduous discharge of all his duties with ability, learning, and success.

Among those who were thought of for the cabinet, Henry Clay, one of Monroe's supporters for the presidency, was conspicuous. He declined the offer of an appointment as secretary of war, but his "friends did not conceal their disappointment that he was not invited to take the office of secretary of state ; nor did he disguise his dissatisfaction at the appointment of Mr. Adams ; " so writes Josiah Quincy. There are many subsequent indications of Clay's hostility to the administration. William Wirt, for example, in counseling with the President in regard to certain allowances claimed for Clay's diplomatic services, where the usage of the government was not clearly established, remarks as follows: " I am aware of the delicacy which connects itself with this question considered personally as it relates to you; but it is a delicacy with a double aspect: if you reject the claim, Mr. Clay and his friends may impute it to hostility to him, on account of the political part which he has occasionally taken against you; and, on the other hand, if you admit the claim and it shall be thought unjust, it may, and by some most probably will, be imputed to a dread of his further opposition and a wish to bribe him to silence. The best way will be to consider the question abstractly without any manner of reference to the character of the claimant, and this I shall endeavor to do." It is one of the curious incidents of political life, that at the close of Monroe's administration the vote of Clay's friends made Adams president, and Adams made Clay his secretary of state.

Jackson had formed a personal attachment to Monroe in 1815, and welcomed his accession to the presidency partly on this account, partly because he disliked Crawford. Several letters exchanged by Jackson and the President elect have long been familiar to the public. They indicate that he, as well as Clay and Shelby, declined the office of secretary of war. They also show that Jackson felt quite at liberty to make confidential suggestions in respect to candidates for the cabinet. For the War Department he urgently recommended Colonel W. H. Drayton, late of the army; Shelby he opposed. The selection of Adams he regarded as the best that could be made for the Department of State. The letters of Monroe to Jackson at this juncture show the principles on which the former meant to select his chief advisers, and also the attitude which he proposed to hold in respect to the Federalists. In the formation of an administration, he thought that the heads of departments (there being four) should be taken from the four great sections of the Union, the East, the Middle, the South, and the West, unless great emergencies and transcendent talents should justify a departure from this plan; and he intimated pointedly that in selecting candidates he should act for the country, and not " for the aggrandizement of any one." The Federalists he regarded as thoroughly routed, the great body of them having become Republicans. To preserve the Republican party and prevent the revival of the Federal, was to be his aim as a politician, for he did not regard the existence of parties as necessary to free governments. Hence he favored moderation toward

those who had acted with the Federal party,
and even a generous policy. The embarrassing
question was, how far to indulge that spirit in
the outset. On the other hand, the course pursued
by him when James Kent was proposed to him
for the vacant position on the supreme bench
does not show that he had entirely forgotten his
animosity toward the Federalists. Wirt urged
the appointment of Kent, and Calhoun concurred
with him, but the President hesitated, and finally
Smith Thompson received the nomination.

The principal subjects which engrossed the
attention of Monroe during his two terms of
office were the defense of the Atlantic seaboard,
the promotion of internal improvements, the
Seminole war, the acquisition of Florida, the
Missouri compromise, and the resistance to foreign interference in American affairs, this last
being formulated in that famous declaration
which is known as the Monroe Doctrine. It may
also be added that his administration began and
ended with a sort of pageantry, which is always
attractive to the masses as it moves over the
scene, though not always approved in the cooler
criticism of democratic second thoughts. The
first of these demonstrations was a presidential
tour, in two parts, to the north and to the south;
the second was a national reception of Lafayette,
the country's guest.

With the present facilities in locomotion, presidential journeys are not uncommon, and have rarely any political significance; but in that generation it was a noteworthy event to see and hear the chief magistrate on his travels. There is little doubt that one of the principal objects of this journey was to conciliate the Federalists, whose opposition to this and the preceding administration was strong; but the primary and ostensible purpose was to examine the fortifications and harbors of the United States. For this reason the President was accompanied by General Joseph G. Swift, chief engineer of the army, and not by the members of his cabinet. The choice of an escort was sagacious. Swift was a New Englander of New Englanders, the first graduate at West Point, and a friend of Eustis, late secretary of war, whom he had accompanied from Boston to Washington in 1809, and " inducted into the mysteries of his new vocation." By his skill in protecting New York during the war he had gained the applause of a " benefactor to the city," and had received more substantial proofs of the gratitude of the people. He was therefore a valuable companion in a professional as well as in a social aspect.[1]

[1] See General G. W. Cullum's *Campaigns and Engineers of 1812.*

Three months and a half were expended on the journey. The party visited the chief cities of the Atlantic seaboard as far as Portland, traversed New Hampshire, Vermont, and New York, went West as far as Detroit, and then returned to Washington by way of Zanesville, Pittsburgh, and Fredericktown. Everywhere there were receptions and speeches, dinners and assemblies, and the record of all these doings was compiled and published in a duodecimo volume by an ardent admirer of the administration in Connecticut. The President's first address was at Baltimore on June 2, 1817. There he indicated, in the following language, his double aim to secure defense against external foes, and to seek the promotion of internal harmony.

" Congress has appropriated large sums of money for the fortification of our coast and inland frontier, and for the establishment of naval dock yards and building a navy. It is proper that these works should be executed with judgment, fidelity, and economy; much depends in the execution on the Executive, to whom extensive power is given as to the general arrangement, and to whom the superintendence exclusively belongs. You do me justice in believing that it is to enable me to discharge these duties with the best advantage to my country that I have undertaken this tour.

" From the increased harmony of public opinion,

founded on the successful career of a government which has never been equaled, and which promises, by a future development of its faculties, to augment in an eminent degree the blessings of this favored people, I unite with you in all the anticipations which you have so justly suggested."

A letter which was written by Crawford to Gallatin, after the close of the President's tour, is a good indication of the politician's view of the results of so great an expenditure of time and force.[1]

" The President's tour through the East has produced something like a political jubilee. They were, in the land of steady habits, at least for the time, ' all Federalists, all Republicans.' If the bondmen and bondwomen were not set free, and individual debts released, a general absolution of political sins seems to have been mutually agreed upon. Whether the parties will not relapse on the approach of their spring elections in Massachusetts can only be determined by the event.

" In this world there seems to be nothing free from alloy. Whilst the President is lauded for the good he has done in the East by having softened party asperity and by the apparent reconciliation which, for the moment, seems to have been effected between materials the most heterogeneous, the restless, the carping, the malevolent men in the Ancient Dominion

[1] October 27, 1817.

are ready to denounce him for his apparent acquiescence in the seeming *man-worship* with which he was venerated by *the wise men of the East*.

" Seriously, I think the President has lost as much as he has gained by this tour, at least in popularity. In health, however, he seems to have been a great gainer."

With these views of the critical Georgian may be placed in contrast the genial reflections of an admirer at the North.[1]

" For the political father of a great, a growing, and an intelligent people, freemen by birth, and resolved to *be* free, to witness such striking proofs of their fidelity and admiration, must have made a deep, a lasting impression upon his mind. He must be something *more* or *less* than man, who would view such a scene with apathy and indifference. A *janizary* of *Turkey* may offer up hosannahs to the *Sultan* until the javelin which the Sultan wields ends his life and his plaudits at a stroke ; an eastern despot may be adored by his slaves, who mingle groans of distress with the accents of praise ; European princes may be followed by a famishing peasantry, whose huzzas are feeble from want of food ; but it is the happiness of the President of the United States to be thronged by an assemblage of happy freemen, acknowledging their gratitude to the only 'legitimate' ruler of a great nation ; legitimate, because he derives his power from the voice of the people he governs."

[1] Waldo, p. 51.

The northern trip was followed by one to the Southern States in 1819. The President went as far south as Augusta, then through the Cherokee region to Nashville, and afterwards to Louisville and Lexington.

Before a year had passed there was a renewal of hostilities with the Seminole Indians. The war was brief and decisive, but the enmities which it excited among those who took part in conducting it lasted many years. This controversy, long dormant, burst forth with fury when Jackson was a candidate for a second presidential term. It is to his life that this story belongs, and the reader may readily find the particulars in the pages of Parton and Sumner.

While Florida was still a Spanish domain, Jackson was sent to Southern Georgia to put a stop to the Indian outrages. Before going he addressed a letter to Monroe (January 6, 1818) intimating that, in his opinion, a vigorous policy ought to be pursued. Amelia Island should be seized " at all hazards," and " simultaneously the whole of East Florida, to be held as an indemnity for the outrages of Spain upon the property of our citizens." It is not clear whether he received an authoritative answer from the President to this important programme, for there are discrepancies in the testimony not now explica-

ble. But he acted as if he possessed the complete support of the authorities in Washington.
He crossed the Florida line in pursuit of the
fugitive red men; he captured and garrisoned a
fortress on Spanish territory; he seized Pensa-
cola and captured the Barrancas; and he approved the summary execution of Ambrister and
Arbuthnot, subjects of Great Britain, who were
charged with exciting the Indians against the
Americans. By all this he brought the United
States to the verge of war with Spain, and likewise offended England. War might have been
produced, said Lord Castlereagh to Mr. Rush,
" if the ministry had but held up a finger."

When Jackson returned to the North it was
a question how far he should be sustained by
the administration. Adams wrote a diplomatic
paper vindicating him, the House of Representatives sustained him, and there was a general
acquiescence in the course he had pursued.
But long afterwards, in the spring of 1830, it
became a matter of partisan controversy to
determine the attitude of Monroe and of the
various members of his cabinet in respect to the
inception and progress of this brief and spirited
campaign. The recollections of Monroe, Calhoun, Adams, Crawford, and others were appealed to. The point of the controversy was,
whether in January, 1818, Mr. Rhea, a member

of Congress and a friend of Jackson's, had communicated to the latter *by authority* the wishes of Monroe in respect to the opening campaign. Monroe did not acknowledge that he had given any such authority; Jackson claimed that he did give it; but "the Rhea letter," said to have been written with Monroe's assent, was never produced. In the public correspondence just after the war, Monroe appears to deprecate the course which had been pursued by Jackson, though not to the extent of blaming him. "In transcending the limit of your orders," he says, "you acted on your own responsibility, on facts and circumstances which were unknown to the government when the orders were given . . . and which you thought imposed on you the measure as an act of patriotism, essential to the honor and interests of your country." He also calls the general's attention to some parts of dispatches, "written in haste and under the pressure of fatigue and infirmity, and in a spirit of conscious rectitude," which may make trouble, and he suggests their correction. "If you think proper to authorize the secretary or myself to correct those passages, it will be done with care, though should you have copies, as I presume you have, you had better do it yourself." A convenient summary of these letters was printed for Calhoun in 1831, but copies of it are now scarce.

The endeavor of the United States to get possession of the Floridas by purchase reached a successful issue February 22, 1819, when a treaty was concluded at Washington through the negotiations of John Q. Adams, secretary of state, and Luis de Onis, the Spanish envoy. Notwithstanding opposition from Mr. Clay and others, the treaty was ratified unanimously by the Senate, and thus the control of the entire Atlantic and Gulf seaboard from the St. Croix to the Sabine was secured to this government.

During most of Monroe's administration, Richard Rush was the American minister in London, and his relations were chiefly with Lord Castlereagh and Mr. Canning. Rush was careful in his diary and correspondence, and has published much that is interesting on the aspect of American affairs between 1818 and 1825. The instructions under which he acted had the sanction of Madison, as well as of Monroe and Adams. The two subjects which he brought forward in one of his first interviews with the British minister were, an alleged violation of the treaty of Ghent by the carrying off of slaves in English ships at the close of the war, and a neglect to carry out exactly the commercial convention of 1815. He afterwards told how the news of Jackson's pursuit was received in the diplomatic circles of the Court of St. James. "We have had nothing of late so exciting: it smacks of war," said one of the plenipotentiaries. Subsequently the old subject of impressment, and the subject, ever old and ever new, of the Newfoundland fisheries, were matters of negotiation.

The admission of Missouri to the Union was the theme of violent controversy from 1819 to 1821, resulting in the famous Compromise, the repeal of which more than thirty years later again agitated the country. Here was the beginning of that wandering in the wilderness for forty years which resulted in emancipation. The particular record of the debates, led by Rufus King upon one side and John Randolph upon the other, must be studied in the legislative rather than the administrative history of the times. The crisis in this debate occurred March 1, 1820, when Congress agreed to abandon the idea of prohibiting slavery in Missouri and to insist upon its prohibition in the public territory north of the line 36° 30′. This determined the admission of Missouri, though it did not close the discussion. It came up again in the following year and resulted in a second compromise. During the winter of 1819–20 the excitement in Washington was intense. "At our evening parties," says Mr. Adams, "we hear of nothing but the Missouri question and Mr. King's

speeches." He records also the conversation
which he held with Calhoun, indicating in both
that prophetic sagacity to which reference has
been made, and also their divergence on a fundamental principle which grew wider and wider as
long as they lived.

Writing under the date of February 15, 1820,
a fortnight before the adoption of the Compromise, Monroe in a private letter declared his conviction that " the majority of States, of physical
force, and eventually of votes in both houses,
would be on the side of the non-slave-holding
States." He thought it probable that they
would succeed in their purpose or the Union be
dissolved. " I consider this," he continued, " as
an atrocious attempt in certain leaders to grasp
at power, and being very artfully laid is more
likely to succeed than any effort having the
same object in view ever made before."

The latter portion of this letter is as follows : [1] —

" As to the part which I may act, in all circumstances in which I may be placed, I have not made
up my mind, nor shall I until the period arrives
when it will be my duty to act, and then I shall weigh
well the injunctions of the Constitution, which, when
clear and distinct to my mind, will be conclusive
with me. The next consideration will be a fixed and

[1] February 15, 1820.

an unalterable attachment to the Union; my decided opinion is, that all States composing our Union, new as well as old, must have equal rights, ceding to the general government an equal share of power, and retaining to themselves the like; that they cannot be incorporated into the Union on different principles or conditions. Whether the same restraint exists on the power of the general government, as to Territories, in their incipient and territorial state, is a question on which my mind is clearly decided. By the Constitution, Congress has power to dispose of and make all needful rules and regulations respecting the territory and other property belonging to the United States, with a provision that nothing in this Constitution should be so construed as to prejudice any claims of the United States, or of any particular State. This provision is the only check on the power of Congress, and (referring only to the old controversy between the United States and individual States respecting vacant lands within their charter of limits, whose relative claims it was intended to preserve) has no operation, as I presume, on the present case. The power itself applies to the territory ceded by individual States to the United States, and to none other. In such portions of the territory so ceded as are altogether uninhabited, the people who move there, under any ordinance of Congress, have no rights in the territorial state except such as they may acquire under the ordinance. The question, therefore, cannot occur in regard to them. If there is any restraint, then, on this power in Congress, it must be found in other parts of the Constitution. Slavery is recognized by the Constitution as five to three; but is not the right thus recognized that only of the States in which the slaves are, as the measure or rate of representation in the House of Representatives and for direct taxes? Is it not a right to the slaves themselves, not as I presume to their owners, out of the State in which they are? By another clause it is provided that if slaves run away they may be pursued, demanded, and brought back; this is a right of the slave-holding States, and of the owners of slaves living in them, and would apply to slaves running into Territories as well as into States. As slavery is recognized by the Constitution it is evidently unjust to restrain the owner from carrying his slave into a Territory and retaining his right to him there, but whether the power to do this has not been granted is the point on which I have doubts, and on which I shall be glad to receive your opinion. If I can be satisfied that the Constitution forbids restraint, I shall, of course, obey it in all cases.

" Should a bill pass admitting Missouri, subject to such restraint, I should have no difficulty in the course to be pursued, nor should I in any future case respecting the admission of any other State. Arkansas, being organized without restriction, and people having moved there, as is understood, stands on the most favorable ground, on constitutional principles, in the view stated above.

" Considerations of injustice and impolicy also merit much attention, and will have their weight with me.

I do not think, supposing the constitutional right to exist, that Congress ought to confine the slaves within such narrow limits, even of territories, as might tend to make them a burden on the old States. How far I may go on this principle will merit great consideration. If the right to impose the restraint exists, and Congress should pass a law for it, to reject it, as to the whole of the unsettled territory, might, with existing impressions in other questions, affect our system. This I should look to with a just sensibility to the part likely to be injured."

Mr. Adams, in recording his impressions of the entire discussion, thus defines his own position : —

" I have favored this Missouri compromise, believing it to be all that could be effected under the present Constitution, and from extreme unwillingness to put the Union at hazard. But perhaps it would have been a wiser and bolder course to have persisted in the restriction on Missouri, until it should have terminated in a convention of the States to revise and amend the Constitution. This would have produced a new Union of thirteen or fourteen States unpolluted with slavery, with a great and glorious object — that of rallying to their standard the other States by the universal emancipation of their slaves. If the Union must be dissolved, slavery is precisely the question upon which it ought to break. For the present, however, this contest is laid asleep."

The promotion of internal improvements and

the defense of the seaboard had naturally come to the front as important questions during the momentous events of Madison's administration. Monroe took up these matters in earnest when the chief responsibility of guiding the national policy devolved upon him, but it was not until 1822 that he felt called upon to announce his views in an elaborate paper. He vetoed the Cumberland Road bill on May 4, and he simultaneously submitted to Congress an exposition of his views. His long statement concludes with the assertion that Congress has not the right under the Constitution to adopt and execute a system of internal improvements, but that such a power, if it could be secured by a constitutional amendment, would have the happiest effect on all the great interests of the Union ; though, in his opinion, it should be confined to great national works, leaving to the separate States all minor improvements.

Near the close of Monroe's presidency, Lafayette made his celebrated visit to the United States as " the nation's guest." These two men had been friends from the days when they were both in the Revolutionary army. When Lafayette was a prisoner in Olmütz and Monroe was American minister in France, efforts were made by the latter to secure the former's release. Several letters are before me[1] which relate to the negotiations. Funds were sent by Washington to Monroe for the benefit of Madame Lafayette. As the United States had no minister near the Austrian court, the mediation of the Danish government was solicited by Monroe. Carefully covered references to " the friend in question " were addressed by Monroe to Mr. Masson, aide-de-camp of Lafayette. But the details of this story belong elsewhere. They are here alluded to because they indicate the recollections shared by these two patriots when they met more than a quarter of a century afterwards, and Monroe, as President and as friend, welcomed Lafayette to the hospitality of the United States.

On May 10, 1824, the French Marquis, " with feelings of respectful, affectionate, and patriotic gratitude," accepted the invitation of Congress, and promised to visit " the beloved land " of which it had been his " happy lot to become an early soldier and an adopted son." Early in October, after his landing in this country, the members of Monroe's cabinet were in doubt as to the etiquette which should be observed at the reception of this illustrious visitor in Washington, and also as to the attitude which the administration should take during the progress of

[1] Gouverneur MSS.

his journey. Calhoun, the secretary of war, addressed a letter of eight pages to Mr. Monroe on this matter, saying that it seemed "hazardous on the one side to connect the government too much with the movements in favor of the general, and on the other not to seem to sympathize with the popular feelings. Of the two, however, the latter is the most hazardous, and in a doubtful case we ought to err on the right side." A few days later Monroe answered some inquiries from Lafayette respecting his route, and added that his arrival "has given rise to a great political movement which has so far taken the direction and had the effect among us, and I presume in Europe, which the best friends to you and to sound principles could desire. It is of great importance that it should terminate in like manner." The letters from the visitor to his host are most familiar. In one of them he says, "I feel, my dear sir, the impropriety to address the President of the United States on a half sheet of paper, but am pressed by time, and the knowledge of the sin will remain between you and me." His closing salutations are varied and glowing, one of the most characteristic being, "from your old, affectionate, obliged brother-soldier and friend." From "on board the Pottowmack steam boat," February 24, 1825, he sends to Monroe "the commentary on Montesquieu, by my friend Tracy, George's father-in-law," which may be of use to one who "contemplates writing a political exposition." "It has been translated under the patronage of Mr. Jefferson, who considers it the best publication of the kind. You will, I believe, find it the most advanced theoretical point of the science, although the practice in every detail be still superior to theories." [1]

After Lafayette's return to France his letters to Monroe were marked by the same confidence and affection, and they show that in private life he was as charming as in public he was popular. Two passages will be quoted. In the first he speaks as follows of the American visitors introduced to him at Lagrange : —

"I am afraid, dear friend, you continue to be uneasy at the number of American visits we are wont to receive. Be assured nothing can be more pleasing to me, and to us all; it is even necessary. You know my American education, feelings, habits, prejudices. . . . Doomed as I am to live on a side of the Atlantic where, to be sure, I am bound by family, friendly, patriotic affections and duties, but in other respects less congenial to my youthful avocations and republican nature, I ever have felt something peculiar and sympathetic in American communications, a dispo-

[1] Gouverneur MSS.

sition which, of course, has been strengthened in my
last visit, when in every man, woman, and child of a
population of twelve millions, I have found a loving,
indeed an enthusiastic friend. You may conceive
what, in addition to my attachments and remem-
brances of more than fifty years, must now be to
me the United States and every sort of communion
with their citizens. The visits we receive are not by
far so numerous as I would like them, and the feeling
is so unanimous in the family that young American
strangers, as they arrive, are received by our girls
with more confidence and familiarity than they would
be disposed to show to most of their older acquaint-
ances, because there is something like family understanding between them; and so I have the delight to
see that when American friends find themselves here
in sight of American colors, American busts and portraits, American manners, and American welcome,
they look as feeling they are at home. Let me add
that the sentiments, behavior, delicacy of all the
young men from the United States are exemplary
to a degree which, to the older part of their fellow-
citizens, is an object of inexpressible and proud gratification." [1]

In the second extract, the reader may see
with what extreme delicacy Lafayette offers
pecuniary assistance to one who had brought
assistance to the Olmütz prisoner three decades
before.

[1] Gouverneur MSS.

"In the meanwhile, my dear Monroe, permit your earliest, your best, and your most obliged friend to be plain with you. It is probable that to give you time and facilities for your arrangements, a mortgage might be of some use.

"The sale of one half of my Florida property is full enough to meet my family settlements and the wishes of my neighbors. There may be occasion for a small retrocession of acres, in case of some claims on the disposed-of Louisiana lands, an object as yet uncertain, at all events inconsiderable, so that there will remain ample security for a large loan, for I understand the lands are very valuable, and will be more so, to a great extent, after the disposal of a part of them. You remember that in similar embarrassment I have formerly accepted your intervention ; it gives me a right to reciprocity. Our friend, Mr. Graham, has my full powers. Be pleased to peruse the inclosed letter, seal it, and put it in the post-office. I durst not send it before I had obtained your approbation, yet should it be denied, I would feel much mortified. I hope, I know, you are too much my friend not to accept what, in a similar case, I would not an instant hesitate to ask." [1]

When Monroe's second term was almost ended the rivalries for the succession became very apparent. Adams, Crawford, and Calhoun in his cabinet, Clay and Jackson outside

[1] Gouverneur MSS. I do not know whether Monroe availed himself of this generous offer, but I presume that he did not.

of it, were all recognized candidates. Monroe
remained neutral in the contest. The biographer of William Wirt,[1] with ample materials at
his command for forming a judgment, says : —

"During the pendency of this contest, Mr. Monroe observed a most scrupulous resolve against all
interference with the freest expression of the public
sentiment in regard to the candidates. In this he
was fully seconded and sustained by his cabinet, by
none more than by those whose names were in the
lists for suffrage. For, at that time, *it was not considered decorous in the Executive to make itself a
partisan in a presidential or any other election.*
Indeed, there was a most wholesome fastidiousness
exhibited on this point, which would have interpreted
the attempt of a cabinet officer, or any other func-
tionary of the government, to influence the popular
vote by speech, by writing, by favor, fear, or affection, as a great political misdemeanor worthy of
sharpest rebuke. These were opinions of that day
derived from an elder age. They are obsolete opinions now."

[1] Hon. J. P. Kennedy, in his *Life of Wirt*, ii. 168.

CHAPTER VII

THERE is an important subject, pertaining
to Monroe's administration, which has been re-
served for a special chapter. The one event of
his presidency which is indissolubly associated
with his name, is an announcement of the policy
of the United States in respect to foreign interference in the affairs of this continent. The
declaration bears the name of the " Monroe
Doctrine." As such it is discussed in works on
public law and in general histories. It is commonly regarded as an epitome of the principles
of the United States with respect to the development of American States.

Everything which illustrates the genesis of
such an important enunciation is of interest, but
very little has come under my eye to illustrate
the workings of Monroe's mind, or to show how
it came to pass that he uttered in such terse sentences the general opinion of his countrymen.
As a rule, he was not very skillful with his pen;
his remarks on public affairs are not often
quoted, like those of Jefferson, Madison, and

others of his contemporaries ; there was nothing racy or severe in his style ; nevertheless, he alone of all the Presidents has announced, without legislative sanction, a political dictum, which is still regarded as fundamental law, and bears with it the stamp of authority in foreign courts as well as in domestic councils.

We must turn to the annual message of December 2, 1823, for the text. The two passages which relate to foreign interference are quite distinct from one another, and are separated by the introduction of other matter. This is the language : —

I

" At the proposal of the Russian imperial government, made through the minister of the emperor residing here, a full power and instructions have been transmitted to the minister of the United States at St. Petersburg, to arrange, by amicable negotiation, the respective rights and interests of the two nations on the northwest coast of this continent. A similar proposal has been made by his imperial majesty to the government of Great Britain, which has likewise been acceded to. The government of the United States has been desirous, by this friendly proceeding, of manifesting the great value which they have invariably attached to the friendship of the emperor, and their solicitude to cultivate the best understanding with his government. In the discussions to which this interest has given rise and in the arrangements by which they may terminate, the occasion has been judged proper for asserting, as a principle in which the rights and interests of the United States are involved, that the American continents, by the free and independent condition which they have assumed and maintain, are henceforth not to be considered as subjects for future colonization by any European powers."

II

" It was stated at the commencement of the last session that a great effort was then making in Spain and Portugal to improve the condition of the people of those countries, and that it appeared to be conducted with extraordinary moderation. It need scarcely be remarked that the result has been so far very different from what was then anticipated. Of events in that quarter of the globe, with which we have so much intercourse and from which we derive our origin, we have always been anxious and interested spectators. The citizens of the United States cherish sentiments the most friendly in favor of the liberty and happiness of their fellow-men on that side of the Atlantic. In the wars of the European powers, in matters relating to themselves, we have never taken any part, nor does it comport with our policy so to do. It is only when our rights are invaded or seriously menaced, that we resent injuries or make preparation for our defense. With the movements in this hemisphere we are, of necessity, more immediately connected and by causes which must be obvious to all enlightened and impartial observers. The political system of the allied powers is essentially different in this respect from that of America. This difference proceeds from that which exists in their respective governments. And to the defense of our own, which has been achieved by the loss of so much blood and treasure, and matured by the wisdom of their most enlightened citizens, and under which we have enjoyed unexampled felicity, this whole nation is devoted. We owe it, therefore, to candor and to the amicable relations existing between the United States and those powers, to declare that *we should consider any attempt on their part to extend their system to any portion of this hemisphere as dangerous to our peace and safety.* With the existing colonies or dependencies of any European power we have not interfered, and shall not interfere. But with the governments who have declared their independence and maintained it, and whose independence we have, on great consideration and on just principles, acknowledged, we could not view any interposition for the purpose of oppressing them, or controlling in any other manner their destiny, by any European power, in any other light than as *the manifestation of an unfriendly disposition toward the United States.* In the war between those new governments and Spain we declared our neutrality at the time of their recognition, and to this we have adhered and shall continue to adhere, provided no change shall occur which, in the judgment of the competent authorities of this government, shall make a corresponding change on the part of the United States indispensable to their security.

" The late events in Spain and Portugal show that Europe is still unsettled. Of this important fact no stronger proof can be adduced than that the allied powers should have thought it proper, on a principle satisfactory to themselves, to have interposed by force in the internal concerns of Spain. To what extent such interposition may be carried on the same principle, is a question to which all independent powers, whose governments differ from theirs, are interested; even those most remote, and surely none more so than the United States. Our policy in regard to Europe, which was adopted at an early stage of the wars which have so long agitated that quarter of the globe, nevertheless remains the same, which is, not to interfere in the internal concerns of any of its powers; to consider the government *de facto* as the legitimate government for us; to cultivate friendly relations with it, and to preserve those relations by a frank, firm, and manly policy; meeting, in all instances, the just claims of every power; submitting to injuries from none. But in regard to these continents, circumstances are eminently and conspicuously different. It is impossible that the allied powers should extend their political system to any portion of either continent without endangering our peace and happiness; nor can any one believe that our southern brethren, if left to themselves, would adopt it of their own accord. It is equally impossible, therefore, that we should behold such interposition, in any form, with indifference. If we look to the comparative strength and resources of Spain and those new governments, and their distance from each other, it must be obvious that she can never subdue them. It is still the true policy of the United States to leave the parties to themselves, in the hope that other powers will pursue the same course."

It appears to me probable that Monroe had but little conception of the lasting effect which his words would produce. He spoke what he believed and what he knew that others believed; he spoke under provocation, and aware that his views might be controverted; he spoke with authority after consultation with his cabinet, and his words were timely; but I do not suppose that he regarded this announcement as his own. Indeed, if it had been his own decree or ukase it would have been resented at home quite as vigorously as it would have been opposed abroad. It was because he pronounced not only the opinion then prevalent, but a tradition of other days which had been gradually expanded, and to which the country was wonted, that his words carried with them the sanction of public law.

A careful examination of the writings of the earlier statesmen of the republic will illustrate the growth of the Monroe Doctrine as an idea dimly entertained at first, but steadily developed by the course of public events and by the reflection of men in public life. I have not made a thorough search, but some indications of the mode in which the doctrine was evolved have come under my eye which may hereafter be added to by a more persistent investigator.

The idea of independence from foreign sovereignty was at the beginning of our national life. The term "continental," applied to the army, the congress, the currency, had made familiar the notion of continental independence. This kept in mind the notion of a continental domain, — not provincial, nor colonial, nor merely national. Moreover, in the writings, both public and private, of the fathers of the republic, we see how clearly they recognized the value of separation from European politics, and of repelling, as far as possible, European interference with American interests.

1. Governor Thomas Pownall, in a work entitled "A Memorial to the Sovereigns of Europe," observed, in 1780, that a people, "whose empire stands singly predominant on a great continent," can hardly "suffer in their borders such a monopoly as the European Hudson Bay Company;" and again, "America must avoid complication with European politics," and "the

entanglement of alliances, having no connections with Europe other than commercial." [1]

2. One of the earliest of like allusions happens to be in a letter of Monroe to Madison, December 6, 1784, when he says that "the conduct of Spain respecting the Mississippi, etc., requires the immediate attention of Congress."

3. A few months later, June 17, 1785, Jefferson, writing to Monroe from Paris, begs him to add his "testimony to that of every thinking American, in order to satisfy our countrymen how much it is their interest to preserve, *uninfected by contagion*, those peculiarities in their government and manners to which they are indebted for those blessings."

4. Washington wrote to Jefferson, January 1, 1788, in the interval which preceded the ratification of the Constitution : [2] "An energetic general government must prevent the several States from involving themselves in the political disputes of the European powers."

5. When Washington's first term drew near its close he submitted to Madison the draft of a farewell address (May 20, 1792), and in it he gives emphasis to the independence of the

---

[1] These citations from Pownall are taken from Sumner's *Prophetic Voices concerning America*, pp. 123, 124.

[2] Quoted by Bancroft from MS., *History of the Constitution*, ii. 299.

United States, in a phrase which with various turns was perpetuated through the subsequent revisions of that paper. His original language was this: " The extent of our country, the diversity of our climate and soil, and the various productions of the States consequent to both, . . . may render the whole, at no distant period, *one of the most independent nations in the world.*"

6. Madison's modification of this draft has the following sentence (June 20, 1792): " The diversities [of this country] may give to the whole *a more entire independence* than has, perhaps, fallen to the lot of any other nation."

7. Four years later (prior to May 10, 1796), Washington submits to Hamilton memoranda for a farewell address, and says again: " If this country can remain in peace twenty years longer . . . such in all probability will be its population, riches, and resources, when combined with *its peculiarly happy and remote situation* from the other quarters of the globe, as to *bid defiance in a just cause to any earthly power whatsoever.*"

8. The address, finally issued, says: " The great rule of conduct for us in regard to foreign nations is, in extending our commercial relations, to have with them as little political connection as possible." " Europe has a set of

primary interests which to us have none or a very remote relation." "Our detached and distant situation." "Why forego the advantages of so peculiar a situation?" (September 17, 1796.)

9. John Adams speaks thus in his first inaugural address (March 4, 1797): "If [the control of an election] can be obtained by foreign nations by flattery or menaces, by fraud or violence, by terror, intrigue, or venality, the government may not be the choice of the American people but of foreign nations. *It may be foreign nations who govern us*, and not we the people who govern ourselves."

10. In the second annual address of Adams this paragraph occurs (December 8, 1798): —

"To the usual subjects of gratitude I cannot omit to add one of the first importance to our well-being and safety — I mean that spirit which has arisen in our country against the menaces and aggressions of a foreign nation. A manly sense of national honor, dignity, and independence has appeared, which, if encouraged and invigorated by every branch of the government, will enable us to view undismayed the enterprises of any foreign power, and become the sure foundation of national prosperity and glory."

11. There are three extracts from Jefferson's writings which show the tendency of his mind

at the beginning of the century. He said to
Thomas Paine (March 18, 1801) : [1] —

"Determined as we are to avoid, if possible, wast-
ing the energies of our people in war and destruction,
we shall avoid implicating ourselves with the powers
of Europe, even in support of principles which we
mean to pursue. They have so many other interests
different from ours, that we must avoid being entangled in them. We believe we can enforce those principles, as to ourselves, by peaceable means, now that
we are likely to have our public councils detached
from foreign views."

A little later he wrote to William Short (October 3, 1801) : [2] —

"We have a perfect horror at everything like con-
necting ourselves with the politics of Europe. It
would indeed be advantageous to us to have neutral
rights established on a broad ground ; but no dependence can be placed in any European coalition
for that. They have so many other by-interests of
greater weight that some one or other will always
be bought off. To be entangled with them would be
a much greater evil than a temporary acquiescence in
the false principles which have prevailed."

Again he says (October 29, 1808) : "We
consider their interests and ours as the same,

---

[1] Jefferson's *Works*, iv. 370.
[2] *Works*, iv. 414.

and that the object of both must be to exclude
all European influence in this hemisphere." [1]

12. At a cabinet meeting, May 13, 1818, President Monroe propounded several questions on
the subject of foreign affairs, of which the
fifth, as recorded by J. Q. Adams,[2] was this:
" Whether the ministers of the United States
in Europe shall be instructed that the United
States will not join in any project of interposition between Spain and the South Americans,
which should not be to *promote the complete
independence of those provinces;* and whether
measures shall be taken to ascertain if this be
the policy of the British government, and if so
to establish a concert with them for the support
of this policy." He adds that all these points
were discussed, without much difference of
opinion.

13. On July 31, 1818, Rush had an important interview with Castlereagh in respect to a
proposed mediation of Great Britain between
Spain and her colonies. The coöperation of
the United States was desired. Mr. Rush informed the British minister that " the United

[1] This quotation is made by Schouler in a note, where he
says: " The germ of the Monroe Doctrine of later development
is early seen in Jefferson's correspondence in view of the Spanish uprising against Bonaparte and its possible effects upon
Cuba and Mexico, which he is well satisfied to leave in their
present dependence." — *History of the United States*, ii. 202.

[2] *Diary*, iv.

States would decline taking part, if they took part at all, in any plan of pacification, except *on the basis of the independence of the colonies.* This," he added, "was the determination to which *his government had come on much deliberation."*

14. August 4, 1820, Jefferson writes to William Short: [1] —

"From many conversations with him [M. Correa, appointed minister to Brazil by the government of Portugal], I hope he sees, and will promote in his new situation, the advantages of a cordial fraternization among all the American nations, and *the importance of their coalescing in an American system of policy, totally independent of and unconnected with that of Europe.* The day is not distant when we may formally require a meridian of partition through the ocean which separates the two hemispheres, *on the hither side of which no European gun shall ever be heard, nor an American on the other ;* and when, during the rage of the eternal wars of Europe, the lion and the lamb, within our regions, shall lie down together in peace. . . . The principles of society there and here, then, are radically different, and I hope no American patriot will ever lose sight of the essential policy of interdicting in the seas and territories of both Americas, the ferocious and sanguinary contests of Europe. I wish to see this coalition begun."

[1] Randall's *Jefferson*, iii. 472.

15. Gallatin writes to J. Q. Adams, June 24, 1823, that before leaving Paris he had said to M. Chateaubriand on May 13 : " The United States would undoubtedly preserve their neutrality provided it were respected, and avoid every interference with the politics of Europe. . . . On the other hand, they would not suffer others to interfere against the emancipation of America." [1]

A year previously, April 26, 1822, he had written from Paris that he had said to Monsieur : " America, having acquired the power, had determined to be no longer governed by Europe, . . . that we had done it [recognized the independence of the Spanish-American provinces] without any reference to the form of government adopted by the several provinces, and that the question, being one of national independence, was really altogether unconnected with any of those respecting internal institutions which agitated Europe."

16. John Quincy Adams, in his diary under date of July 17, 1823, makes a note which the editor of that work regards as " the first hint of the policy so well known afterwards as the Monroe Doctrine." [2]   In a conversation with Baron Tuyl, the Russian minister, on the Northwest

---

[1] *Writings of Gallatin*, by Adams, ii. 271 ; ii. 240.
[2] *Diary*, vi. 163.

Coast question, Mr. Adams, then secretary of state, told him that " we should contest the right of Russia to *any* territorial establishment on this continent, and that we should assume distinctly the principle that the American continents are no longer subjects for any new European colonial establishments."

17. After Canning had proposed to Rush (September 19, 1823) that the United States should coöperate with England in preventing European interference with the Spanish-American colonies, Monroe consulted Jefferson as well as the cabinet, on the course which it was advisable to take, and with their approbation prepared his message. Jefferson's reply to the President (October 24, 1823) was as follows:[1] —

" The question presented by the letters you have sent me is the most momentous which has ever been offered to my contemplation since that of independence. That made us a nation, this sets our compass and points the course which we are to steer through the ocean of time opening on us. And never could we embark on it under circumstances more auspicious. Our first and fundamental maxim should be, *never to entangle ourselves in the broils of Europe. Our second, never to suffer Europe to intermeddle with cis-Atlantic affairs.* America, North and South,

[1] Randall, iii. 491.

has a set of interests distinct from those of Europe, and peculiarly her own. She should therefore have a system of her own, separate and apart from that of Europe. While the last is laboring to become the domicile of despotism, our endeavor should surely be, to make our hemisphere that of freedom."

An extract, dated 1824, and recently published, from the diary of William Plumer, who was a member of Congress during Monroe's administration, gives to John Quincy Adams the credit of drafting the important portions of the message. He says that a day or two before Congress met Monroe was hesitating about the allusion to the interference of the Holy Alliance with Spanish America, and consulted the secretary of state about omitting it. Adams remained firm, replying, "You have my sentiments on the subject already, and I see no reason to alter them." "Well," said the President, "it is written, and I will not change it now." [1]

Enough has been quoted to show that Mr. Sumner [2] is not justified in saying that the "Monroe Doctrine proceeded from Canning," and that he was "its inventor, promoter, and champion, at least so far as it bears against European intervention in American affairs."

[1] *Pennsylvania Magazine of History and Biography*, vol. vi. No. 3, p. 358.

[2] See his *Prophetic Voices*, pp. 157–160.

Geo Canning

Nevertheless, Canning is entitled to high praise for the part which he took in the recognition of the Spanish republics, a part which almost justified his proud utterance, " I called the New World into existence to redress the balance of the Old."

If memoranda of Monroe's upon this subject are still extant they have eluded me. There is a letter to him from one of his family (December 6) praising the message, and adding these sentences, which show the expectations of the friends of the administration.[1]

" You have a full indemnification for all the time and attention it may have cost you, in the sentiment which has accompanied it throughout the nation, and I mistake greatly if it do not excite a feeling in Europe as honorable to our country as it may be unacceptable to many there. You will have the merit of proposing an enlightened system of policy, which promises to secure the united liberties of the New World, and to counteract the deep laid schemes in the Old for the establishment of an universal despotism. The sentiments and feelings which the message expresses, you may be assured, will be echoed with pride and pleasure from every portion of our widely extended country, and will be esteemed to have given to our national character new claims upon the civilized world.

[1] Gouverneur MSS.

"The operation of your message also upon the reputation of your own administration cannot be mistaken. Effecting higher objects, it will also be distinctly traced in the prostration of those limited views of policy which have infected so many of those who have been intrusted of late with a portion of the powers and character of our country, and in the diffusion among our citizens of a great confidence in the general administration, so essential to the prosperity of our system. By giving a new and exalted direction to the public reflections, a tone of feeling and expression must succeed as fatal to the pretended patriots of the two last years as it will be honorable to those who, at the risk of popularity, have been the objects of their clamorous abuse." [1]

The Monroe Doctrine came before Congress less than three years later, when the propriety of sending ministers to the Congress of Panama was debated. Mr. McLane was opposed to any course which should bind the United States to resist interference from abroad in the concerns of the South American governments, and Mr. Rives wished to declare still more explicitly that the United States was not pledged to maintain by force the principle that no part of the American continent was henceforward subject to colonization by any European power. Daniel Webster made a speech, April 11, 1826, on the

[1] I am indebted to Mr. Morse, the editor of this series of volumes, for these citations.

Panama mission, in which he came boldly to
the defense of the Monroe Doctrine. The country's honor, he said, is involved in that declaration; "I look upon it as a part of its treasures
of reputation, and for one I intend to guard it."
After reviewing the political history from the
Congress of Verona onward, he continued : "I
look on the message of December, 1823, as forming a bright page in our history. I will help
neither to erase it nor tear it out; nor shall it
be by any act of mine blurred or blotted. It
did honor to the sagacity of the government,
and I will not diminish that honor." [1]

The origin of the Monroe Doctrine is regarded
by a recent English writer [2] as of "more than
speculative importance;" for, in his opinion,
"the history of the doctrine shows that its literal
interpretation is far from clear. Phrases which
in the mouth of one man might be the obscure
expression of confused thought would not be
uttered by another without a deep political meaning." This leads the writer to an elaborate and
very interesting investigation of the authorship.
He speaks of Monroe "as the mild and venerable patriarch of whom little but good is known,
and who may the more easily be reputed a
hero;" and he conjectures that the popular ven-

[1] *Works*, iii. 205.
[2] Reddaway: *The Monroe Doctrine*, p. 74.

eration for the doctrine is due to "its supposed
parentage by Monroe." On the other hand,
he argues that if this famous pronunciamento
"were proved to be the offspring of Adams,
much of the glamour encircling it might fade
away, and its interpretation might pass more
completely from the sphere of sentiment into
that of reason." This introduces an acute analysis of the opinions and views of Monroe and
of his secretary of state, John Quincy Adams,
and involves the conclusion that "the conception
of the Monroe Doctrine and much of its phrase-
ology came from Adams, and that the share of
Monroe did not extend beyond the revision."

To me this discussion seems more important
to the antiquary than to the historian; for if
further research should establish beyond question the authorship as that of Adams, the fact
will still remain that the President and not the
secretary of state announced the doctrine. It
was his official sanction which gave authority to
the phrases, by whomsoever they were written,
and lifted them far above the plane of personal
opinions. Monroe spoke from the chair of the
Chief Executive; and to him statesmen and his-
torians have continuously attributed the doctrine. His official station, at a critical moment,
and not his personal characteristics and opinions,
gave to his words authority; and their pro-

nounced acceptance by the people of the United States shows how accurately they express the sentiments of the people. It would require a volume to trace the effects of the Monroe Doctrine upon political discussions in the United States, from the date of its enunciation to the beginning of the Cuban war in the spring of 1898. No attempt is here made to engage in this review, but in the appendix will be found a comprehensive bibliography by means of which the course of events and of debates may be readily traced.

CHAPTER VIII

SYNOPSIS OF MONROE'S PRESIDENTIAL MESSAGES [1]

PRESIDENT MONROE'S inaugural addresses and annual messages are of greater length than those of any of his predecessors. His fifteen special messages are almost all brief; one, however, that of May 4, 1822, on internal improvements, is of extraordinary length.

In his first inaugural address, delivered on March 5, 1817, he dwells upon the happy condition into which the country had been brought by the excellence of its political institutions and the bounty of Nature. Protection of its liberty and prosperity against dangers from within could be secured only by maintaining the excellence of the national character. To secure it against dangers from without, the coast and frontier defenses, the army, the navy, but especially the militia, should be maintained in a state of efficiency. Attention is drawn to the advantages

---

[1] The following summary of the speeches and messages of James Monroe, printed in the *Statesman's Manual*, has been prepared for insertion here by Professor J. F. Jameson, Ph. D.

of developing the resources of the country and
drawing the various parts of the Union more
closely together by the construction of roads and
canals, to the extent sanctioned by the Constitution ; of increasing the independence and
strength of the industrial system of the country
by the care of the government; of paying the
national debt at an early period ; and, in general,
of making those improvements for which peace
gives the best opportunity. He promises that
the new administration will do all in its power
to secure efficiency in all departments of the
public service, to maintain peace with other nations, and to promote the increased harmony
then pervading the Union.

In the first annual message of President Monroe, dated December 2, 1817, which opens with
congratulations on the progress of the national
defenses and the increase of harmony, he speaks
of the diplomatic relations with England, and
with Spain and her revolted colonies, the national revenue and the rapid extinguishment
of the debt, recent purchases of lands from the
Indians, our relations with them, the method
of sale of public lands, the constitutionality of
executing at national expense, improvements in
inter - communication, American manufactures,
public buildings at the federal capital, pensions
for soldiers of the Revolution, and the repeal

of the internal taxes. Under the first head he reports the completion of arrangements for reducing naval forces on Lake Erie, the progress of various minor negotiations pursuant to the provisions of the treaty of Ghent, and the failure of our proposals for the opening of the ports in the West Indies and other British colonies to American vessels; how this shall be met he leaves to Congress. He complains of violations of our neutrality by both Spain and her colonies, but expresses the belief that the occupation and hostile use of portions of territory claimed by us, at Amelia Island and Galveston, were not authorized by the latter, and defends the suppression of these resorts. He recommends provision for the better civilization of the Indians upon the Western frontier, whose lands have recently been bought, and such regulation of the sale of the tracts thus opened to immigrants as shall most benefit the general government and the settlers. Concerning the right to make internal improvements he says: " Disregarding early impressions, I have bestowed on the subject all the deliberation which its great importance and a just sense of my duty required, and the result is a settled conviction in my mind that Congress does not possess the right." But he suggests a constitutional amendment giving the right to do this, and to institute seminaries of learning. He recommends the repeal of the internal taxes, believing them no longer necessary.

A special message of January 13, 1818, informs Congress that the settlement at Amelia Island, and probably that at Galveston, has been broken up. The President considers this justified by their character, and declares that nothing has been or will be done to injure Spain.

The second annual message, dated November 17, 1818, opens with a statement by the President of the arrangements which had been made with reference to a continuation of the convention with Great Britain. He discusses the troubles in Florida, mentions the progress of the South American revolutions and the mediation proposed by the allied powers, notices the excellent condition of the national finances, and recommends further protection. He dwells with satisfaction upon the progress of the system of defenses, and upon the admission of a new State, Illinois, believing that the rise of new States within our borders will produce the greatest benefits, both material and political. He recommends such provision for the Indians as will, if possible, prevent their extinction, accustom them to agriculture, and promote civilization among them; and the establishment of a government for the District of Columbia more agreeable to principles of self-government. His statements

as to events in Florida ought, perhaps, to be
represented more fully. He draws a strong
picture of the impotence of the Spanish authorities, of the lawless character of the adventurers
who seized upon various positions in the province,
and of the dangers to which the citizens of the
United States were subjected, at sea by the de-
predations of the adventurers and on land by
the attacks of the Indians incited by them.   As
Spain could not govern the region, and would
not transfer it, the only course open to our government, says the President, was to suppress the
establishment at Amelia Island, and to carry
the pursuit of the Indians so far as to prevent
further disturbance from them, or from their in-
citers, English or Spanish; but care, he said, has
been taken to show due respect to the government of Spain.

The negotiations of our government with that
of Spain form the chief subject of the annual
message of December 7, 1819. A treaty by
which the Spanish government ceded to the
United States the province of Florida, while the
United States renounced its claims to the part
of Louisiana west of the River Sabine, known
as Texas, and its claims to compensation for
injuries sustained by its citizens from Spanish
cruisers some twenty years before, had, early in
this year, been concluded at Washington and

ratified by the government there. It was then sent to Madrid, but, unexpectedly, the Spanish government delayed ratifying it, alleging not only that attempts had been made by United States citizens against Texas, but that our minister at Madrid had, as instructed, when presenting the treaty for ratification, accompanied it by a declaration explaining the meaning given to one of its articles. In the present message the President comments severely upon the conduct of the Spanish court, denies its first charge absolutely, and explains that the second refers to a correction enabling the treaty to cover, as both governments agreed that it should cover, all cases of land grants of a specified sort. He declares that the conduct of Spain is perfectly unjustifiable, and is so regarded by European governments, and that it would be right for our government to carry out the treaty fairly, alone ; but suggests forbearance until the expected envoy shall have arrived from Madrid. Other matters, new and old, which the President discusses in this message are, the preservation of our neutrality in the South American conflict, the Canadian and West Indian commerce, the treasury, the contraction of bank circulation and depression of industry, the coast survey, the increase of the navy, and the maintenance of the Mediterranean squadron.

A special message, sent a few days later, December 17, describes, and submits to amendment by Congress, the arrangements which the Executive had made for the transference to Africa of negroes captured in accordance with the act for the abolition of the slave-trade.

In the last annual message of his first term, that of November 14, 1820, President Monroe takes occasion to review the present situation of the Union. He expresses the greatest satisfaction at our wonderful prosperity. While certain interests have suffered depression because of the long European wars and the consequent industrial derangements, he regards these as mild and instructive admonitions, and as accumulating " multiplied proofs of the great perfection of our most excellent system of government, the powerful instrument in the hands of an all merciful Creator, in securing to us these blessings." He reports that the treaty with Spain is not yet ratified, while Florida is constantly made a basis of smuggling operations ; that the restrictions on commerce to and from the West Indies continue ; and that negotiations have been commenced for a commercial treaty with France, and recommends legislation making more just the recent tonnage duties on French vessels. South American affairs are, as usual, mentioned. The rapid reduction of the public debt is noted,

as showing the extent of the national resources.
The President then recommends legislation to
relieve those who have bought public lands on
credit in days of higher prices. He reports progress in the preparation of the extensive system
of fortifications, and sets forth the great advantages to be expected from them, and more briefly
those derivable from the frontier posts among
the Indians and the naval squadrons abroad.

In his second inaugural address, delivered
March 4, 1821, President Monroe first expresses
his gratitude for the confidence of his fellow-citizens, and his satisfaction at the general accord
with which it has been expressed. " Having
no pretensions," says he, " to the high and
commanding claims of my predecessors, whose
names are so much more conspicuously identified
with our Revolution, and who contributed so
preëminently to promote its success, I consider
myself rather as the instrument than the cause
of the union which has prevailed in the late
election. . . . It is obvious that other powerful causes, indicating the great strength and sta-
bility of our Union, have essentially contributed
to draw you together." He then reviews the
acts of the government in the previous term,
and, first of all, the progress made in fortification. Upon matters of foreign policy, the chief

opinions expressed by him are, that our neutrality in the South American conflict should by all
means be preserved, that the troubles in Florida
could not be ended in any other way than that
pursued, that the treaty with Spain and the
acquisition of the peninsula will prove highly
advantageous to our country, and that our naval
squadrons in foreign waters have been most efficient in suppressing the slave-trade and piracy.
He recommends, in view of the public exigencies,
the restoration of the internal duties and excises, the removal of which he had, under other
circumstances, suggested in a former message.
He further recommends that the Indians, instead of being treated as independent nations,
be settled upon lands granted to them as individuals, and helped to improvement in agriculture
and civilization; and that measures be taken to
make us always capable of self-defense. He
then compares the excellence and success of our
government with the defects and failures of those
of thé ancient republics, and expresses the belief
" that our system will soon attain the highest
degree of perfection of which human institutions
are capable." The address closes with remarks
upon the increase of the area and population of
the United States, and with acknowledgments
of the ability and uprightness of the President's
cabinet advisers.

The principal subjects of the fifth annual message, that of December 3, 1821, are, commercial relations arising under the act of March 3, 1815, and the transference and government of Florida. Besides these, the President briefly discusses Portuguese and South American affairs, the treasury and revenue, incidental protection to manufactures, internal taxation, now no longer deemed necessary, surveys, fortifications, and war vessels, and the efficiency of the Mediterranean squadron in restraining the Barbary powers, and of the naval forces elsewhere in suppressing piracy and the slave-trade. The act of March 3, 1815, had provided that the manufactures and productions of any foreign nation, imported into the United States in vessels of the same nation, should be exempted from the payment of any further duties than would be paid upon the same merchandise if imported in our ships, whenever the Executive should be satisfied that the nation in question had conferred the like privilege upon our commerce. It was thought, says the President, that the proposal was liberal, and that any power acceding to it would also throw open the trade of its colonies to foreign vessels on a similar basis. But England, while accepting it for her European dominions, has declined it for the West Indies, and France has declined it altogether; direct

trade with the West Indies and France in our
vessels and their has therefore ceased. He
expresses regret at the extreme interpretation
put by the French government upon the most-
favored-nation clause in the treaty of 1803, and
defends the seizure of the Apollo, on the nomi-
nally Spanish side of the St. Mary's River, on
the ground that the sole purpose of its presence
there was to elude our revenue laws. He reports
the extension of the reciprocity system of the act
of 1815 by treaties with several powers. In announcing the transfer of Florida, he comments
severely upon the refusal of the Spanish officials
in charge to transfer the land records of the
province. He describes the measures taken for
the provisional government of the district, re-
grets the dissensions which have occurred in it,
recommends the prompt establishment of a territorial government for it, and reports progress
in the satisfaction of the claims of our citizens
against Spain.

During this same session several special messages were sent to Congress. The first, on February 25, 1822, suggests a larger appropriation
for a treaty with the Cherokees; the second,
dated March 8, 1822, relates to the contest
between Spain and her colonies. The opinion
is expressed that recent events have made it
manifest that the colonies not only possess inde-

pendence, but are certain to retain it, and that the recognition of their independence by us should now be made, that it cannot be regarded by Spain as improper, and may help to shorten the struggle. A longer special message of March 26 refers to the fortifications at Dauphin Island at the mouth of Mobile Bay, and, incidentally, to the subject of fortifications in general. The President demonstrates the necessity of extensive fortifications at that point for the protection not only of Mobile but of New Orleans, and thus of the whole valley of the Mississippi. He ends the message with a strong vindication of the policy of fortification adopted by Congress soon after the late destructive war with England; he shows that the amount of loss which, in any similar emergency, would be thus prevented, far exceeds the cost of the works themselves, and that the latter has been, and is being, defrayed without sensibly increasing the burdens resting upon the people.

By far the most important of the special messages of President Monroe are those vetoing the Cumberland Road Bill, and giving the reasons therefor. In the former he briefly declares his opinion that the power to pass such a law implies the power to adopt and execute a complete system of internal improvement, and that such a power is neither specifically nor incidentally granted by the Constitution. The session being too advanced to permit him to include his reasons in this message, he instead transmits to Congress an exposition of his views on the subject previously committed to paper, and having a form somewhat different from that which would have been adopted in a message. The paper so transmitted forms a special message of great length, setting forth fully the President's views on internal improvements.

This message may be divided into four parts. In the first he discusses the general subject of the division of powers between the general government and the State governments; in the second he describes the powers which the general government would have to exercise if it possessed the right claimed for it; in the third he controverts in detail the arguments of those who seek to derive the power in question from various powers conceded to Congress by the Constitution; in the fourth he declares the advantages of the possession of such a power by them, if carefully confined to great works of national importance, and recommends an amendment to secure that end.

The subjects of the first portion are, the origin of the state governments and their endow-

ments when first formed; the origin of the
national government and the powers vested in
it, and the powers which are admitted to have
remained to the state governments. The views
disclosed in it are substantially the following:
When the power of the crown was abrogated,
the authority which had been held by it vested
exclusively in the people of the colonies. These
appointed a Congress. They also formed state
governments, to which all necessary powers of
government, not vested in Congress, were im-
parted, the sovereignty still residing in the people. Meanwhile the powers of Congress, though
vast, were undefined. Hence the plan of confederation ratified in 1781. Now it may fairly
be presumed that where grants of certain powers were transferred in the same terms from
this to the Constitution of 1788, they should be
construed in the same sense in the latter which
they bore in the former. Its principal provisions are therefore here inserted. Its incompetence being demonstrated, the new Constitution
was formed and ratified, the state governments
themselves taking the lead in this forward movement. A compact was thus formed, which cannot be altered except by those who formed it,
and in the mode in it described. Thus there
were two separate and independent governments
established over the Union, one for local pur-

poses over each State, by the people of the
State; the other for national purposes over all
the States, by the people of the United States.
Both governments have a common origin or
sovereign, the people, whose whole power, on
the representative principle, is divided between
them. As a result of this survey, two important facts are disclosed; the first is, that the
power or sovereignty passed from the crown
directly to the people; the second, that it passed
to the people of each colony, and not to the
people of all the colonies in the aggregate.
Had it been otherwise, had the people not had
equal rights and a common interest in the struggle, or had the sovereignty passed to the aggregate, the Revolution might not have succeeded.
But, clearly, power passed to the people of
each colony, for the chartered rights, whose violation produced the Revolution, were those secured by the charters of each colony; and the
composition and conduct of Congress confirm
this position. The powers granted by the Constitution to the government of the United States
are then detailed. On the powers remaining to
the governments of the States, it is observed,
that the territory contemplated by the Constitution is the territory of the several States, and
under their jurisdiction; the people is the people
of the several States; the militia, the holding

of property, the administration of justice, the criminal code, are all under the control of the state governments, except in cases otherwise specially provided for. The right of the general government is, in short, a power to perform certain specified acts and those only.

The second division of the message discusses briefly the nature and extent of the powers requisite to the general government in order to adopt and execute a system of internal improvement, a necessary preliminary to the decision whether it has this power. First, says the President, it must be able to buy the land even in spite of the owner's refusal to sell ; secondly, it must be able to punish those who injure the road or canal, by having not only jurisdiction over it but power to bring them to justice, wherever caught ; thirdly, it must be able to establish tolls and provide for their collection and for the punishment of those infringing such regulations.

If, he continues, the United States possess this power, it must, since it has not been specifically granted, be derived from one of the following sources : First, the right to establish post-offices and post-roads ; second, to declare war ; third, to regulate commerce among the several States ; fourth, from the power to pay the debts and provide for the common defense and general welfare of the United States ; fifth, from the power

to make all laws necessary and proper for carrying into execution all the powers vested by the
Constitution in the government of the United
States, or in any department or officer thereof;
sixth, from the power to dispose of and make
all needful rules and regulations respecting the
territory and other property of the United States.
From some one or other of these the advocates
of the power derive it, and all these the President proceeds, in this third part of his message,
to consider in detail.

As to the first grant, it is contended that it
cannot, in the ordinary sense of the word "establish," be held to mean anything more than the
use of existing roads by the mail-carrier in passing over them as others do; that the phrase
must be held to mean just what it did in the
Articles of Confederation; that, its object being
the carriage of the mails, only what is absolutely necessary to that object is conceded; and
that the proposed interpretation would give Congress the same jurisdiction over all the roads
already existing in every State.

The claim under the second grant mentioned
would extend to canals as well as to roads. If
internal improvements are to be carried to the
full extent to which they may be useful for military purposes, the power must extend to all
roads in the Union. Further, the Constitution

makes a special grant of several rights, like that of raising an army, which might much more certainly be derived from that of declaring war than could the power in question; omission to mention the latter, therefore, proves that it is not granted, as does also the specification of a grant of jurisdiction over land ceded for fortifications; we are obliged to infer that in this case alone is the power given.

Next, the President takes up the third argument, from the power to regulate commerce between the States. The history of this grant and of the discussions which preceded it make it evident, he says, that it was intended merely to give power to impose duties on foreign trade and to prevent any on trade between the States.

The fourth claim is founded on the second part of the first clause of Art. I. Sec. 8 of the Constitution, which reads: "The Congress shall have power to lay and collect taxes, duties, imposts, and excises, to pay the debts and provide for the common defense and general welfare of the United States; but all duties, imposts, and excises shall be uniform throughout the United States." The reasoning upon this point is in substance the following: The second phrase here used gives a right to appropriate the public money, and it gives this power alone. For, first, if the right of appropriation is not given by this

clause it is not given at all; secondly, this part
of the grant has none of the characteristics of a
distinct and original power, but is manifestly incidental to the first part; thirdly, if this is not
its real meaning it has a scope so wide as to
make unnecessary all the other grants in the
Constitution, for they would be included in this;
further, the place which this phrase occupies is
exactly the one most fitting for a grant of the
right of appropriation.   If, then, this is the
power here granted, it remains to inquire what
is the extent of this power.   One construction
is, that the government has no right to expend
money except in the performance of acts authorized by the other specific grants, according to
a strict construction of their nature.   "To this
construction," says President Monroe, "I was
inclined in the more early stage of our government; but, on further reflection and observation,
my mind has undergone a change, for reasons
which I will frankly unfold."   The power to
raise money and the power to appropriate it are
both, in this grant, conveyed in terms as general
and unqualified as, for instance, those conceding
to Congress the power to declare war.   More
comprehensive terms than " to pay the debts and
provide for the common defense and general
welfare " could not have been used.   And so
intimately connected with and dependent on

each other are the two branches of power granted, that a limitation of one would have had the like effect upon the other. But indeed it was impossible to have created a power within the government, distinct from Congress and the Executive, which should control the movement of the government in respect to expenditures, and not destroy it. This, then, must be the nature of the grant of appropriation. Have Congress, then, a right to raise and appropriate the public money to any and to every purpose, according to their will and pleasure ? They certainly have not. The government of the United States is a limited government, instituted for great national purposes, and for those only. Good roads and canals will, however, promote many very important national purposes. To the appropriation of the public money to such improvements there seems to be no well founded constitutional objection ; to do anything further than this the general government is not competent. This has also been the practice of our government; for instance, in the case of the Cumberland Road, all the acts of the United States have been based on the principle that the sovereignty and jurisdiction belonged not to the general government but to the States ; Congress has simply appropriated money from the public treasury, thus aiding a work of great national utility.

The conclusion reached upon this point is, therefore, that the right to make internal improvements has not been granted by the power to "provide for the common defense and general welfare," but only the right to appropriate the public money; that the government itself being limited, the power to appropriate is also limited, the extent of the government, as designated by the specific grants, marking the extent of the power, which should, however, be extended to every object embraced by the fair scope of those grants, and not confined to a strict construction of their respective powers (it being safer to aid the purposes of those grants by the appropriation of money than to extend, by a forced construction, the grant itself); and that, though the right to appropriate is indispensable, it is insufficient as a power if a great scheme of improvements is contemplated.

Against the fifth source suggested, the power to make all laws necessary and proper for carrying into execution all powers vested by the Constitution in the general government, it is urged that such a power is not by that instrument so vested.

Sixthly, the second clause of Art. II. Sec. 3 of the Constitution is shown, by the first clause and by the history of the cessions of land to the United States by the States, to refer to such

lands only. The power to make all needful regulations respecting the territory and other property of the United States has, therefore, no
bearing upon the subject of internal improvements to be made by the general government.

Therefore it is concluded that the desired
power is not possessed. Much more than the
right to appropriate is required ; territorial jurisdiction over the roads is not, however, necessary,
but may be left to the States, if the government
have the power to protect its works.

The great advantages of such improvements
are easily seen, while no other region can, from
its configuration, be improved so vastly by roads
and canals at so slight expense. The inter-
change of our varied productions would be rendered more easy and commerce increased ; the
efficiency of both the general and the state
governments, the intelligence of the people, the
strength of the Union, and the expansion of our
system, would be greatly promoted. It cannot
be doubted that such improvements can be made
by the general government better than by the
local governments, liable to jealousies and influences not felt by the former. The Cumberland Road, in particular, has a pressing need
of the use of this power by the national government.

" If it is thought proper," concludes the Pre-

sident, " to vest this power in the United States,
the only mode in which it can be done is by an
amendment of the Constitution. On full consideration, therefore, of the whole subject, I am
of opinion that such an amendment ought to be
recommended to the several States for their
adoption. It is, however, my opinion that the
power should be confined to great national works
only, since, if it were unlimited, it would be
liable to abuse and might be productive of
evil."

President Monroe in his sixth annual message, dated December 3, 1822, touches upon a
great variety of subjects. He reports the conclusion of a satisfactory commercial convention
with France, the opening of trade with the
British colonies, and a decision by the Emperor
of Russia upon Article I. of the Treaty of Ghent,
and recommends the legislation which these
events require. He announces the formation of
a territorial government for Florida ; states the
prosperous condition of the finances ; summarizes the report of the secretary of war, especially as to the Academy at West Point, and that
of the secretary of the navy ; and recommends
the removal of the Seminoles. Referring to
his message upon the Cumberland Road, he suggests that if Congress do not see fit to propose

the amendment there advised, it can certainly take measures to repair and protect the road; he further recommends increased protective duties. The remainder of the message deals with foreign affairs. The President expresses his hope that Spain will soon give up the contest with her colonies, and exhibits strong sympathy with the cause of Greece. In view of the complications in Europe which make war imminent, he exhorts the nation, while it congratulates itself upon its exemption from the causes which disturb peace elsewhere, to keep itself ever in a position to defend its liberties in any emergency.

At the beginning of his seventh annual message, December 2, 1823, the President explains the purpose of his messages, declaring that, as with us the people are exclusively the sovereigns, they should be informed on all public matters, especially foreign affairs and finance. Progress is reported in various negotiations. Our government having begun to negotiate with the Russian emperor and with England in regard to the northwest boundary, " the occasion has been judged proper for asserting, as a principle in which the rights and interests of the United States are involved, that the American continents, by the free and independent condition which they have assumed and maintain, are

henceforth not to be considered as subjects for
future colonization by any European powers."
He mentions the proposals of our government
that the slave-trade be declared piracy, and that
privateering be abolished, and expresses strong
approval of both these measures.   The condition of the finances, the war department, the
militia, the navy, piracies in the Gulf, the post-
office department, the tariff, the public accounts,
and the Cumberland Road, is described, without
recommendations of special significance.   The
project for the Chesapeake and Ohio Canal is
mentioned with approval, and an appropriation
for a survey is recommended, as well as for other
public works.   The most ardent wishes for the
success of Greece in winning independence are
expressed.   Then follows a celebrated passage,
already reproduced in the text of this book.[1]

The message closes with a comparison of the
present state of the country with that at the
close of the Revolution, touching upon the ad-
ditions to our territory, the expansion of our
population, the accession of new States, and the
strengthening of our system to such an extent
that consolidation and disunion are both im-
practicable.

A special message, sent to Congress on February 24, 1824, submitted to their consideration

[1] See p. 158.

the claim of a portion of the Massachusetts militia to compensation for services in the late war. The decision of the Governor of Massachusetts, that the power to call out the militia of a State was conditional upon the consent of its Executive, and that when called out they could not be placed under the command of an officer of the regular army, had previously made it impossible for the national Executive to make such compensation. Now, however, the principle in dispute being conceded by that State, favorable action is recommended to Congress.

The important matters mentioned in the last annual message of President Monroe, that of December 7, 1824, aside from those which appear in the same form in previous messages, are: the slave-trade, the rights of neutrals, the engineers' surveys, the visit of General Lafayette, the relations of our government with those of South America, the Supreme Court, and the Indians. A convention between the United States and Great Britain, declaring the slave-trade piratical, has been concluded but not yet ratified. An effort has been made, on occasion of the war between France and Spain, to put upon a more just basis the rights of neutral vessels in time of war, and it is hoped will prove successful. In view of the extensive roads and canals now projected, it is recommended that the corps of engineers be increased. The arrival of General Lafayette and his warm welcome are mentioned, and it is suggested that in consideration of his services a suitable provision be tendered him by Congress. The independent states of South America are reported to be following the example of our prosperity, in spite of some presumably temporary disturbances; the most friendly feelings toward them are expressed. The President recommends an organization of the Supreme Court which will relieve the judges of that court from any duties not connected with it, and will be more suited to the requirements of the present day; that some wise and humane arrangement be made for the Indians, — perhaps settling them in the territory toward the Rocky Mountains, — which will lead to their permanent settlement in agricultural pursuits, and ultimately to their civilization, for which it is our solemn duty to provide; and that the propriety of establishing a military station on the Pacific Coast be considered. He again reminds the nation of the many blessings it enjoys, and exhorts it to preserve them from dangers without and dissensions within, and concludes this, his last annual message, with expressions of gratitude for the public confidence and the generous support received from his fellow-citizens.

During the session of 1825 several brief special messages were sent to Congress. In the first, dated January 5, the President requests a full investigation of his accounts with the government during his long public service, with a view to a decision upon them hereafter. In the second, dated January 10, he gives reasons for withholding the documents, called for by the House of Representatives, concerning the conduct of Commodore Stewart and Mr. Provost in South America. With the third, also addressed to the House and dated January 27, he transmits a report of the secretary of war in regard to the removal of Indians to the West, and recommends that some scheme of good government for them be adopted. With the fourth, of February 14, he transmits to the House a report of the secretary of war on certain surveys for internal improvements. The fifth, of February 17, concerns special affairs of the District of Columbia. The sixth, of February 21, again refers the claims of the Massachusetts militia to Congress, to whom, and not to the Executive, belongs the decision of the matter. The last message, dated February 26, 1825, concerns a matter of mere routine, the unintentional neglect to sign a certain bill.

CHAPTER IX

PERSONAL ASPECT AND DOMESTIC RELATIONS

LITTLE has been said hitherto of Monroe's domestic and personal characteristics, but I cannot close the narrative without some reference to them, — beginning with a mention of his happy marriage and his family ties. While attending Congress in New York, he became engaged to Miss Eliza Kortwright, daughter of Lawrence Kortwright of that city, a lady of high social standing and of great beauty. He consulted his relative and life-long friend, Judge Jones, on this important matter, and received from him this counsel, which, however admirable for its discretion and caution, was certainly not likely to influence a man of twenty-eight who was ardently in love.

JUDGE JONES TO JAMES MONROE

" You will act prudently (so soon as you determine to fix yourself to business) to form the connection you propose with the person you mention or some other, as your inclination and convenience shall dictate. Sensibility and kindness of heart, good-nature without levity, a moderate share of good sense, with some portion of domestic experience and economy, will generally, if united in the female character, produce that happiness and benefit which results from the married state, and is the highest human felicity a man may enjoy, and he cannot fail to enjoy it when he is blessed with a companion of such a disposition and behavior, unless he is so weak and imprudent as to be his own tormentor. You have reached that period of life to be capable of thinking and acting for yourself in this delicate and interesting business, and I can only assure you that any accommodation I shall be able to afford you, to render yours and her situation agreeable and easy, will be cheerfully afforded, which, should fortune be wanting, will be more embarrassing in the commencement than any after period."

It does not appear how carefully the lover weighed these words of wisdom, but the result of his own reflections appears in a letter to Madison, in which he announces his intended marriage.

"If you visit this place shortly I will present you to a young lady who will be adopted a citizen of Virginia in the course of this week."

Three months later he writes to Jefferson: —

"You will be surprised to hear that I have formed the most interesting connection in human life with a young lady in this town, as you know my plan was to visit you before I settled myself ; but having formed an attachment to this young lady — a Miss Kortwright, the daughter of a gentleman of respectable character and connections in this State, though injured in his fortunes by the late war — I have found that I must relinquish all other objects not connected with her. We were married about three months since. I remain here until the fall, at which time we remove to Fredericksburg in Virginia, where I shall settle for the present in a house prepared for me by Mr. Jones, to enter into the practice of the law."

The young lawyer had doubted where to make his permanent home, and his friendly relative went over the field carefully, and pointed out to him the comparative advantages of Fredericksburg and Richmond, with particular reference to his profession. The former is at length determined on, and the choice is thus announced to Jefferson, August 19, 1786: —

"I shall leave this about the 1st of October for Virginia, — Fredericksburg. Believe me, I have not relinquished the prospect of being your neighbor. The house for which I have requested a plan may possibly be erected near Monticello ; to fix there, and to have yourself in particular, with what friends we may collect around, for society is my chief object; or rather, the only one which promises to me, with the connection I have formed, real and substantial pleasure ; if, indeed, by the name of pleasure it may be called."

There were two children of this marriage, Eliza, who married Judge George Hay of Virginia; and Maria, who married Samuel L. Gouverneur of New York. When Monroe was in Paris his elder daughter was at school with Hortense Beauharnais, who became Queen of Holland, and their teacher was the celebrated Madame Campan. The acquaintance thus formed became a warm friendship. The child of Monroe's daughter was named Hortense or Hortensia, after Queen Hortense, who retained a warm interest in her namesake through her life. In a Baltimore family interesting mementos of this intimacy are carefully preserved. Portraits in oil of Hortense and Eugene Beauharnais and of Madame Campan were sent to Hortensia Hay by the former queen, with an affectionate letter, and there are reasons to think that she remembered in her last will her American namesake.[1]

Monroe's interest in the various members of his family connection is marked by more than ordinary affection. He took great pains to further their material welfare, and make them comfortable in their outward affairs, but he was always on his guard against using his official

[1] The gentleman, Charles Wilmer, Esq., who owns these valuable pictures, has also a charming miniature of Mrs. Monroe, painted when she resided in Paris.

station for the benefit of any relative.   In June,
1794, just as he was about to sail for Europe,
he gave the following advice to a nephew.[1]   It
indicates, more accurately than any other letter
which I recall, Monroe's moral principles.

" You may by your industry, prudence, and studi-
ous attention to your business, as well as to your
books, make such exertions as will advance your fortune and reputation in the world, whereby alone your
happiness or even tranquillity can be secured.   Not
only the reality of these virtues must be possessed,
but such an external must be observed as to satisfy
the world you do possess them, otherwise you will
not enjoy their confidence.   You will recollect, likewise, that heretofore your youth and inexperience
were an excuse for any apparent levity or irregular-
ity, but now that you are advancing in life, have a
family and children, the case is altered.   Solid merit
and virtue alone will support and carry you with
credit through the world.

" The principal danger to which a young man commencing under limited resources is exposed, and in
which, if he errs, he inflicts the most incurable wound
on his reputation, is the abuse of pecuniary confidence.   Let me, therefore, warn you never to use your
client's money.   No temptation is greater to a person
possessed of it than that which daily arises in the
occurrences of a private family, to use this money,
especially when the prospect of reimbursement fur-

[1] Gouverneur MSS.

nishes the hope it may not be called for. But as the commencement of this practice breaks down to a certain degree that chaste and delicate refinement, which forms the strongest barrier for the protection of virtue, it should never be commenced.

"I would make it one of those sacred rules of my life which should not be violated, never to use it. I believe you have no passion for anything of that kind. I sincerely hope you have not. I suggest this hint, therefore, rather to guard you against a danger which assails every young man, than that I believe you likely to suffer by it. I mean the vice of gambling. I recollect there is a billiard table near you. Let me warn you against it. A passion of this kind will control, as it always has, every other. If it seizes you, your client's money will not be safe in your hands."

Several sketches of Monroe, written at different periods of his life, by different persons, will next be given.

1799–1802.

William Wirt, in the "Letters of a British Spy," which were published in a newspaper in 1803, and afterwards reprinted in various forms, drew the portrait of Monroe at the time when first he was governor. It is an interesting sketch by itself, but still more so in connection with a pendent likeness of the illustrious Marshall, whose career began with that of Monroe,

in the College of William and Mary, and whose
life was almost exactly contemporaneous.

"In his stature," says Wirt, "he is about the middle height of men, rather firmly set, with nothing
further remarkable in his person, except his muscular
compactness and apparent ability to endure labor.
His countenance, when grave, has rather the expression of sternness and irascibility; a smile, however
(and a smile is not unusual with him in a social
circle), lights it up to very high advantage, and gives
it a most impressive and engaging air of suavity and
benevolence.

"His dress and personal appearance are those of a
plain and modest gentleman. He is a man of soft,
polite, and even assiduous attentions; but these, although they are always well-timed, judicious, and
evidently the offspring of an obliging and philan-
thropic temper, are never performed with the striking
and captivating graces of a Marlborough or a Boling-
broke. To be plain, there is often in his manner an
inartificial and even an awkward simplicity, which,
while it provokes the smile of a more polished person,
forces him to the opinion that Mr. Monroe is a man
of a most sincere and artless soul."

This is but a portion of the description.

1825.

A letter from Mrs. Tuley, then of Virginia,
recently published,[1] gives the following picture

---

[1] *Philadelphia Times*

of the last levee at the White House, on New
Year's day, during Monroe's administration.
When she entered the reception-room,

" Mr. Monroe was standing near the door, and as
we were introduced we had the honor of shaking
hands with him and passing the usual congratulations
of the season. My impressions of Mr. Monroe are
very pleasing. He is tall and well formed. His
dress plain and in the old style, small clothes, silk
hose, knee-buckles, and pumps fastened with buckles.
His manner was quiet and dignified. From the frank,
honest expression of his eye, which is said to be 'the
window of the soul,' I think he well deserves the
encomium passed upon him by the great Jefferson, who said, ' Monroe was so honest that if you
turned his soul inside out there would not be a spot
on it.'

" We passed on and were presented to Mrs. Monroe
and her two daughters, Mrs. Judge Hay and Mrs.
Gouverneur, who stood by their mother and assisted
her in receiving. Mrs. Monroe's manner is very
gracious and she is a regal-looking lady. Her dress
was superb black velvet; neck and arms bare and
beautifully formed; her hair in puffs and dressed
high on the head and ornamented with white ostrich
plumes; around her neck an elegant pearl necklace.
Though no longer young, she is still a very handsome woman. You remember Mrs. —— told us that,
when Mr. Monroe was sent as Minister to France,
Mrs. Monroe accompanied him, and in Paris she was

called '*la belle Américaine*.' She also told us that
she was quite a belle in New York in the latter part
of the Revolutionary War. Her maiden name was
Kortwright. Mrs. Judge Hay (the President's eldest
daughter) is very handsome also — tall and graceful,
and, I hear, very accomplished. She was educated
in Paris at the celebrated boarding-school kept by
Mme. Campan, and among her intimate school friends
was the beautiful Hortense de Beauharnais, step-
daughter of the Emperor Napoleon. Her dress was
crimson velvet, gold cord and tassel round the waist,
white plumes in the hair, handsome jewelry, bare
neck and arms. The other daughter, Mrs. Gouverneur, is also very handsome — dress, rich white satin,
trimmed with a great deal of blonde lace, embroidered
with silver thread, bare neck and arms, pearl jewelry
and white plumes in the hair. By the bye, plumes in
the hair seem to be the most fashionable style of
head-dress for married ladies.

"All the lower rooms were opened, and though
well filled, not uncomfortably so. The rooms were
warmed by great fires of hickory wood in the large
open fireplaces, and with the handsome brass and-
irons and fenders quite remind me of our grand old
wood fires in Virginia. Wine was handed about in
wine-glasses on large silver salvers by colored waiters,
dressed in dark livery, gilt buttons, etc. I suppose
some of them must have come from Mr. Monroe's
old family seat, 'Oak Hill,' Virginia."

1830.

Here is an autographic sketch of the ex-President's literary work, addressed to Mr. Gouverneur : [1] —

" I am engaged in a work which will be entitled 'A biographical and historical view of the great events to which Mr. Monroe was a party and of which he was a spectator in the course of his public service,' — commencing with my service in the army, in the legislature and council of the State, in the Revolutionary Congress and in the Senate. I have brought it to the conclusion of my first mission to France, which would, if printed, make about one hundred and twenty pages, and with the appendix, should it be thought advisable to add one, perhaps as many more. This work to this stage might be published at an early period as introductory to the sequel, though, I being closely engaged in it, I could, if I have health, complete the whole in five or six months. I have composed in part another work, a comparison between our government and the ancient republics, and likewise with the government of England. Of this I have already extended it to a view of the government of Athens and Lacedemon, of Greece, of Carthage, with notes on that of Rome, to which I have drawn an introductory view of government and society as the basis of the work. This work I could also finish in about the same time, by devoting myself to it. What I have already written would occupy more pages than that above mentioned.

[1] Gouverneur MSS.

My correspondence, when in the war department, of three hundred and ninety-four pages folio, I mean my own letters only, is another work which I intend at a proper time to publish. If my claims are rejected I should wish to take the preparatory steps to a publication, by suitable notices in the public papers at the proper time. I think no part had better be published until that part is finished ; and to accomplish which, that I had better devote myself to one of the works mentioned, exclusively in the first instance, the biographical one, for instance. I shall place occurrences and develop principles by a faithful attention to facts, manifesting no hostility to any one. The publication of any part cannot, I presume, be made till the fall, and no notice had better be taken of it till just before."

1830.

During the latter part of his life a gentleman who is now living in Charlottesville, Va., Judge E. R. Watson, was a member of Monroe's family, and retains a very vivid recollection of his appearance, occupations, and characteristics. He has been so kind as to prepare for insertion here the following reminiscences.

Judge Watson's Recollections.

" In person Mr. Monroe was about six feet high, perhaps rather more ; broad and square-shouldered and raw-boned. When I knew him he was an old man (more than seventy years of age), and he looked

perhaps even older than he was, his face being
strongly marked with the lines of anxiety and care.
His mouth was rather large, his nose of medium size
and well-shaped, his forehead broad, and his eyes
blue approaching gray. Altogether his face was a
little rugged ; and I do not suppose he was ever
handsome, but in his younger days he must have
been a man of fine physique, and capable of great
endurance. As an illustration of this, I remember
hearing him say that immediately preceding the occupation of Washington by the British, and just after
their retreat from the city, during the war of 1812,
with the burden of three of the departments of the
government resting upon him, — State, Treasury, and
War, — he did not undress himself for ten days and
nights, and was in the saddle the greater part of the
time. There was no grace about Mr. Monroe, either
in appearance or manner. He was, in fact, rather an
awkward man, and, even in his old age, a diffident
one. Nevertheless, there was a calm and quiet dignity about him with which no one in his presence
could fail to be impressed, and he was one of the
most polite men I ever saw to all ranks and classes.
It was his habit, in his ride of a morning or evening,
to bow and speak to the humblest slave whom he
passed as respectfully as if he had been the first gentleman in the neighborhood. I have heard him de-
fine true politeness as 'right feeling controlled by
good common sense.'

"I do not know that I ever witnessed in Mr. Monroe any actual outbreak of temper, but I was always

impressed with the idea that he was a man of very
strong feelings and passions, which, however, he had
learned to control perfectly.   I never heard him use
an oath, or utter a word of profanity, and hence I
was quite astonished when, on one occasion, I was
talking with an old family servant about a gentleman
who swore very hard, and he remarked, ' Bless your
soul, you ought to hear old master! He can give
that man two in the deal and beat him.'   In his
intercourse with his family he was not only unvary-
ingly kind and affectionate, but as gentle as a woman
or a child.   He was wholly unselfish.   The wishes,
the feelings, the interests, the happiness, of others
were always consulted in preference to his own.

"Being quite young at the time, I was not a very
competent judge, but my recollection is that Mr.
Monroe's conversational powers were not of a high
order.   He always used the plainest, simplest language, but was not fluent, and was, it seemed to me,
wholly wanting in imagination.   He lacked the ver-
satility, and I should say also the general culture,
requisite for shining in the social circle, but was
always interesting and instructive ; when with good
listeners he led in conversation, and talked of the
scenes and events through which he had passed, *et
quorum magna pars fuit.*   Whilst I was a member
of Mr. Monroe's family it was his habit, when the
weather and his health would allow, and the presence
of visitors did not prevent, to ride out morning and
evening, and I was very often his only companion.
On these occasions he always talked of the past, and

I was strongly impressed with the idea that he must have been in his public career essentially a man of action ; content even that others might share the credit really due to him, if he could only enjoy the consciousness of doing his duty and rendering his country service. Love of country and devotion to duty appeared to me the explanation of his success in life and the honors bestowed upon him. There was not the least particle of conceit in Mr. Monroe, and yet he seemed always strongly to feel that he had rendered great public service. From Washington to John Quincy Adams, he was the associate and co-laborer of the greatest and best men of his day. Yet he had no feeling of envy towards any of them ; and though he felt that some had not always treated him justly, he took far more pleasure in commending their high qualities and patriotic services than in referring to his wrongs, real or imaginary.

"One striking peculiarity about Mr. Monroe was his sensitiveness, his timidity in reference to public sentiment. I do not mean as it respected his past public life. As to that he appeared to feel secure. But in retirement his great care seemed to be to do and say nothing unbecoming in an ex-President of the United States. He thought it incumbent on him to have nothing to do with party politics. This was beneath the dignity of an ex-President, and it was unjust to the people, who had so highly honored him, to seek to throw the weight of his name and character on either side of any contest between them. Hence Mr. Monroe, after retiring from office, rarely, if ever, expressed his opinions of public men or measures, except confidentially. Over and over again, in the early days of Jackson's administration, did he speak freely to me of that remarkable man, of Mr. Calhoun, Mr. Webster, Mr. Clay, and others scarcely less prominent, as well as of the principles and measures with which they were respectively identified ; but always with the injunction that what he said was never to be repeated. I recollect well to this day some of his opinions as then expressed, and have often regretted that I did not make some note of them all. But the truth is, I was so much afraid that in some unguarded moment I might betray the confidence reposed in me, that I sought rather to forget than to treasure up what he said about men and measures of the day.

"I cannot recall more than a single instance in which, in company, he expressed any opinion as to the character or conduct of prominent public men, except in so far as he could approve and commend them. On one occasion John Randolph of Roanoke was the subject of discussion among several gentlemen present, who differed widely in their estimates of his character and services. Finally Mr. Monroe was appealed to for his opinion by one of Mr. Randolph's admirers, in a way which indicated that the party addressing him scarcely expected any direct answer. Very promptly, however, Mr. Monroe replied, 'Well, Mr. Randolph is, I think, a capital hand to pull down, but I am not aware that he has ever exhibited much skill as a builder.'

"Mr. Monroe's official life was marked by the same deference to and fear of offending public sentiment. My impression is that during his whole presidential term he appointed no relative or near connection to office. His two sons-in-law were George Hay of Virginia, and Samuel L. Gouverneur of New York. The former was a lawyer of eminent ability and a man of the very highest character, and was promptly appointed to a federal judgeship (the same now held by Judge Hughes of Virginia) by John Quincy Adams ; but he received nothing at the hands of Mr. Monroe. And so with Mr. Gouverneur ; he was a talented and popular young man, of one of the best families of New York, but he received no federal appointment till Mr. Adams had succeeded Mr. Monroe. Then Adams made him postmaster of New York. Judge Hay had a son (by his first marriage), Charles Hay, who was made chief clerk of the Navy Department under Mr. Adams, but held no office under Mr. Monroe. The latter, as I heard from his own lips, was not willing, in making any appointment, to lay himself liable even to the suspicion of being influenced by any other consideration than the public good.

"Though Mr. Monroe in early life practiced law, I feel very sure he could not have been a very good speaker. He wrote with no great facility, but with pains. His handwriting was very bad. Some time in 1829, possibly in 1830, by his horse falling with him, he sprained his right wrist very badly, and for some time could not write at all. I often acted as his

amanuensis. His correspondence was immense, and
with the best and wisest men of his day. I do not
remember whether he kept copies of his letters. I
rather think he did not. But I have often thought
that from those written to him there might be gathered
a vast amount of valuable material bearing upon the
history of the country, and the character and conduct
of its public men.

"I have intimated that Mr. Monroe was probably
deficient in general culture. If this be true, it is
equally true that he was a student of history, especially of ancient history. Whilst I was with him he
completed the manuscript of a little work entitled, I
think, 'A Comparison of the American Republic with
the Republics of Greece and Rome.' Every line of
this I copied for him. On its completion he showed it
to Judge Hay (who, with his family, lived with him),
and asked him to read it and tell him what he thought
of it. I well remember that, after examining it,
Judge Hay said to Mr. Monroe, 'I think your time
could have been better employed. If the framers of
our Constitution could have had some work, from a
modern standpoint, on the Constitutions of Greece
and Rome, it might have been of value to them. I do
not think yours is of practical value now. A history
of your Life and Times, written by yourself, would
really be interesting and valuable.' The idea seemed
quite new to Mr. Monroe. Such was his modesty
and self-depreciation that he had never thought of
it before. The suggestion, however, had controlling
weight, and Mr. Monroe immediately began to pre-

pare such a work, and made some progress in it, but how much I cannot say. His memory of past events was remarkable ; and as, from the very beginning of the Revolution, when he became a member of Washington's military family, to the close of his presidency, he was intimately associated with the government and those who controlled it, it is greatly to be deplored that his life and health were not spared to enable him to complete the work. It might not have been distinguished by literary merit, but it would have been marked, in my humble judgment, by a degree of truth, impartiality, and justice which never have been and never will be surpassed by any human production. I have often wondered what had become of this fragment of Mr. Monroe's ' Life and Times,' as well as the little work which I copied for him.

" Mr. Monroe was warmly attached to his friends. He never forgot a service rendered him, whether in public or private life. But in his friendship and affection for Mr. Madison there was something touching and beautiful. Washington and Jefferson he greatly admired, but Mr. Madison he loved with his whole heart. They were once rival candidates for office, but, from what I have heard Mr. Monroe say, I do not suppose there was ever, for a single moment, the slightest feeling of estrangement or unkindness between them.

" I have several times seen them together at Montpelier, and, as it seemed to me, it was only in Mr. Madison's society that Mr. Monroe could lay aside his usual seriousness and indulge in the humorous jest and merry laugh, as if he were young again.

" Mrs. Monroe was Eliza Kortwright of New York, the niece, I think, of General Knox, of Revolutionary fame. Even in old age and feeble health she bore traces of having been very beautiful in early life. She survived Judge Hay but a short time. I was at Oak Hill, on a visit, when she died. She was not buried for several days, the delay being occasioned by the construction of a vault, designed not only for her remains but for those also of Mr. Monroe, as he himself told me. I shall never forget the touching grief manifested by the old man on the morning after Mrs. Monroe's death, when he sent for me to go to his room, and with trembling frame and streaming eyes spoke of the long years they had spent happily together, and expressed in strong terms his conviction that he would soon follow her. In this connection he spoke of his purpose to build a vault for the remains of both of them ; and I have often thought it would have been well if, when Virginia caused his remains to be removed to Richmond, those of Mrs. Monroe had been also removed and laid side by side with them.

" The death of Mr. Monroe occurred on the 4th of July of the next year (1831), at the residence of his son-in-law, Mr. Gouverneur, in the city of New York. I have a strong impression that Mr. Monroe either told me in person, or wrote to me, that his purpose in going to New York was not only to visit his daughter, but especially to see his friend William Wirt, to whom he was devotedly attached."

Here are two almost pathetic letters, one from Monroe to Madison, the other from Madison to Monroe, written in the spring of 1831.

MONROE TO MADISON [1]

I have intended for some time to write and explain to you the arrangement I have made for my future residence, and respecting my private affairs with a view to my comfort, so far as I may expect it, but it has been painful to me to execute it.

My ill state of health continuing, consisting of a cough, which annoys me by night and by day with considerable expectoration, considering my advanced years, although my lungs are not affected, renders the restoration of my health very uncertain, or indeed any favorable change in it. In such a state I could not reside on my farm. The solitude would be very distressing, and its cares very burdensome. It is the wish of both my daughters, and of the whole connection, that I should remain here and receive their good offices, which I have decided to do. I do not wish to burden them. It is my intention to rent a house near Mr. Gouverneur, and to live within my own resources so far as I may be able. I could make no establishment of any kind without the sale of my property in Loudoun, which I have advertised for the 8th of June, and given the necessary power to Mr. Gouverneur and my nephew James. If my health will permit, I will visit it in the interim and arrange affairs there for that event and my removal

[1] Monroe MSS.

here.   The accounting officers have made no decision on my claims, and have given me much trouble.   I have written them that I would make out no account adapted to the act, which fell far short of making me a just reparation, and that I had rather lose the whole sum than give to it any sanction, be the consequences what they may.   I never recovered from the losses of the first mission, to which those of the second added considerably.

It is very distressing to me to sell my property in Loudoun, for, besides parting with all I have in the State, I indulged a hope, if I could retain it, that I might be able occasionally to visit it, and meet my friends, or many of them, there.   But ill health and advanced years prescribe a course which we must pursue.   I deeply regret that there is no prospect of our ever meeting again, since so long have we been connected, and in the most friendly intercourse, in public and private life, that a final separation is among the most distressing incidents which could occur.   I shall resign my seat as a visitor at the Board in due time to enable the Executive to fill the vacancy, that my successor may attend the next meeting.   I beg you to assure Mrs. Madison that I never can forget the friendly relation which has existed between her and my family.   It often reminds me of incidents of the most interesting character.   My daughter, Mrs. Hay, will live with me, who, with the whole family here, unite in affectionate regards to both of you.

Very sincerely, your friend,

J. M.

New York, *April* 11, 1831.

MADISON TO MONROE [1]

MONTPELIER, *April* 21, 1831.

DEAR SIR, — I have duly received yours of [April
11]. I considered the advertisement of your estate
in Loudoun as an omen that your friends in Virginia
were to lose you. It is impossible to gainsay the
motives to which you yielded in making New York
your residence, though I fear you will find its climate unsuited to your period of life and the state of
your health. I just observe, and with much pleasure,
that the sum voted by Congress, however short of
just calculations, escapes the loppings to which it was
exposed from the accounting process at Washington,
and that you are so far relieved from the vexations
involved in it. The result will, I hope, spare you at
least the sacrifice of an untimely sale of your valuable property ; and I would fain flatter myself that,
with an encouraging improvement of your health,
you might be brought to reconsider the arrangement
which fixes you elsewhere. The effect of this, in
closing the prospect of our ever meeting again, afflicts
me deeply ; certainly not less so than it can you.

The pain I feel at the idea, associated as it is with
a recollection of the long, close, and uninterrupted
friendship which united us, amounts to a pang which
I cannot well express, and which makes me seek for
an alleviation in the possibility that you may be
brought back to us in the wonted degree of intercourse. This is a happiness my feelings covet, not-

[1] Madison's *Writings*, vol. iv. pp. 178–179.

withstanding the short period I could expect to enjoy it; being now, though in comfortable health, a
decade beyond the canonical three-score and ten, an
epoch which you have but just passed.

As you propose to make a visit to Loudoun previous to the notified sale, if the state of your health
permits, why not, with the like permission, extend
the trip to this quarter? The journey, at a rate of
your own choice, might coöperate in the reëstablish-
ment of your health, whilst it would be a peculiar
gratification to your friends, and, perhaps, enable you
to join your colleagues at the university once more
at least. It is much to be desired that you should
continue, as long as possible, a member of the Board,
and I hope you will not send in your resignation in
case you find your cough and weakness giving way
to the influence of the season and the innate strength
of your constitution. I will not despair of your being able to keep up your connection with Virginia
by retaining Oak Hill and making it not less than an
occasional residence. Whatever may be the turn of
things, be assured of the unchangeable interest felt
by Mrs. Madison, as well as myself, in your welfare,
and in that of all who are dearest to you.

In explanation of my microscopic writing, I must
remark that the older I grow the more my stiffening
fingers make smaller letters, as my feet take shorter
steps, the progress in both cases being, at the same
time, more fatiguing as well as more slow.

CHAPTER X

MONROE retired from his high office March 4, 1825, and during the seven years which remained of his life divided his time between his home at Oak Hill, in Loudoun County, Virginia, and the residence of his daughter, Mrs. Gouverneur, in the city of New York. He accepted the post of regent in the University of Virginia, which was instituted in 1826, and gave his personal attention to the duties of the office, with Jefferson and Madison. He was asked to serve on the electoral ticket of Virginia in 1828, but declined to do so, on the ground that an ex-President should refrain from an active participation in political contests. He consented, however, to act as a local magistrate and to become a member of the Virginia constitutional convention, which assembled a little later. He maintained an active correspondence with friends at home and abroad, and, what is much more remarkable, he undertook to compose a philosophical history of the origin of free governments, for which his literary training was quite inadequate. This treatise was published in 1867.

Monroe, throughout his later days, was somewhat embarrassed in his pecuniary circumstances, and spent a great deal of time in endeavoring to secure from Congress a just reimbursement for the heavy expenses in which he had been involved during his prolonged services abroad. It is truly pitiful to perceive the straits to which so patriotic a servant of the country, against whose financial integrity not a word was uttered, was reduced; particularly when the expenditures he had incurred were, to a very large amount, required by the positions to which his countrymen had called him, and for which they made inadequate remuneration. No private subscription came to honor or relieve him. Lafayette, with a generous impulse and with great delicacy of procedure, offered him relief.[1] Some allowance was at length made by Congress, and after his death his heirs received a moderate sum for the papers he had preserved. His old age was much given to retrospection, doubtless quickened by the necessity of reviewing his accounts in justification of his claims. A letter to Judge McLean may be found in his manuscripts, with a note

[1] *Ante*, page 154.

that the form was altered, though the spirit was preserved.[1] It reads as follows : —

OAK HILL, *December* 5, 1827.

I have read with great interest your letter of the 15th ult. The course which you have pursued in the administration corresponds with that which I had anticipated. I am satisfied that you had done your duty to your country, and acquitted yourself to the just claims of those with whom you were officially connected.

It has afforded me great pleasure to find that the department had considerably improved, under your management, in all the great objects of the institution, the more extensive circulation of political and commercial intelligence among the great body of our fellow-citizens and the augmentation of the revenue. This sentiment seems to be general throughout the community, which it would not be if it was not confirmed by unquestionable evidence. By the faithful and useful discharge of your public duties you have given the best support which could be rendered to the administration of Mr. Adams, and of which he must be sensible. No person at the head of the government has, in my opinion, any claim to the active partisan exertions of those in office under him. Justice to his public acts, friendly feelings, and a candid and honorable deportment towards him, without forgetting what is due to others, are all that he has a

[1] Monroe MSS.

right to expect, and in those I am satisfied you have never failed. Your view, in regard to my concerns, corresponds also with my own. I shall never apply again to Congress, let my situation be what it may. The only point on which my mind has balanced is, whether the republication of my memoir, remarks, and documents, in a pamphlet, would be proper and useful. Those papers relate to important public events in both my missions and in the late war, and since, while I held an office in the administration. I was charged with a failure to perform my duty in my first mission, and recalled from it and censured.

The book which I published on my return home, with the official documents which it contained, vindicated me against the charge, and on that ground I then left it. The parties are since dead, and I am now retired to private life. I never doubted the perfect integrity of General Washington, nor the strength or energy of his mind, and was personally attached to him. I admired his patriotism, and had full confidence in his attachment to liberty and solicitude for the success of the French Revolution.

It being necessary to advert to that occurrence, in my communication to the committee which was first appointed on my claims, I availed myself of the occasion to express a sentiment corresponding with the above in his favor, as I likewise did in the memoir since published. The documents published with it prove, in minute detail, not only that I faithfully performed my duty to my country, but exerted my best faculties, on all occasions, in support of his character and fame.   The letters of Major Mountflorence, which I had forgotten that I possessed, are material on both points.   They prove that the French government charged me with having prevented it from taking measures which it deemed due to the honor of France, for eight months, and that it had withdrawn its confidence from, and ceased to communicate with me at the very moment when I was recalled by my own government.   Major Mountflorence was no particular friend or associate of mine.   I found him in France, on my arrival there.   He was the friend of Mr. Morris, my predecessor, and, as I understand, from Tennessee.   Mr. Skipwith employed him as the chancellor in his office, on account of his acquaintance with our affairs and knowledge of the French language.   He passed daily, on the business of the consulate, through the several departments of the government, and was acquainted with the principal officers, especially the clerks in each, and on that account I instructed him to make the inquiries to which his reports relate.   All the other documents correspond with and support his statement, which they extend to other objects that are very interesting.

I was likewise charged in that mission with speculation, in consequence of a purchase which I made of a house.   The documents published show clearly the motive which led me into that measure, as they do my intention to offer it to my government, on my resignation and return, on the terms on which I bought it; being recalled, and the minister sent to replace me not received, such an offer would have been absurd.   Besides, I was forced to sell it to enable me to leave the country; and even then I lost one half of the price given for it, as I believe, in consequence of my recall and the circumstances under which I left it.   An important examination of the state of our affairs on my arrival in France, the seizure of our vessels, jealousy of our views, and distress of our citizens there, and the change produced on my appeal and presentation to the convention, with the offer of a house, etc., will, I think, enable any candid person, aided by the documents referred to, to decide whether my motive in making that purchase was a private or a public one.   That it had the desired effect was the opinion of all my fellow-citizens there, who had earnestly advised me to it.

The documents relating to my second mission are likewise very interesting.   The call made on me by Mr. Jefferson, the manner of the call, and circumstances under which I left the country, with the losses attending it, are fully shown, as are the consequences, resulting from the mission.   Those were not known before, and the latter had been misrepresented and were by many misunderstood.   They were never used to promote my election to any office.

This memoir, with the remarks and documents, form a case between my country and me, and, being collected in a pamphlet, will be better understood and more easily preserved.   If not true in a single instance, let it be shown.   I know that they are true in every one, and am not afraid of the severest scrutiny, should the proof presented be deemed inadequate in any circumstance. The preservation of them may tend to give a coloring, or rather character, to some of the wants to which they relate.

With my conduct in the offices in the city, at the most difficult periods, you are well acquainted in the outline, having been a large portion of the time in Congress, and in confidential communication with me. You know that I was called into the Department of War on a great emergency, and by that emergency, not by any desire of mine. Many circumstances, however, occurred while I was in that department, with which I wish to make you acquainted, and especially those which relate to the measures taken for the defense of New Orleans in the late war. Representations have been given of my conduct in that instance very injurious to me.

To the gallantry and very meritorious conduct of General Jackson there, I have always done, and shall do, full justice. I wish, however, to make you fully acquainted with the part I have acted towards him in that and some other instances, which have since occurred. By such a view you will be able to judge whether I have acted fairly towards him, and taken responsibility on myself for him, from motives of friendship, or acted a different part. The papers, which I wish to show you, are original. I do not wish you to come here at this time, and am inclined to think you had better not. If you see no impropriety in it, I will inclose to you the papers which, after perusing them, I wish you to return to me immediately, and without showing or letting it be known to any person existing that you had ever seen them.

On the question of republication and the subject to which it relates, above referred to, I shall be glad to receive your opinion when convenient.

In these last years his quiet was disturbed by a controversy, already mentioned, as to the action of his cabinet in respect to the proceedings of General Jackson. The irritation appears to have begun in 1827.

His son-in-law, Mr. Gouverneur, referring to an article which had appeared in a Tennessee paper, and reflected discredit on Monroe's administration, expressed to Monroe great surprise that such an article should have been written with Jackson's approbation.

"That injustice might be attempted," he says (May 24, 1827), "by the heated partisans of the day for their own purposes, I can readily conceive, but that General Jackson, with whom you have so long preserved the most intimate relations of friendship, and whose public character you have so frequently sustained during the most perilous periods of your administration, should authorize that injustice, I should not only be slow to believe but most deeply regret. It certainly is at variance with all the feelings I have ever entertained of his character, which I thought had been fully justified in all the incidents of his life. It is undoubtedly desirable that you should collect such evidences as are in your possession, and to which you may now have access, as relate to the period in question. It is among the most interesting of our history, and must be so regarded by posterity. How far it may be advisable to use them in any shape at this time, I think depends on what may occur hereafter, and the circumstances which may arise to call for it. Your position is one of a defensive character, if necessary, and I do not think requires anything from you which may invite attack. When it comes I should consider you at full liberty to meet it by all the evidences of which you may be able to avail yourself."

His dread of any financial action which should endanger the Union is clearly brought out in a letter to John C. Calhoun, February 16, 1830,[1] in reply to one which he had received from his former secretary.

" Nothing can be more distressing to me than the approach or possibility of a crisis, which may, in its consequences, endanger our Union. I trust, however, that the patriotism, intelligence, and virtue of the people, and of those who may fill our public councils at the epoch you refer to, will rescue us from such a danger. Satisfied I am that nothing can be so calamitous to every section of the Union as a dismemberment. With such an event our republican system would soon go to wreck; wars would take place between the new States as they did between the

[1] Gouverneur MSS.

ancient republics, and now do between the powers of
Europe ; and we to the south, where so large a portion of the population consists of slaves, would by domestic conjunctions be most apt to fall the victims.

"From the close of our Revolution we have looked
to the extinction of the public debt as a period of
peculiar felicity. There is, I believe, no other government or people in existence who are thus blessed.
That this epoch should lay the foundation for such
a calamity would be an event without example. I
think with you that the interesting questions which
you state will, in the discussion, excite much feeling,
and may, in the view which the different sections
may take of their local interests, put them for a
while in a marked opposition to each other. Each
however will, I trust, weigh the subject calmly, and
be willing to make some concession and even sacrifices to save our republican system."

There are many estimates of Monroe to be
met with in the memoirs of his contemporaries.
Washington's early praise has already been
quoted. Jefferson said of him, "He is a man
whose soul might be turned wrong side outwards
without discovering a blemish to the world."
Madison used this language : "His understanding was very much underrated ; his judgment
was particularly good ; few men have made more
of what may be called sacrifices in the service
of the public." John Quincy Adams delivered
a eulogy, the last pages of which glow with

praise "of a mind, anxious and unwearied in the pursuit of truth and right, patient of inquiry, patient of contradiction, courteous even in the collision of sentiment, sound in its ultimate judgments, and firm in its final conclusions." John McLean gave emphasis to the purity of his action in making executive appointments: — "Personal motives, either as they regarded the President himself or the person appointed, were lost in higher considerations of duty." Webster, in 1825, declared that "the administration now closed had been in general highly satisfactory to the country. It could not be said," he continued, "that that administration had either been supported or opposed by any party associations, or on any party principles." Calhoun, the stern and stately Calhoun, is effusive in the terms which he employs when speaking of the President in whose cabinet he served. One of the most elaborate estimates of Monroe's career is that of Benton, which deserves to be quoted.

"Mr. Monroe had none of the mental qualities which dazzle and astonish mankind ; but he had a discretion which seldom committed a mistake ; an integrity that always looked to the public good ; a firmness of will which carried him resolutely upon his object ; a diligence which mastered every subject ; and a perseverance that yielded to no obstacle or reverse.

" He began his patriotic career in the military service at the commencement of the war of the Revolution, went into the General Assembly of his native State at an early age, and thence, while still young, into the Continental Congress. There he showed his character, and laid the foundation of his future political fortunes in his uncompromising opposition to the plan of a treaty with Spain, by which the navigation of the Mississippi was to be given up for twenty-five years in return for commercial privileges. It was the qualities of judgment and perseverance which he displayed on that occasion which brought him those calls to diplomacy in which he was afterwards so much employed with three of the then greatest European powers, — France, Spain, Great Britain. And it was in allusion to this circumstance that President Jefferson afterwards, when the right of deposit at New Orleans had been violated by Spain, and when a minister was wanted to recover it, said, 'Monroe is the man; the defense of the Mississippi belongs to him.' And under this appointment he had the felicity to put his name to the treaty which secured the Mississippi, its navigation and all the territory drained by its western waters, to the United States forever. Several times in his life he seemed to miscarry and to fall from the top to the bottom of the political ladder, but always to reascend as high or higher than ever. Recalled by Washington from the French mission, to which he had been appointed from the Senate of the United States, he returned to the starting point of his early career, the

General Assembly of his State, served as a member
from his county, was elected Governor, and from that
post was restored by Jefferson to the French mission,
soon to be followed by the embassies to Spain and
England. Becoming estranged from Mr. Madison
about the time of that gentleman's first election to
the presidency, and having returned from his missions
a little mortified that Mr. Jefferson had rejected his
British treaty without sending it to the Senate, he
was again at the foot of the political ladder, and ap-
parently out of favor with those who were at its top.
Nothing despairing he went back to the old starting
point, served again in the Virginia General Assembly, was again elected Governor, and from that post
was called to the cabinet of Mr. Madison, to be
his double secretary of state and war. He was the
effective power in the declaration of war against Great
Britain. His residence abroad had shown him that
unavenged British wrongs were lowering our character with Europe, and that war with the 'mistress of
the seas' was as necessary to our respectability in
the eyes of the world, as to the security of our citizens and commerce upon the ocean. He brought up
Mr. Madison to the war point. He drew the war
report which the Committee on Foreign Relations
presented to the House, that report which the absence of Mr. Peter B. Porter, the chairman, and the
hesitancy of Mr. Grundy, the second on the committee, threw into the hands of Mr. Calhoun, the third
on the list and the youngest of the committee, and
the presentation of which immediately gave him a

national reputation. Prime mover of the war, he was also one of its most efficient supporters, taking upon himself, when adversity pressed, the actual duties of war minister, financier, and foreign secretary at the same time. He was an enemy to all extravagance, to all intrigue, to all indirection in the conduct of business. Mr. Jefferson's comprehensive and compendious eulogium upon him, as brief as true, was the faithful description of the man — 'honest and brave.' He was an enemy to nepotism, and no consideration or entreaty, no need of the support which an office would give, or intercession from friends, could ever induce him to appoint a relative to any place under the government. He had opposed the adoption of the Constitution until amendments were obtained ; but these had, he became one of its firmest supporters, and labored faithfully, anxiously, and devotedly to administer it in its purity."

On reviewing all that I have been able to read in print and in manuscript, and all I have been able to gather from the writings of others, the conclusion is forced on me that Monroe is not adequately appreciated by his countrymen. He has certainly been insufficiently known, because no collection has been made of his numerous memoirs, letters, dispatches, and messages. That want is now [1898] about to be supplied by the collection already mentioned. He has suffered also by comparison with four or five

illustrious men, his seniors in years and his supe-
riors in genius, who were chiefly instrumental in
establishing this government on its firm basis.
He was not the equal of Washington in prudence, of Marshall in wisdom, of Hamilton in
constructive power, of Jefferson in genius for
politics, of Madison in persistent ability to
think out an idea and to persuade others of its
importance. He was in early life enthusiastic
to rashness, he was a devoted adherent of partisan views, he was sometimes despondent and
sometimes irascible ; but as he grew older his
judgment was disciplined, his self-control became
secure, his patriotism overbalanced the considerations of party. Political opponents rarely as-
sailed the purity of his motives or the honesty of
his conduct. He was a very good civil service re-
former, firmly set against appointments to office
for any unworthy reason. He was never exposed
to the charge of nepotism, and in the choice of
officers to be appointed he carefully avoided the
recognition of family and friendly ties. His hands
were never stained with pelf. He grew poor in
the public service, because he neglected his private affairs and incurred large outlays in the
discharge of official duties under circumstances
which demanded liberal expenditure. He was
extremely reticent as to his religious sentiments,
at least in all that he wrote. Allusions to his

belief are rarely if ever to be met with in his correspondence. He was a faithful husband, father, master, neighbor, friend. He was industrious, serious, temperate, domestic, affectionate. He carried with him to the end of his life the good-will and respect both of his seniors and juniors. Many of those who worked with him, besides those already quoted, have left on record their appreciation of his abilities and their esteem for his character.

His numerous state papers are not remarkable in style or in thought, but his views were generally sound, the position which he took in later life on public questions was approved by the public voice, and his administration is known as the "era of good feeling." His attention does not seem to have been called in any special manner to the significance of slavery as an element of political discord, or as an evil in itself. If he foresaw, he did not foretell the great conflict. He does not seem expert in the principles of national finance, though his views are often expressed on such matters.

The one idea which he represents consistently from the beginning to the end of his career is this, that America is for Americans. He resists the British sovereignty in his early youth; he insists on the importance of free navigation in the Mississippi; he negotiates the purchase of Louisiana and Florida; he gives a vigorous impulse to the prosecution of the second war with Great Britain, when neutral rights were endangered; finally he announces the " Monroe doctrine."

It is clear that he was under great obligations to Jefferson. The aid and counsel of this saga-cious man are apparent from the time when Monroe began the study of law, in adverse and in prosperous times, in public and in private matters, throughout their long lives. Madison's friendship was also a powerful support. But both these men could not have sustained Mon-roe through his varied career, in circumstances which required popular approbation, if he had not possessed some very uncommon qualities. As a youth he must have been bright and attrac-tive. In early manhood he was devoted to his party beyond reasonable requirements, so that he nearly involved the country in war. As he grew older he was less of a partisan. He retained an accurate remembrance of the men and mea-sures with which he had been associated, and he acquired experience in almost every variety of public station, the judiciary excepted, until he reached the very highest office in the land. He was trained for the presidency in the school of affairs and not in a ring. An ideal prepara-tion for the duties of that high station would hardly involve any kind of discipline to which the business of life had not subjected him. He made enemies; the Federalists, South as well as North, disliked him and undervalued him; but notwithstanding their hostile criticism he sustained himself so well that but one electoral vote was given against his reëlection, and it is said that this was cast by an elector who did not wish to see a second President chosen with the same unanimity which had honored Washington.

When the collected writings of Monroe come before the public, as they soon will, his work will be more accurately estimated, and I think more highly valued. Partisan as he was, often exposed to censure from the Federalists, never rising to the highest statesmanship except when he announced the Monroe doctrine, he will always appear patriotic, indefatigable, and unselfish. As a legislator, envoy, cabinet minister, and president, he was true, often under trying circumstances, to the idea of American independence from European interference.

Monroe died in New York, July 4, 1831, and was buried there with appropriate honors. Years afterward Virginians desired that his dust should mingle with the soil of his native State. His body was carried to Richmond, under the escort of a favorite regiment of New York, and re-interred in the public cemetery just one hundred years after his eyes first saw the light.

APPENDIX

I

GENEALOGY

I HAVE not been successful in tracing the pedigree of James Monroe. Mr. R. C. Brock, of the Virginia Historical Society, has kindly searched the Virginia archives, and finds that successive grants of land were made to Andrew Monroe from 1650 to 1662, and to John Monroe from 1695 to 1719. He has also come upon an old statement that Andrew Monroe came to this country in 1660, after the defeat of the royal army, in which he had the rank of major, and settled in Westmoreland County, Virginia. With this citation it is well to compare a recent paragraph, in respect to the Monroes of Eastern Massachusetts, in F. B. Sanborn's " Life of Thoreau : "—

" The Monroes of Lexington and Concord are descended from a Scotch soldier of Charles II.'s army, captured by Cromwell at the battle of Worcester in 1651, and allowed to go into exile in America. His powerful kinsman, General George Monro, who commanded for Charles at the battle of Worcester, was, at the Restoration, made commander-in-chief for Scotland." [1]

Mr. Brock suggests that the family of Jones, to which the mother of James Monroe belongs, was the same with that of Adjutant-General Robert Jones, Commodore Thomas Catesby Jones, General Walker Jones, and other distinguished Americans.

The private residence of Monroe during the latter part of his life was at Oak Hill, near Aldie, Loudoun County, Virginia, on a turnpike running south from Leesburg to Aldie, about nine miles from the former and three from the latter place.

Major R. W. N. Noland has been so kind as to prepare, at the suggestion of Professor J. M. Garnett of the University of Virginia, a sketch of Oak Hill, as follows: —

The Oak Hill house was planned by Mr. Monroe, but the building superintended by Mr. William Benton, an Englishman, who occupied the mixed relation to Mr. Monroe of steward, counselor, and friend. The house is built of brick in a most substantial manner, and handsomely finished ; it is, perhaps, about 90 x 50 feet, three stories (including basement), and has a wide portico, fronting south, with massive Doric columns thirty feet high, and is surrounded by a grove of magnificent oaks covering several acres. While the location is not as commanding as many others in that section, being in lower Loudoun where the rolling character of the Piedmont region begins to loose itself in the flat lands of tide water, the house in two directions commands an attractive and somewhat ex-

[1] Compare Savage, *New England Genealogical Dictionary*, iii. 256, 257.

tensive view, but on the other sides it is hemmed in by mountains, for the local names of which, " Bull Run " and " Nigger Mountain," it is to be hoped the late President is in no wise responsible, and, indeed, the same may be said of the river or creek which breaks through these ranges within a mile or two of Oak Hill. Tom Moore, in a poetic letter as brilliant as it is ill-natured, satirizing Washington city, writes, " And what was Goose Creek once is Tiber now ; " but the fact is that no such stream is found in the neighborhood of the national capital. The little stream that washes the confines of the Oak Hill estate once bore the Indian name *Gohongarestaw* (the River of Swans), and is now called *Goose Creek*. The following anecdote connected with Oak Hill is, perhaps, worthy of preservation. On the occasion of Lafayette's visit to Loudoun, a large number of distinguished guests were entertained at Oak Hill. It was at the dinner in Leesburg, given to Lafayette, that Mr. Adams drank the celebrated toast to the " Patriots of the Revolution — like the Sibylline leaves, the fewer they become, the more precious they are." In riding back to Oak Hill, Mr. Adams, Major William Noland, and Mr. Hay were thrown together, when the last-named gentleman, with an apology for the seeming impertinence, asked Mr. Adams where he conceived the beautiful sentiment he had that day drunk. Mr. Adams said that the toast was inspired that morning by a sight of the picture of the Sibyl that hung in the Oak Hill hall. " How strange ! " said Mr. Hay, " *I* have been looking at that picture for years, and that thought never *occurred to me*."

There are several quite good pictures of the Oak Hill house extant — one on Taylor's map of Loudoun County, and others in the histories of Virginia (for example, in Howe's " Historical Collections of Virginia," p. 356).

II

WASHINGTON'S NOTES UPON THE APPENDIX TO MON-
ROE'S "VIEW OF THE CONDUCT OF THE EXECU-
TIVE," NOW FIRST PRINTED

[From the copy by Mr. Sparks now owned by the
Library of Cornell University. The figures indicate the
pages in the appendix to Monroe's "View," from which
catch-words are taken, introducing the notes written by
Washington on his copy.]

Page 119 — "*jealousy and distrust.*"

Principally because he asserted our rights and
claimed redress.

On what ground the suspicion, when it was a notorious fact that (we) were upon the worst terms short
of open war with G. Britain?

His communications with the French Govt. con-
tradict this, and accounts [*sic*] satisfactorily for the
delay of the reception, as may be seen by reference
thereto.

Page 120 — "*that I should pursue?*"

As nothing but justice, and the fulfillment of a contract was asked, it dictated firmness conducted with
temperance [*sic*] in the pursuit of it.

Page 120 — "*were closed against me.*"

This appears nowhere but in his own conjectures
and *after*-assertions, for from his own account *at the*

time the delay of his reception was satisfactorily explained, and had been the cause of another waiting of
six weeks.[1] See his letter of the 25 of Aug., p. 16.

Page 120 — "*place a greater confidence?*"

By whom were they advised? and what evidences
are alluded to?

Page 122 — "*and then defy us.*"

Was a good understanding to be interrupted because we were endeavoring to live in peace with all
the world? and were only asking from France what
we were entitled to by treaty?

Page 122 — "*in favour of that administration:*"

It is not understood what is here meant by *concession.* None was asked, or any [*sic*] thought of being
made.

Page 122 — "*decisively on the decline.*"

It will not be denied, it is presumed [*sic*], that
there had been and might again be great viscissitudes
in their affairs, bothe [*sic*] externally and internally.
Prudence and policy therefore required, that the
Govt. of the U. S. should move with great circum-
spection.

Page 123 — "*the point in question.*"

A very singular mode truly to obtain it, but look

[1] This "waiting of six weeks" refers to the delay in receiving the minister of Geneva. — EDITOR.

to letter of Nov. 7th, 1794, pp. 58, 59, and judge whether it would not have been accomplished sooner if he had desired it ; — and what can he mean by not conceding, when in explicit terms he has declared that the point, if upon consideration they desired it, would have been given up with pleasure !

Page 123 — "*upon the slightest intimation.*"

That is to say, if we would not press *them* to do us justice, but have yielded to *their* violations, they would [*sic*] aided us in every measure, which would have cost them *nothing.*

Page 124 — "*from the western posts,*"

By what means were the British to be expelled from the Western posts, without first conquering Canada, or passing thro' the territory of the U. S., and would not the latter, by the law of nations, have been a cause of war ?   The truth is Mr. Manroe [*sic*] was cajoled, flattered, and made to believe strange things.   In return he did, or was disposed to do, whatever was pleasing to that nation ; reluctantly urging the rights of his own.

Page 140 — " *in the second the whole.*"

This is a mistake, — no such promise to be found in the 2[d] letter.   See p. 105, Nov. 25th.

Page 140 — "*to me on the subject?*"

The intention was to enable him on the veracity and authority of the negotiator of the Treaty to assert, that there was nothing contained in it repugnant to our engagement with France, and that was all that they or he had a right to expect.

Page 147 — "*power alone to make it, etc.*"

And this ought to have satisfied the French Govt. It was as much as that Govt. would have done for us or any other nation.

Page 148 — "*my secretary, Mr. Gauvain*"

Here is a striking instance of his folly. This secretary of his was a foreigner — it is believed a Frenchman — introduced no doubt to his confidence and papers for the sole purpose of communicating to the Directory the secrets of his office.

Page 160 — "*with you in June next.*"

The sufferings of our citizens are always a secondary consideration when put in competition with the embarrassments of the French.

Page 161 — "*reasons above suggested.*"

Hence is a disregard shown to repeated orders of his government to press this matter.

Page 207 — "*me to do it here.*"

What inference is to be drawn from this declaration? What light is it in Philadelphia, that is to discover the sense of the French Govt. in Paris, before it was divulged there? — except the conduct of the French party by whom the wheels were to be moved?

Page 210 — "*of this government,*"

If he does not mean himself here, it is not difficult to guess who the other character is marked out by this description.

Page 210 — "*of what kind must it be ?*"

War was the suggestion, and is here repeated. This has no horrors when waged in *favor* of France, but dreadful even in thought when it is against her.

Page 297 — "*decide in his case.*"

Mr. Fenwick was accused of covering by the American flag French money under false invoices, but Mr. M. could readily excuse this breach of faith in his office.

Page 313 — "*furnished lose its force.*"

England before the late treaty with the U. S. and France were different in their commercial relations with America.

Page 314 — "*than in precise terms ;*"

For the best reason imaginable ; because none could be urged that had any weight in them.

Page 321 — "*the United States have taken,*"

Only in cases where the captors have contravened the treaty — acting contrary to the laws of nations — or our own municipal laws.

Page 322 — "*prizes into those ports.*"

A single instance *only* of a prize being brought in
is recollected, and against it a strong remonstrance
was made ; — without prizes, ships of war are not
restrained by the Treaty.

Page 322 — "*executing their judgments.*"

No interruption has been given to this. To carry
their own judgments into effect has constituted the
difficulty, — and in its nature it is nearly impossible
to do it.

Page 322 — "*certified by the consuls.*"

This is the French construction of the Act. The
Judiciary of the U. S. interpret it otherwise ; over
whom the Executive have [*sic*] no control.

Page 322 — "*safeguard of their flag.*"

This arrestation was for an offense committed
against the law of nations and those of the U. S.
and has been explained over and over again. See
the Sec[ty] of State's Letter, 13th of June, p. 364.

Page 323 — "*merited an example.*"

What more could the U. S. do than was done ? See
the Sec[ty] of State's Letter, Sept. 14th, 1795, p. 292.

Page 323 — "*least contested, of neutrality.*"

These are assertions upon false premises. Strange
indeed would it be if the U. S. could not make a

treaty without the consent of the French Govt. when that treaty infracted no prior engagements, but expressly recognizes and confirms them.

Page 323 — " *the principles of neutrality ?* "

They have given *nothing*, but left those principles precisely upon the ground they stood [*sic*] before the Treaty ; with some explanations favorable to the U. S. and not injurious to France. They have made nothing contraband, that was not contraband before ; — nor was it in their power to obtain from G. B. a change, which the Armed Neutrality, (as it was called) could not when combined accomplish.

Page 345 — " *and without delay.*"

How strangely inconsistent are his accounts !

Page 356 — " *most strict reciprocity.*"

From hence it follows, that if A makes a contract with B, and C will not make a similar contract with him, B will not be bound by his contract, although the cases are unconnected with each other [*sic*].

Page 359 — " *course of the present war.*"

All this he ought to have done, and was instructed to do in the beginning ; and had it been urged with firmness and temperance, might have prevented the evils which have taken place since.

Page 359 — " *my duty would permit ;* "

And a great deal more than his duty permitted

Page 371 — "*the merit of this delay ;*"

By implication he has done this in a variety of instances.

Page 371 — "*was the true cause of it.*"

That is, by not pressing the execution of the Treaty; and for compensation to our suffering citizens. This no doubt was accommodating and pleasing one party at the expense of the other.

Page 374 — "*be passed by unnoticed.*"

Did France expect, that the U. S. could compel G. B. to relinquish this right under the law of nations, while [*sic*] the other maritime powers of Europe (as has been observed before), when combined for the purpose were unable to effect [*sic*]. Why then call it an abandonment?

Page 377 — "*what they did avow.*"

This is all external and a flimsy covering of their designs. Why else send their emissaries through that country to inculcate different principles among the inhabitants, a fact that could be substantiated.

Page 390 — "*nations had sworn to.*"

Yes, *Citizen*, and every one else who can read are [*sic*] acquainted with [*sic*] facts ; and your violations of our rights under the Treaty prove (?) it also.

Page 391 — " *be made through you.*"

The treatment of our minister, Gen¹ Pinckney, is a pretty evidence of this ; — the thot' [*sic*] of parting with Mr. Monroe was insupportable by them.

III

BIBLIOGRAPHY OF MONROE, AND THE MONROE DOCTRINE

PREPARED FOR THIS WORK BY J. F. JAMESON, PH. D.

THE following bibliography has been prepared with a view to the needs of persons specially studying the career of Monroe, rather than to those of the general reader. Hence it does not ordinarily include references to the most familiar sources, such as the State Papers, the published correspondence of Washington, etc., and the standard histories. It aims to include nothing that does not bear directly upon Monroe or the Monroe Doctrine ; nor, in even the limited area thus marked out, can it hope to be complete. The titles under A are arranged alphabetically by authors ; those under B chronologically ; those under C first chronologically, according to the period of Monroe's public life to which they refer, and then alphabetically by authors. At least one locality of a book or pamphlet, unless it be a common one, has been designated when known. In such designations, at the end of the title, A indicates the existence of a copy in the Astor Library ; B, in the

Boston Public Library; BA, in that of the Boston
Athenæum; C, in the Library of Congress; H, in
that of Harvard College; JCB, in the John Carter
Brown Library; JH, in that of the Johns Hopkins
University; M, in the Massachusetts State Library;
MH, in that of the Massachusetts Historical Society;
N, in the New York State Library; NH, in that of
the New York Historical Society; P, in that of the
Philadelphia Library Company; S, in that of the
Department of State; W, in that of the American
Antiquarian Society at Worcester. The Maryland
Historical Society is supplied with most of the works
to which reference has been made in the preparation
of this volume.

SYNOPSIS.

A. BIOGRAPHICAL.

B. PUBLISHED WRITINGS OF MONROE.

C. PUBLICATIONS RELATING TO THE PUBLIC CAREER OR
    THE WRITINGS OF MONROE.

  1. First Diplomatic Service and the " View."

  2. Louisiana Purchase and Spanish Mission.

  3. Diplomatic Efforts in England.

  4. Period of Cabinet Office.

  5. Presidency.

  6. Subsequent Period.

D. THE MONROE DOCTRINE.

  1. Its Immediate Origin.

  2. Discussion of it in Treatises on International Law.

  3. In more Special Treatises and Articles.

    a. American.   *b.* European.

  4. Occasions on which it has been applied.

    a. The Panama Congress.

    b. Yucatan.

c. The Clayton-Bulwer Treaty.

d. Central America, 1845–1860.

e. Cuba, etc., 1850–1898.

f. French Intervention in Mexico.

g. The Inter-oceanic Canal.

h. America North of the United States.

i. The Pan-American Conference.

j. The Venezuela-Guiana Boundary.

BIBLIOGRAPHY.

A. BIOGRAPHICAL.

John Quincy Adams: An Eulogy on the Life and Character of James Monroe, Fifth President of the United States, . . . delivered at . . . Boston, August 25, 1831. Boston, 1831. 8vo, pp. 100. BA, N. (See [John Armstrong] under C. 6, p. 277.)

John Quincy Adams: Lives of Celebrated Statesmen. [Madison, Lafayette, and Monroe.] New York, 1846. 8vo, pp. 105. N.

John Quincy Adams: The Lives of James Madison and James Monroe, Fourth and Fifth Presidents of the United States. With Historical Notices of their Administrations. Buffalo, 1850. 12mo, pp. 432. C. +[1] Philadelphia, 1854. M.

S. L. Gouverneur: Introduction to "The People, the Sovereigns," by James Monroe. See under B.

S. L. K[napp]: *in* James B. Longacre and James Herring, National Portrait Gallery of Distinguished Americans, vol. 3. Philadelphia, 1836. 8vo.

[S. L. Knapp]: James Monroe. [n. p., n. d.] 8vo, pp. 10. (Portrait.)

Lippincott's Magazine, first series, vol. 9, p. 359.

A Narrative of a Tour of Observation, made during the Summer of 1817, by James Monroe, President of the United States, through the North-Eastern and North-Western Departments of the Union; with a View to the Examination of

---

[1] The sign + indicates another edition.

their several Military Defenses. With an Appendix. Philadelphia, 1818. 12mo, pp. 228, xxxvi. B, C, N.

New England Magazine, vol. 1, p. 178.

New York Mirror, vol. 12 [1834–5], p. 41. (Portrait.)

Niles' Register, vol. 10, p. 4, March 2, 1816; from the National Advocate. Also, December 3, 1825, and vol. 35, p. 68. Also, vol. 40, p. 369, July 23, 1831.

Order of Exercises at the Old South Church, Commemorative of . . . James Monroe. . . . August 25, 1831. Boston, 1831. 8vo, pp. 8. B.

T. Paine: Anecdote of James Monroe and Rufus King, in Political Writings. London, 1844. BA, C.

Portfolio, vol. 19, p. 251: fourth series, vol. 5. Philadelphia, April, 1818. (Portrait.)

William O. Stoddard: The Lives of the Presidents: James Madison, James Monroe, and J. Q. Adams. pp. 128–224. New York, 1887. Pp. 331. 12mo, 20 cm.

R. W. Thompson: Personal Recollections of Sixteen Presidents. Indianapolis, 1894.

S. Putnam Waldo: Tour of James Monroe, President of the United States, in the year 1817, through the States of Maryland, Pennsylvania, New Jersey, New York, Connecticut, Rhode Island, Massachusetts, New Hampshire, Vermont, and Ohio; together with a Sketch of his Life. Hartford, 1818. 12mo, pp. 300. BA.

S. P. Waldo: Tour of James Monroe, President of the United States, through the Northern and Eastern States, in 1817; his Tour in 1818, with a Sketch of his Life. Hartford, 1819. 12mo. C.

In Edwin Williams: The Statesman's Manual. New York, 1847. 8vo, vol. 1.

Udolpho Wolfe: Grand Civic and Military Demonstration in Honor of the Removal of the Remains of James Monroe, Fifth President of the United States, from New York to Virginia. New York, 1858. 12mo, pp. 324. C.

(And numerous unimportant notices in lives of the presidents, cyclopædias, and biographical dictionaries.)

B. Published Writings of Monroe,

(in addition to the messages, dispatches, and letters which
may be found in familiar sources. Manuscripts of Monroe's
public papers are in the possession of the Department of
State; much of his private correspondence is in the possession
of Mrs. S. L. Gouverneur, Jr., of Washington.)

The Writings of James Monroe. Edited by Stanislaus Murray
Hamilton. [In six or seven volumes.] New York. G. P.
Putnam's Sons, 1898, *et seq.*

　　The first volume of this collection, — the only one that
has yet appeared, July, 1898, — contains reprints of the two
following : —

Some Observations on the Constitution. Pp. 24, small quarto.
(A copy, thought to be unique, was recently found by
Mr. John P. Weissenhagen, of the Bureau of Rolls and
Library, in the Department of State.)
Observations upon the Proposed Plan of Federal Government.
With an Attempt to answer some of the Principal Objections
that have been made to it. By a Native of Virginia. Peters-
burg. Printed by Hunter and Prentis. 1788. Pp. 64,
small quarto. (A copy, supposed to be unique, is in the
Library of the Department of State.)
A View of the Conduct of the Executive, in the Foreign
Affairs of the United States, connected with the Mission to
the French Republic in the years 1794, '5, and '6. By James
Monroe. . . . Illustrated by his Instructions and Correspond-
ence and other Authentic Documents. Philadelphia, 1797.
8vo, pp. lxvi., 407. + *Same*, the Second Edition. London,
1798. 8vo, pp. viii., 117. + *Same*, the Third Edition.
London, 1798. 8vo, pp. xvi., 117. (See London Monthly
Review, vol. 25, p. 232.)
Governor's Letter to the Speaker and House of Delegates of
Virginia, 6th December, 1802. Richmond, 1802. 12mo. C.
A Letter from the Minister Plenipotentiary of the United

States to Lord Mulgrave, late Secretary of State for Foreign Affairs. *With* [James Madison] : An Examination of the British Doctrine which subjects to Capture a Neutral Trade not open in Time of Peace. [n. p.] 1806. 8vo, pp. 204. + Second Edition. London, 1806. B, C.

Correspondence between . . . Thomas Jefferson, President of the United States, and James Monroe, Esq. . . . Boston, 1808. 4to, pp. 8. BA.

Letter from the Secretary of State to Mr. Monroe, on the subject of the attack on the Chesapeake. The Correspondence of Mr. Monroe with the British Government ; and also Mr. Madison's Correspondence with Mr. Rose, on the same subject. Washington, 1808. 8vo. (Peabody Library, Baltimore.)

Letters of James Madison . . . to Mr. Monroe on . . . Impressments, etc. Also Extracts from, and Enclosures in, the Letters of Mr. Monroe to the Secretary of State. Washington, 1808. 8vo, pp. 130. B, MH.

Defence of the Mission to England. . . . Washington, 1808. 8vo.

Letters between James Monroe, Esq., Secretary of State of the United States, and Augustus J. Foster, Esq., . . . Minister Plenipotentiary of his Britannic Majesty ; in relation to the Orders in Council, and the Affair of the Little Belt. To which is added, the Declaration of War. New York, 1812. 12mo, pp. 59. B.

To all who are honestly searching after the Truth. Mr. Monroe's Letter on the Rejected Treaty between the United States and Great Britain, concluded by Messrs. Monroe and Pinkney. Also the Treaty itself, and Documents connected with it. Portland, 1813. 8vo, pp. 52. BA, C.

Commercial Regulations of Foreign Countries. [Message.] Washington, 1819. BA.

Message from the President, transmitting Sundry Papers relating to Transactions in East and West Florida. April 19, 1822. [Washington, 1822.] Pp. 46. P.

Message transmitting a Digest of the Commercial Regulations

of the Different Foreign Nations. Washington, 1824. 18th
Congress, 1st Session, House Doc. No. 130. BA, M.

Message transmitting a Report of the Secretary of the Navy.
Washington, 1824. 8vo. C.

Correspondence between Gen. Jackson and Mr. Monroe, as
published in the National Intelligencer. Washington, 1824.
12mo. N.

The Memoir of James Monroe, Esq., relating to his Unsettled
Claims upon the People and Government of the United
States. [With documents.] Charlottesville, Va., 1828.
8vo, pp. 60. BA, C, NH.

A Letter from James Monroe, in Answer to . . . Questions
[on War and Slavery, etc.] . . . [n. p., 1863 ?] 8vo, pp.
32. H.

The People, the Sovereigns, Being a Comparison of the Government of the United States with those of the Republicks,
which have existed before, with the Causes of their Deca-
dence and Fall. By James Monroe. Edited by S. L. Gouverneur. Philadelphia, 1867. 12mo, pp. 274. (See, under
C 6, C. C. Hazewell, p. 277.)

Calendar of the Correspondence of James Monroe. [Bulletin
of the Bureau of Rolls and Library of the Department of
State, No. 2.] Washington, 1893. Pp. 371.

C. PUBLICATIONS RELATING TO THE PUBLIC CAREER OR
THE WRITINGS OF MONROE.

1. *First Diplomatic Service and the " View."*

Alexander Addison: Observations on the Speech of Albert
Gallatin on the Foreign Intercourse Bill. Washington, Pa.,
1798. 8vo.

An Address on the Past, Present, and Eventual Relations of
the United States to France. By Anticipation. New York,
[1803]. 8vo, pp. 20. A.

P. A. Adet: Notes adressées par le citoyen Adet, Ministre
Plénipotentiaire de la République Française près les États-

Unis d'Amérique, Au Secrétaire d'État des États-Unis. Philadelphia, 1796. 8vo, pp. 95. + *Same*, translated.

[P. A. Adet]: Authentic Translation of a Note from the Minister of the French Republic to the Secretary of State of the United States. New York, 1796. 8vo, pp. 38. N. (See, also, Wm. Cobbett.)

The Anti-Gallican; or, The Lover of his own Country; in a Series of Pieces . . . wherein French Influence, and False Patriotism, are fully and fairly displayed. By a Citizen of New England. Philadelphia, 1797. 8vo, pp. 82. (Includes Letters on Pseudo-Patriots, by Ascanius; of which No. VI. is on James Monroe.) H.

Camillus, *pseud.*: History of French Influence in the United States. Philadelphia, 1812. M.

[William Cobbett]: A History of the American Jacobins, commonly denominated Democrats. By Peter Porcupine. *In* Wm. Playfair, The History of Jacobinism. Philadelphia, 1795. P.

[William Cobbett]: The Gros Mosqueton Diplomatique; or, Diplomatic Blunderbuss, containing Citizen Adet's Notes to the Secretary of State, as also his Cockade Proclamation. With a Preface by Peter Porcupine. Philadelphia, 1796. 8vo, pp. 72. C.

William Cobbett: Porcupine's Works. London, 1801. 8vo. [Vol. iv. contains The Diplomatic Blunderbuss (Oct. 31, 1796); Political Censor, No. vi. (Nov. 1796); A Brief Statement of the Injuries and Insults received from France (Feb. 1797). In vol. v. pp. 131–138; vol. vi. pp. 12, 13, 92–98, 116–124, 358–376, 414–417; vol. vii. pp. 90–95, 151–156, are notices of Monroe's doings, from Porcupine's Gazette, 1797. Vol. x., Dr. Morse's Exposition of French Intrigue in America.]

Coup d'œil sur la situation des affaires entre la France et les États-Unis de l'Amérique. 1798. 8vo, pp. 28. BA.

J. Dennis: Address on the Origin, Progress, and Present State of French Aggression. Philadelphia, 1798. BA.

Wm. Duane: A History of the French Revolution, with a

free Examination of the Dispute between the French and
American Republics. Philadelphia, 1798. 4to.

Joseph Fauchet : Coup d'œil sur l'état actuel de nos rapports
politiques avec les États-Unis de l'Amérique Septentrionale ;
par J. Fauchet, Ex-ministre de la République à Philadelphie. Paris, an V. [1797.] 8vo, pp. 42. H.

Joseph Fauchet : A Sketch of the Present State of our Po-
litical Relations with the United States of North America.
. . . Translated by the Editor of the " Aurora." [Wm. J.
Duane.] Philadelphia, 1797. 8vo, pp. 31. BA.

A Five Minutes' Answer to Paine's Letter to Washington,
London, 1797. 8vo, pp. 44. MH. (See below, T. Paine.)

[Albert Gallatin] : An Examination of the Conduct of the
Executive of the United States toward the French Republic ; . . . In a Series of Letters. By a Citizen of Pennsylvania. Philadelphia, 1797. 8vo, pp. vi., 72. BA.

Albert Gallatin : The Speech of Albert Gallatin, delivered in
the House of Representatives . . . on the First of March
1798. Upon the Foreign Intercourse Bill. [n. p., 1798.]
8vo, pp. 48. (And other Editions.) BA, H, MH, P, JCB.

[A. G. Gebhardt] : Actes et Mémoires concernant les négociations qui ont eu lieu entre la France et les États-Unis
d'Amérique. [1793–1800.] Londres, 1807. 3 vols. 12mo.
BA.

A. G. Gebhardt : State Papers relating to the Diplomatick
Transactions between the American and French Governments. [1793–1800.] London, 1816. 3 vols. 8vo. BA.

L. Goldsmith : An Exposition of the Conduct of France to
America, illustrated by Cases decided in the Council of
Prizes in Paris. [1793–1808.] London, 1810. 8vo, pp. 133.
(Various other editions.) B, BA, H.

[Alexander Hamilton.] See [Uriah Tracy], below.

R. G. Harper : Observations on the Dispute between the
United States and France, addressed by Robert Goodloe
Harper, Esq., of South Carolina, to his Constituents in
May, 1797. Philadelphia, 1797. 8vo, pp. 102. (And
twenty other editions.) B, BA, H, NH, P.

R. G. Harper : Mr. Harper's Speech on the Foreign Intercourse Bill, in Reply to Mr. Nicholas and Mr. Gallatin. Delivered in the House of Representatives of the United States, on the second of March, 1798. [n. p., n. d.] 8vo, pp. 43. (And other editions.) B, H, MH, NH, P.

R. G. Harper: A short Account of the principal Proceedings of Congress in the late Session, and a Sketch of the State of Affairs between the United States and France, in July, 1798, in a Letter to one of his Constituents. Philadelphia, 1798. 8vo.

P. Kennedy : An Answer to Mr. Paine's Letter to General Washington ; or, Mad Tom convicted of the Blackest Ingratitude. London, 1797. 8vo, pp. 55. JCB.

A Letter to Thomas Paine, in Answer to his Scurrilous Epistle . . . to Washington . . . By an American Citizen. New York, 1797. 8vo, pp. 24.

L'Indépendance absolue des Américains des Etats-Unis, prouvée par l'état actuel de leur Commerce avec les Nations Européennes. Paris, 1798. 8vo, pp. 149. (Written by an American merchant, in answer to Fauchet, Coup d'œil, above.)

Thomas Paine : A Letter to George Washington, President of the United States, on Affairs Public and Private. Philadelphia, 1796. 8vo, pp. 76. (And other editions.) B, BA, H. (Also in vol. i. of Works. Philadelphia, 1854. 12mo.)

E. C. J. Pastoret : Conseil des Cinq-Cents : motion d'ordre sur l'état de nos rapports politiques et commerciaux avec les Etats-Unis de l'Amérique septentrionale. Paris, an V. [1797]. 8vo, pp. 26. BA.

[Timothy Pickering] : Lettre du Secrétaire d'Etat des Etats-Unis de l'Amérique au Général Charles C. Pinckney, Ministre Plénipotentiaire des dits Etats-Unis près la République Française ; en reponse aux différentes plaintes faites contre le gouvernement des Etats-Unis par le Ministre Français . . . 1796. Paris, 1797. 8vo, pp. 62.

Timothy Pickering and P. A. Adet : Review of the Administration of the United States since '93. Boston, 1797. BA.

C. C. Tanguy de la Boissière: Observations sur la dépêche écrite le 16 jan., 1797, par M. Pickering, Secrétaire d'Etat des Etats-Unis de l'Amérique, à M. Pinkney, Ministre Pléni- potentiaire des Etats-Unis près la République Française. Philadelphie, 1797. Also, translated. BA, C.

[Uriah Tracy, or (?) Alexander Hamilton]: Reflections on Monroe's View, . . . as published in the Gazette of the United States under the Signature of Scipio. [n. p., n. d.] 8vo, pp. 88. BA, P.

[Uriah Tracy, or (?) Alexander Hamilton]: [Scipio's] Reflec- tions on Monroe's View. . . . Boston, 1798. 8vo, pp. 140. C, H, M.

George Washington: Notes on Monroe's View, Sparks, xi. 504–529. (His Notes on the Appendix to the View are printed in Appendix III of this book.)

[R. Walsh]: An Enquiry into the Past and Present Relations of France and the United States of America. [London, 1811.] 8vo, pp. 87. (Reprinted from the American Review, vol. i.)

2. *Louisiana Purchase and Spanish Mission.*

Analysis of the Third Article of the Treaty of Cession of Louisiana. [Washington (?)], 1803. 8vo, pp. 8.

Atlantic Monthly, vol. 32, p. 301. The Louisiana Purchase.

Samuel Brazer, Jr.: Address pronounced at Worcester, May 12, 1804, in Commemoration of the Cession of Louisiana to the United States. Worcester, 1804. 8vo, pp. 15. MH.

[Charles Brockden Brown]: An Address to the Government of the United States on the Cession of Louisiana to the French, and on the late Breach of Treaty by the Spaniards. Philadelphia, 1803. 8vo, pp. 92. C, N.

[Charles Brockden Brown]: Monroe's Embassy; or, The Conduct of the Government in relation to our Claims to the Navigation of the Mississippi, considered, by the Author of the Address to the Government. . . . [Signed " Poplicola."] Philadelphia, 1803. 8vo, pp. 57. BA, C.

Camillus, *pseud.* See Duane, below.

James Cheetham: Letters on our Affairs with Spain. New York, 1804. 8vo, pp. 59. C.

S. M. Davis: The Purchase of Louisiana. Chautauquan, vol. 14, p. 658. 1891.

Wm. Duane: Mississippi Question. Report of a Debate in the Senate of the United States, on the 23d, 24th, and 25th Feb., 1803, on Certain Resolutions concerning the Violation of the Right of Deposit in the Island of New Orleans. Philadelphia, 1803. 8vo, pp. 198. BA, H.

[Wm. Duane]: Camillus, *pseud.* The Mississippi Question fairly stated, and the Views and Arguments of those who clamor for War, examined. In Seven Letters. Philadelphia, 1803. 8vo, pp. 48. BA.

[Wm. Fessenden]: The Political Farrago, or a Miscellaneous Review of the Politics of the United States, . . . including . . . Remarks on the "Louisiana Purchase," by Peter Dobbin, Esq., R. C. U. S. A. Brattleboro', Vt., 1807, pp. 59. W.

C. Gayarré: The Cession of Louisiana to the United States. De Bow's Mag., n. s., vol. 1, pp. 256 and 404. 1866. (See also his History of Louisiana.)

Wm. Maclure: To the People of the United States on the Convention with France of 1803. Philadelphia, 1807. P.

A. B. Magruder: Reflections on the Cession of Louisiana to the United States. Lexington, 1803. BA.

F. de Barbé-Marbois: Histoire de la Louisiane et de la Cession de cette Colonie par la France aux Etats-Unis de l'Amérique septentrionale. Paris, 1829. 8vo, pp. 485. BA, H.

F. de Barbé-Marbois: The History of Louisiana, particularly of the Cession of that Colony to the United States of America. Translated from the French by an American Citizen. [William Beach Lawrence.] Philadelphia, 1830. 8vo, pp. xviii., 455. C, H. (See Sparks, below.)

Mémoires sur la Louisiane et la Nouvelle-Orléans, accompagné d'une Dissertation sur les avantages que le commerce de l'Empire doit tirer de la stipulation faite par l'article 7 du

Traité de cession, du 30 avril 1803; par M. * * * Paris, an
XII. [1804]. 8vo, pp. 176.

G. Morris. See Ross, below.

Geo. Orr: The Possession of Louisiana by the French, considered as it affects the interests of those Nations more immediately concerned, viz.: Great Britain, America, Spain, and
Portugal. London, 1803. 8vo, pp. 45. BA.

J. M. Peck: The Annexation of Louisiana. Christian Review,
vol. 16, p. 555.

Political, Commercial, and Statistical Sketches of the Spanish
Empire in both Indies; and a View of the Questions between
Spain and the United States respecting Louisiana and the
Floridas. London, 1809. 8vo, pp. 156. BA.

David Ramsay: Oration on the Cession of Louisiana to the
United States; delivered May 12, 1804, in Charleston, S. C.
Charleston, 1804. 8vo, pp. 27. BA.

C. F. Robertson: The Louisiana Purchase and its Influence
on the American System. New York, 1885. (Am. Hist.
Asso. Pap., vol. 1, No. IV.)

J. Ross and G. Morris: Speeches in Support of Ross's Resolutions relating to the Free Navigation of the Mississippi.
Philadelphia, 1803. BA.

Jared Sparks: The History of the Louisiana Treaty. North
American Review, vol. 28, p. 389 (April, 1829), and vol. 30,
p. 551 (April, 1830). (Reviews of Marbois and of the
translation of it.)

Sylvestris, *pseud.*: Reflections on the Cession of Louisiana to
the United States. Washington, 1803. BA, P.

B. Vaughan: Remarks on a Dangerous Mistake made as to
the East Boundary of Louisiana. Boston, 1814. 8vo, pp.
28. BA.

3. *Diplomatic Efforts in England.*

American Candour, in a Tract lately published at Boston, entitled "An Analysis," . . . etc. (See [J. Lowell], below.)
London, 1809. 8vo.

American State Papers and Correspondence between Messrs.

Smith, Pinkney, Marquis Wellesley, General Armstrong, M. Champagny, M. Turreau, Messrs. Russell, Monroe, Foster, etc. London, 1812. 8vo, pp. 187, 116. H.

Nathaniel Atcheson : American Encroachment on British Rights. London, 1808, pp. xiii., cxiii., 250. Also in Pamphleteer, vol. 6, pp. 33–98, 361–400. BA.

A. B. : Six Letters of A. B. on the Difference between Great Britain and the United States of America, with a Preface by the Editor of the Morning Chronicle. London, 1807. 8vo, pp. 48. BA.

Alex. Baring : An Inquiry into the Causes and Consequences of the Orders in Council ; and an Examination of the Conduct of Great Britain towards the Neutral Commerce of America. London, 1808 (and other editions). C, H, P. (See T. P. Courtenay, below.)

[Charles B. Brown, or G. Morris] : The British Treaty [of 1806. n. p., 1807.] 8vo, pp. 86. BA. + The British Treaty with America, with an Appendix of State Papers ; which are now first published. London, 1808. 8vo, pp. 147. N.

James Cheetham : Peace or War ? or, Thoughts on our Affairs with England. New York, 1807. 8vo, pp. 44. B, BA, MH.

[T. P. Courtenay] : Observations on the American Treaty, in Eleven Letters. First published in The Sun, under the Signature of " Decius." London, 1808. 8vo, pp. 75.

T. P. Courtenay : Additional Observations on the American Treaty, with some Remarks on Mr. Baring's Pamphlet ; being a Continuation of the Letters of Decius. To which is added an Appendix of State Papers, including the Treaty. London, 1808. 8vo, pp. viii., 94, lxix. N.

[Alexander J. Dallas] : An Exposition of the Causes and Character of the Late War with Great Britain. Baltimore, 1815. (And other editions.) BA, C.

Decius, pseud. See [T. P. Courtenay], above.

A Farmer, pseud. See Senex, pseud., below.

Thos. G. Fessenden : Some Thoughts on the Present Dispute between Great Britain and America. Philadelphia, 1807. 8vo, pp. 91. P.

An Inquiry into the Present State of the Foreign Relations of the Union, as affected by the Late Measures of Administration. Philadelphia, 1806. 8vo, pp. 183. BA.

Wm. Lee: Les Etats-Unis et l'Angleterre, ou, Souvenirs et Reflexions d'un Citoyen Américain. [1791–1814.] Bordeaux, 1814. 8vo, pp. 346. BA, C, H.

[J. Lowell]: Analysis of the Late Correspondence between our Administration and Great Britain and France. With an Attempt to show what are the Real Causes of the Failure of the Negotiations between France and America. [Boston, 1808.] BA. (See American Candour, above.)

[J. Lowell]: Supplement to the late Analysis of the Public Correspondence between our Cabinet and those of France and Great Britain. [Boston, 1808.] 8vo, pp. 28. BA.

[J. Lowell]: Thoughts upon the Conduct of our Administration in Relation both to Great Britain and France, more especially in Reference to the Late Negotiation, concerning the Attack on the Chesapeake; by a Friend to Peace. [1808.]

[J. Madison.] See under B, pp. 264, 265, A Letter, etc., 1806.

[James McHenry]: Three Patriots, [Jefferson, Madison, and Monroe,] or, the Cause and Cure of Present Evils. Baltimore, 1811. 8vo. M.

B. Mihir, *pseud.*: Considerations in Answer to the Pamphlet containing Madison's Instructions to Monroe. Albany, 1807. BA.

[G. Morris]: An Answer to "War in Disguise;" or, Remarks upon the New Doctrine of England concerning Neutral Trade. New York, 1806. 8vo, pp. 76. (See, also, [Charles B. Brown], above.)

Timothy Pickering: Letters addressed to the People of the United States of America on the Conduct of the Past and Present Administrations of the American Government towards Great Britain and France. London, 1812. 8vo, pp. 168.

The Present Claims and Complaints of America briefly and fairly considered. London, 1806. 8vo, pp. 56.

Remarks on the British Treaty with the United States. Liverpool, 1807. BA.

Report of the Committee to whom was referred the Correspondence between Mr. Monroe and Mr. Canning, and between Mr. Madison and Mr. Rose, relative to the Attack on the Chesapeake. April 16, 1808. Washington, 1808.

Senex, *pseud.* : Letters under the signatures of "Senex" and of "A Farmer," comprehending an examination of the conduct of our Executive toward France and Great Britain, out of which the present crisis has arisen. Originally published in the North American. Baltimore, 1809. 8vo, pp. 108. BA.

[James Stephen], War in Disguise; or, the Frauds of Neutral Flags. London, 1805. 8vo, pp. 215. (See [G. Morris], above.)

The Tocsin; an Inquiry into the Late Proceedings of Great Britain, etc. Charleston, 1807. P.

4. *Period of Cabinet Office.*

(See [John Armstrong], under 6, below.)

Major-General George W. Cullum: The Attack on Washington City in 1814. *In* Papers of the American Historical Association. Vol. 2, pp. 54–68. 1888.

E. D. Ingraham: A Sketch of the Events which preceded the Capture of Washington by the British on the Twenty-fourth of August, 1814. Philadelphia, 1849. 8vo, pp. 66. A, B, BA, C.

Remarks on "An Enquiry," etc. (See next title.) Baltimore, 1816. 8vo. BA.

Spectator, *pseud.* : Enquiry respecting the Capture of Washington by the British. Washington, 1816. 8vo. BA.

United States, 13th Congress, 3d session. Report of Committee to inquire into the Causes and Particulars of the Invasion of the City of Washington by the British Forces, August. Washington, 1814. 8vo. BA.

J. S. Williams: History of the Invasion and Capture of Washington. New York, 1857. 12mo. BA.

5. *Presidency*.

Exposition of the Motives for opposing the Nomination of Mr. Monroe for the Office of President of the United States. Washington, 1816. 8vo, pp. 14. B, BA.

[C. Pinckney]: Observations to show the Propriety of the Nomination of Col. J. Monroe to the Presidency. Charleston, 1816. BA.

Edward T. Channing: Oration delivered at Boston, July 4, 1817. Boston, [1817]. 8vo, pp. 24. BA, MH, W.

J. L. M. Curry: The Acquisition of Florida. Magazine of American History, vol. 19, p. 286. 1887.

[J. Forsyth]: Observaciones sobre la Memoria del Señor Onis, relativa à la Negociacion con los Estados Unidos. (See fifth title below.) Madrid, 1822. 8vo.

T. W. Higginson: The Administration of James Monroe. Harper's Magazine, vol. 68, p. 936. 1883.

J. R. Ireland: The Republic. History of the United States in the Administrations. Chicago, 1888. 18 v.

Joshua Leavitt: The Administration of Monroe. Harper's Monthly Magazine, vol. 29, p. 461. September, 1864.

Official Correspondence between Don Luis de Onis, Minister from Spain, . . . and John Quincy Adams, in relation to the Floridas and the Boundaries of Louisiana, etc. London, 1818. 8vo, pp. 130. C.

Luis de Onis: Memoria sobre las negociaciones entre España y los Estados-Unidos de América, que dieron motivo al Tratado de 1819; con una noticia sobre la estadística de aquel pais, [i. e. Florida]. Acompaña un Apéndice. Madrid, 1820. 8vo. H.

[L. de Onis]: Memoirs upon the Negotiations between Spain and the United States of America, which led to the Treaty of 1819. With a Statistical Notice of that Country, [Florida]. Accompanied by an Appendix. [Translated by Tobias Watkins.] Washington, 1821. 8vo. H.

John Overton: A Vindication of the Measures of the President and his . . . Generals, in the Commencement and

Termination of the Seminole War. Washington, 1819. 8vo. N.

Wm. Patterson: Letter to Peter Van Schaack, Kinderhook, N. Y., on President Monroe and his Cabinet (1822). *In* Magazine of American History, vol. 6, p. 217.

J. F. Rattenbury: Remarks on the Cession of the Floridas to the United States of America, etc. London, 1819. 8vo. C. (Also in Pamphleteer, vol. 15.)

J. Schouler: Monroe and the Rhea Letter. Magazine of American History, vol. 12, p. 308. 1884.

United States, 18th Congress, 2d Session. [1825.] Reports of Committees, 79. On President Monroe's Accounts. B.

Verus, *pseud.*: Observations on the Existing Differences between Spain and the United States. Philadelphia, 1817. BA.

6. *Subsequent Period.*

[John Armstrong]: Notice of Mr. Adams' Eulogium on the Life and Character of James Monroe. [Washington, 1832.] 8vo, pp. 32. C, M, N.

United States, 30th Congress, 2d Session. [1849.] Senate Miscellaneous Documents, 10. On President Monroe's Manuscript Papers.

C. C. Hazewell: Review of "The People, the Sovereigns." North American Review, vol. 105, p. 634. (Also noticed in the Nation, vol. 5, p. 109.)

D. THE MONROE DOCTRINE.

President Monroe's Seventh Annual Message, December 2, 1823. *In* Williams' Statesman's Manual, vol. 1, pp. 460, 461; State Papers, Foreign Affairs, vol. 5, pp. 245–250.

Edward Channing and A. B. Hart, eds. Extracts from Official Declarations of the United States embodying the Monroe Doctrine, 1789–1891. [American History Leaflets, No. 4.] New York, 1892.

S. M. Hamilton: Hamilton Fac-similes of Manuscripts in the National Archives relating to American History. Pt. I. The Monroe Doctrine. New York, 1896.

1. *Its Immediate Origin.*

The Principles of the Holy Alliance; or Notes and Manifestoes of the Allied Powers. London, 1823.

North American Review, vol. 17, p. 340, October, 1823. (Review of the above. See especially pp. 373–375.)

Diplomatic Review, vol. 13, pp. 65–69 (August 2, 1865), 73–74 (September 6, 1865), 81–86 (October 4, 1865).

F. R. de Chateaubriand, Congrès de Vérone. Guerre d'Espagne. Négociations. Colonies espagnoles. 2e éd. Paris, 1838. 2 vols. 8vo. C. + (Translated), Memoirs of the Congress of Verona. London, 1838. 2 vols. 8vo. C, N.

Briefwechsel zwischen Varnhagen von Ense und Oelsner. Vol. 3.

A. G. Stapleton : The Political Life of the Right Honorable George Canning, 1822–1827. 3 vols. London, 1831.

Conference of Mr. Canning with Prince Polignac, October 9, 1823 ; in Annual Register, vol. 66, p. 99.

[G. Canning] : Official Correspondence, Notes by E. J. Stapleton. 2 vols. Longmans, 1887.

George Canning : Speech in the House of Commons, December 12, 1826. *In* Hansard's Parliamentary Debates, New Series, vol. 16, pp. 390–398 ; Annual Register, vol. 68, p. 192 ; Canning's Speeches, vol. 6, pp. 108, 109.

Richard Rush : Memoranda of a Residence at the Court of London. Philadelphia, 1845. 2 vols.

John Quincy Adams : Diary. Vols. 4 and 6, *passim.*

John T. Morse, Jr.: John Quincy Adams. [American Statesmen Series.] Pp. 130–137.

Mr. Adams to Mr. Rush, July 22, 1823. State Papers, Foreign Affairs, vol. 5, pp. 791–793, etc.

Mr. Clay's Resolution, offered January 20, 1824. Annals of Congress, 18th Congress, 1st Session, vol. 1, p. 1104; Benton's Abridgment, vol. 8, p. 650 ; Niles' Register, vol. 25, p. 335.

President Monroe's Eighth Annual Message, December 7, 1824. *In* Statesman's Manual, vol. 1, pp. 476, 479, 480; State Papers, Foreign Affairs, vol. 5, pp. 353–359.

Jefferson to Monroe, October 24, 1823. Works, vol. 7, pp.
315–317.

Madison to Monroe, October 30, 1823. Works, vol. 3, p. 339.

Pennsylvania Magazine of History and Biography. No. 23.
1882. Extracts from the Letters and Diary of William
Plumer, Jr.

2. *Discussion of it in the Chief Treatises on International Law.*

J. C. Bluntschli: Droit International Codifié. Paris, 1870.
Pp. 253, 254. S, JH.

Carlos Calvo: Derecho Internacional Teórico y Práctico de
Europa y América. Paris, 1868. Vol. 1, pp. 142–154, and
note (from Dana's Wheaton). S. + French translation,
Droit International, etc. 3e éd., Paris, 1880. JH.

Sir Edward S. Creasy: First Platform of International Law.
London, 1876. Pp. 120–124. S, JH.

A. W. Heffter: Das Europäische Völkerrecht der Gegenwart.
Berlin, 1873. Pp. 96–98. S, JH.

Wm. Beach Lawrence: Commentaire sur les Éléments du
Droit International et sur L'Histoire des Progrès du Droit
des Gens de Henry Wheaton. Leipzig (4 vols.), 1868–1880.
Vol. 2 (1869), pp. 297–394. S, JH.

G. F. de Martens: Précis du Droit des gens moderne de l'Europe; augmenté des notes de Pinheiro-Ferreira. Paris,
1864. Vol. 1, pp. 208–214. S.

Robert Phillimore: Commentaries upon International Law.
London, 1854–1857. Vol. 1, p. 433. JH.

F. Snow: Treaties and Topics in American Diplomacy, (pp.
237–356). Boston, 1894. 8vo.

Henry Wheaton: Elements of International Law. Lawrence's edition (1855), p. 97; Dana's edition (1866), p. 112.

3. *In more Special Treatises and Articles.*

a. AMERICAN.

John Quincy Adams. See Edward Everett, below.

America for Americans. Democratic Review, vol. 32, pp. 187,
193; vol. 37, p. 263.

J. G. Patterson: The Passing of the Monroe Doctrine. Independent, vol. 10, p. 664. May 19, 1898.

H. A. Boardman: New Doctrine of Intervention, tried by the Writings of Washington. Philadelphia, 1852. 8vo, pp. 63. C.

W. F. Borrough: The Monroe Doctrine and Its History. American Magazine of Civics, vol. 8, p. 47, 1895.

James Buchanan: Article on the Monroe Doctrine, in Mr. Buchanan's Administration on the Eve of the Rebellion. New York, 1866. 8vo. BA.

H. C. Bunts: The Scope of the Monroe Doctrine. Forum, vol. 7, p. 192, 1889.

J. W. Burgess: Recent Pseudo-Monroeism. Political Science Quarterly, vol. 11, p. 44, 1896.

A. C. Casset: The Monroe Doctrine: Defense not Defiance. Forum, vol. 20, p. 456, 1895.

Catholic World, vol. 31, p. 116. April, 1880.

[Wm. Duane]: The Two Americas, Great Britain, and the Holy Alliance. Washington, 1824. 8vo. P.

M. P. Dunnell: The Monroe Doctrine. American Law Review, vol. 29, p. 829, 1894.

[A. H. Everett]: America, or a General Survey of the Political Situation of the Several Powers of the Western Continent. . . . By a Citizen of the United States. Philadelphia, 1827.

Edward Everett, John Quincy Adams, and others: The Monroe Doctrine. New York, 1863. 8vo, pp. 17. Also, as No. 34 of the Loyal Publication Society. 1863. 8vo, pp. 11. [Contains Mr. Everett's letter of September 2, 1863, in the New York Ledger, and Mr. Adams' letter of August 11, 1837, to the Rev. Dr. Channing.] H, M.

W. Gammell: The Monroe Doctrine. In Selected Writings, edited by J. O. Murray, pp. 178–198. Cambridge, 1890.

E. L. Godkin: The Development of the Monroe Doctrine. Nation, vol. 62, p. 490, 1895. More about the Monroe Doctrine. Nation, vol. 61, p. 304, 1895.

J. C. Green: Americanism and the Monroe Doctrine. Westminster Magazine, vol. 149, pp. 237–247, March, 1898.

Gunton's Magazine, vol. 10, p. 1, 1896. The Philosophy of the Monroe Doctrine. Vol. 10, p. 81, 1896. The Monroe Doctrine : Definition and Interpretation.

Harper's Monthly, vol. 18, p. 418. (Easy Chair.) The Monroe Doctrine Abroad.

G. Hosmer : D. C. Gilman on the Monroe Doctrine. Open Court, vol. 10, p. 4801, 1896.

Intervention of the United States : The Crisis in Europe. Democratic Review, vol. 30, pp. 401 and 554, May, June, 1852.

Thomas E. Jevons : The Monroe Doctrine. Bachelor of Arts, vol. 2, p. 437, 1895.

J. A. Kasson : The Monroe Declaration. North American Review, vol. 133, pp. 241–254, September, 1881.

J. A. Kasson : The Monroe Doctrine in 1881. North American Review, vol. 133, pp. 523–533, December, 1881.

Gustav Körner : The True Monroe Doctrine. Nation, January 5, 1882, vol. 34, p. 9.

Joshua Leavitt: The Monroe Doctrine. New York, 1863. 8vo, pp. 50. H. (Reprint of article, New Englander, vol. 22, p. 729, October, 1863. See, also, Joshua Leavitt, under A, above, a part of that article.)

J. F. McLaughlin : The Monroe Doctrine. Richmond, 1896.

J. B. McMaster : The Origin, Meaning, and Application of the Monroe Doctrine. Philadelphia, 1896.

National Quarterly Review, vol. 13, p. 114. (1866.) The Monroe Doctrine and the South American Republics.

New Review, vol. 14, p. 47, 1895. The Monroe Doctrine.

R. Ogden ; Some of the Myths of the Monroe Doctrine. Nation, vol. 60, p. 356, 1894.

R. Olney : International Isolation of the United States. Atlantic Monthly, vol. 81, pp. 577–588, May, 1898.

Providence Public Library Monthly Bulletin, vol. 1, No. 6, 1895. The Monroe Doctrine.

W. F. Reddaway. The Monroe Doctrine. Cambridge, England, 1898. Pp. 162.

T. Roosevelt: The Monroe Doctrine. *In his* American Ideals. New York, 1897.

W. L. Scruggs : The Monroe Doctrine. Magazine of American History, vol. 26, p. 39, 1891.

W. G. Sumner : The Monroe Doctrine : Proposed Dual Organization of Mankind. Popular Science Monthly, vol. 49, p. 433, 1896.

G. F. Tucker : The Monroe Doctrine. Its Origin and Growth. Boston, 1885. 138 pp.

J. C. Welling : The Monroe Doctrine on Intervention. North American Review, vol. 82, p. 478. (1856.)

J. A. Woodburn : The Monroe Doctrine and Some of its Applications. Chautauquan, vol. 22, p. 549, 1895.

Theodore D. Woolsey. Article " Monroe Doctrine " in Johnson's Cyclopædia.

b. EUROPEAN.

G. Carnazza Amari : Nuova Esposizione del Principio del non Intervento. Catania, 1873. Pp. 16–24. S. *In French, in* Revue de Droit International, 1873, pp. 352–390, 531–566.

Benner : Article, " Intervention," in Bluntschli's Staatswörterbuch.

Carlos Calvo: Une page de droit international, ou l'Amérique du Sud devant la science du droit des gens moderne. Paris, 2e éd., 1870. 2 vols.

Diplomatic Review, vol. 15, p. 92.

L. B. Hautefeuille : Le principe de Non-Intervention et ses applications aux évènements actuels. Paris, 1863. 8vo. (Reprinted from Revue Contemporaine, vol. 34, p. 193.)

Heiberg : Das Princip der Nicht-Intervention. Leipzig, 1842.

L. count Kamarowsky: The Principle of Non-Intervention (in Russian). Moscow, 1874.

M. Kapoustine : Le droit d'intervention. 1876.

Don Rafael Manuel de Labra : De la representacion y influencia de los Estados-Unidos de América en el derecho internacional. Madrid, 1877. 38 pp.

D. D. de Pradt : Vrai système de l'Europe relativement à

l'Amérique. . . . 1825. C. $+$ *In* Pamphleteer, vols. 25
and 26. BA.

H. von Rotteck : Das Recht der Einmischung in die inneren
Angelegenheiten eines fremden Staates. Freiburg, 1845.

Carl Rümelin : Die Monroe-Doctrin. *In* Zeitschrift für die
gesammte Staatswissenschaft. Tübingen, 1882. Heft 2.

Hermann Strauch : Zur Interventions-Lehre. Eine völker-
rechtliche Studie. Heidelberg, 1879. See especially pp.
17, 18.

4. *Occasions on which it has been applied.*

a. THE PANAMA CONGRESS.

Mr. Adams' Messages of February 2, 1826 (St. P., V. 794–
797) and March 21 (V. 834–897). (Those of December 26,
1825, and March 15, 1826, are to be found in United States,
etc., below.)

American Annual Register, 1826, chap. iv.

Benton's Thirty Years, vol. i. p. 65.

Henry Clay's Dispatch to Mr. Poinsett, March 25, 1825 : *In*
State Papers, Foreign Affairs, vol. 5, pp. 908, 909.

Coronel Don Bernardo Monteagudo : Ensayo sobre la Necesi-
dad de una Federacion Jeneral entre los Estados Hispano-
Americanos, y Plan de su Organisacion. Obra Póstuma del
H. Coronel D., etc. Lima, 1825. (See Sparks, below.)

Niles' Register, vols. 30, 36, *passim.*

D. D. de Pradt : Congrès de Panama. Paris, 1825. BA.

Revue Britannique, mars, 1826, pp. 159–176. Congrès de
Panama.

[Jared Sparks] : Alliance of the Southern Republics. *In*
North American Review, vol. 22, p. 162, January, 1826.
(Review of Coronel, above.)

J. M. Torres Caicedo : Union latina americana, etc. Union
latine-américaine ; la pensée de Bolivar, son origine et ses
développements. Paris, 1875. (Reviewed by A. Villamus,
in Revue Politique et Littéraire, 30 sept., 1876.)

United States, 19th Congress, 1st Session. [68.] The Execu-

APPENDIX

tive Proceedings of the Senate of the United States, on the subject of the Mission to the Congress at Panama, together with the Messages and Documents relating thereto. Washington, 1826. Pp. 160. B, P.

United States, 19th Congress, 1st Session. House of Representatives. [Document No. 129.] Congress of Panama. Message from the President of the United States, . . . in relation to the Proposed Congress to be held at Panama. Washington, 1826. Pp. 90.

United States. Congressional Debates, 19th Congress, 1st Session, vol. 2. Benton's Abridgment, viii. 417–472, 637–675 (Senate); ix. 48–50, 62–76, 90–218 (House of Representatives).

United States: The Congress of 1826 at Panama, and Subsequent Movements toward a Conference of American Nations. Historical Appendix (vol. 4) to the Report of the International American Conference. Washington, 1890. Pp. 375.

Don Manuel Lorenzo de Vidaurre : Speech on opening the Congress. Niles' Register, vol. 31, pp. 44–47.

Von Holst: Constitutional History of the United States, vol. 1, pp. 409–432.

Webster's Speech, in Works, vol. 3, pp. 178–217.

———

C. Lefebvre de Bécour : Des rapports de la France et de l'Europe avec l'Amérique du Sud. Revue des Deux Mondes, juil., 1838.

b. YUCATAN.

Mr. Polk's Annual Message of December 2, 1845 (Statesman's Manual, iii. 1458); his Special Message on Yucatan, of April 29, 1848 (iii. 1737). (Benton, xvi. 187, 188.)

Congressional Globe, vol. 18, and Appendix. 30th Congress, 1st Session. Benton's Abridgment, xvi. 188, 189 (House); 189, 190, 196–204 (Senate).

Calhoun's Speech, May 15, 1848, in Works, iv. 454–479.

Von Holst, iii. 448–453.

c. THE CLAYTON-BULWER TREATY.

Treaty with New Granada, December 12, 1846, especially Art. 35. In Statutes at Large, vol. viii.

Clayton and Bulwer Convention, 19th April, 1850, between the British and American Governments, concerning Central America, with Correspondence. 1856.

Joseph P. Comegys: Memoir of John M. Clayton. (Papers of the Historical Society of Delaware, iv.) Wilmington, 1882. Pp. 190–202, 211–234. JH.

Congressional Globe. 32d Congress, 2d Session, vol. 26, 1853. 33d Congress, 1st Session, vol. 28, 1853. Appendix, vol. 29. 34th Congress, 1st Session, 1855–1856, and appendix. 35th Congress, 1st Session.

Clarendon-Dallas Treaty, 1856.

G. W. Hobbs: The Clayton-Bulwer Treaty. Bay State Monthly, vol. 3, p. 17. 1885.

T. J. Lawrence: Essays on Some Disputed Questions in Modern International Law. Essay III, pp. 89–162; The Panama Canal and the Clayton-Bulwer Treaty. Cambridge, England, 1885. (And other editions.)

Nation, vol. 34, p. 92, 1881. J. G. Blaine and the Clayton-Bulwer Treaty.

W. L. Scruggs: The Clayton-Bulwer Treaty. North American Review, vol. 145, p. 313, 1887.

Treaty with Nicaragua, June 21, 1867.

United States. 34th Congress, 1st Session. Senate Ex. Doc. 35. Messages of the President . . . on the construction of the Treaty of July 4, 1850. (1856).

See also next section, and the last.

d. CENTRAL AMERICA, 1845–1860.

N[apoléon] L[ouis] B[onaparte] : Canal of Nicaragua, or a Project to connect the Atlantic and Pacific Oceans by means of a Canal. London, 1846. [Not published.]

Louis Napoléon Bonaparte : Le Canal de Nicaragua, ou projet de jonction des océans Atlantique et Pacifique. Revue Britannique, mai, 1849.

[Sir Henry Bulwer] : Great Britain and the United States. Edinburgh Review, vol. 104, pp. 267–298. July, 1856.

Canal interocéanique par l'isthme de Darien, Nouvelle Granade (Amérique du Sud). Canalisation par le colonisation. Paris, 1860. Pp. 203. A.

Correspondence with the United States respecting Central America. Printed by order of Parliament. London, 1856–1860. Pp. 344.

Democratic Review, Oct. 1852. Vol. 31, p. 337. Our Foreign Relations. Central America.

A. Denain : Intérêts qui se rattachent à l'isthme de Panama, et aux différentes isthmes de l'Amérique Centrale. Paris, 1845. C.

Question Anglo-Américaine. Documents officiels échangés entre les Etats-Unis et l'Angleterre au sujet de l'Amérique Centrale et du traité Clayton-Bulwer. Paris, 1856. S.

Xavier Raymond : Diplomatie Anglo-Américaine ; les Américains et les Anglais au Mexique et dans l'Amérique Centrale. Revue des Deux Mondes, 15 avril, 1853.

E. G. Squier: Letter to the Hon. H. S. Foote, Chairman of the Committee of Foreign Relations of the United States Senate, on the Nicaragua Treaty, 1850. N.

[E. G. Squier] : The Mosquito Question. Whig Review, February, March, 1850.

[E. G. Squier] : The Islands of the Gulf of Honduras. Their Seizure and Organization as a British Colony. Democratic Review, vol. 31, p. 544. (November, December, 1852.)

E. G. Squier : The States of Central America and the Honduras Interoceanic Railway. New York, 1858. Pp. 782. N.

e. CUBA, ETC., 1850–98.

G. d'Alaux, Cuba et la propagande annexioniste. Revue des Deux Mondes, 15 juil., 1850.

Charles Benoist: Cuba, l'Espagne et les Etats-Unis. Revue des Deux Mondes, vol. 141, p. 112, mai 1, 1897.

Buchanan, Mason and Soulé : the "Ostend Manifesto." Diplomatic Correspondence, 1854–1855. Buchanan : Message, December 3, 1860.

General Cass to Lord Napier, May 12, May 29, 1857, . . . November, 1858; to Mr. Dodge, October 2, 1858. (Spanish invasion of Mexico.)

J. Chanut, La Question de Cuba aux Etats-Unis et en Europe. Revue Contemporaine, vol. 8, p. 470. (1859.)

G. Colmache: How Cuba might have belonged to France. Fortnightly, vol. 64, p. 747, 1895.

Congressional Globe. 33d Congress, 2d Session. (1854–1855.) (Ostend Manifesto.) 35th Congress, 2d Session. (1859.) (Cuba.)

A. B. Hart: A Century of Cuban Diplomacy. Harper's Magazine, vol. 97, pp. 127–134, June, 1898.

A. B. Hart: The Ostend Manifesto. American History Leaflet, No. 2. 1892.

M. W. Hazeltine: Possible Complications of the Cuban Question. North American Review, vol. 162, p. 406, April, 1896.

V. W. Kingsley: Spain, Cuba, and the United States. Recognition and the Monroe Doctrine. New York, 1870. 34 pp.

J. K. Latane: The United States Intervention in Cuba. North American Review, vol. 166, p. 350, 1898.

F. J. Matheson: The United States and Cuban Independence. Fortnightly, vol. 66, pp. 816–832, May, 1898.

Revue Britannique, août, 1854; pp. 257–290. La question de Cuba, jugée au point de vue Américaine.

[E. G. Squier?]: The Cuban Debate. Democratic Review, vol. 31, pp. 433, 624. (November, December, 1852.)

S. Webster: Mr. Marcy: the Cuban Question: and the Ostend Manifesto. Political Science Quarterly, vol. 8, p. 1, March, 1893.

f. FRENCH INTERVENTION IN MEXICO.

F. Bancroft: The French in Mexico and the Monroe Doctrine. Political Science Quarterly, vol. 11, p. 30, 1896.

Congressional Globe. 37th Congress, 3d Session, Appendix, p. 94. 38th Congress, 1st Session; the House resolution of April 4, 1864, and debate. 39th Congress, 1st Session; message on the sending of Austrian troops to Mexico, and debate. 39th Congress, 2d Session; on Mexican affairs.

Democratic Review, vol. 32, p. 39. Mexico and the Monroe Doctrine.

Fraser's Magazine, vol. 64, p. 717. December, 1861. Mexico.

Free Press, Urquhart, vol. 9. November 6, 1861. Collective Intervention in the New World.

Hunt's Merchants' Magazine, vol. 50, p. 415, vol. 51, p. 106. (June, August, 1864.) The Conquest of Mexico by France.

V. W. Kingsley, French Intervention in Mexico, 1863, pph. N.

A. Laugel: France and the United States. Nation, vol. 1, p. 302. (September 7, 1865.)

Joshua Leavitt: The Key of the Continent. New Englander, vol. 23, p. 517. (July, 1864.)

E. Lefèvre : Histoire de l'intervention française au Mexique. Vol. 2, ch. 18, etc. Bruxelles et Londres. 1869.

H. Mercier de Lacombe : Le Mexique et les Etats-Unis. 2e éd. Paris, 1863. 8vo. B.

Mexico and the Monroe Doctrine. [n. p. 1862 ?] Pp. 24.

Nation, vol. 1, p. 678. November 30, 1865. The Solution of the Mexican Problem.

Revue Britannique, septembre, 1863, pp. 213–224. Le Mexique au point de vue américaine, avant et depuis l'expédition française.

G. Reynolds : Mexico. Atlantic Monthly, vol. 14, p. 51. July, 1864.

J. H. Robinson : The Mexican Question. North American Review, vol. 103, pp. 106–142. July, 1866.

J. M. Schofield : The Withdrawal of the French from Mexico. Century, vol. 54, pp. 128–137. May, 1897.

United States: Message and Documents, Department of State, 1863–1864.

United States : Messages of the President of the United States to Congress, with accompanying documents relating to the Mexican Question.

Justus Strictus Veritas, *pseud. :* Nuevas Reflexiones sobre la Cuestion Franco-Mexicana. Folleto publicado en Paris, el 30 de setiembre de 1862 por supplemento al Correo de ultramar. Mexico, 1862. Pp. 192. C.

APPENDIX 289

Westminster Review, vol. 80, p. 313. October, 1863. The French Conquest of Mexico. Same art., Eclectic Magazine, vol. 61, p. 36. Same art., Living Age, vol. 79, p. 251.

g. THE INTER-OCEANIC CANAL — (OFFICIAL)

Congressional Record, vol. 9, p. 2312. Senator Burnside's resolution, June 25, 1879. (46th Congress, 1st Session. S. R. No. 43.) Further discussion in vol. 10.

President Hayes: Message, March 8, 1880. In Congressional Record, vol. 10, p. 1399. Since printed with documents.

Papers relating to the Foreign Relations of the United States, 1881. Mr. Blaine to Mr. Lowell (circular), June 24, 1881, pp. 537–540. Lord Granville to Mr. Hoppin, November 10, 1881, p. 549. Mr. Blaine to Mr. Lowell, November 19, 1881, pp. 554–559; November 29, 1881, pp. 563–569.

Earl Granville to Mr. West, January 14, (7 ?) 1882.

Correspondence respecting the projected Panama Canal. Presented to both Houses of Parliament by command of Her Majesty. 1882.

Mr. Frelinghuysen to Mr. Lowell, May 8, 1882.

Don Antonio Aguilar, Marquis de la Vega de Armijo, to Don Francisco Barca, Spanish Minister at Washington, March 15, 1882. In " the Red Book," Madrid, 1882.

Congrès International d' Etudes du Canal Interocéanique. Compte Rendu des Séances. Paris, 1879.

Bulletin du Canal Interocéanique, Nos. 1 to 60+. (September 1, 1879, to February 15, 1882.) Paris.

(UNOFFICIAL)

D. Ammen: M. de Lesseps and his Canal. (See Lesseps, below.) North American Review, vol. 130, pp. 130–146, February, 1880.

Cassell's, December, 1879. Panama and the Isthmus.

C. DeHalb: The Nicaragua Canal — Ours or England's? Forum, vol. 19, p. 690, 1894.

A Delawarean: The Clayton-Bulwer Treaty and the report of the Committee of the House on Foreign Relations against it. May 1, 1880. S.

Edinburgh Review, April, 1882. The Panama Canal.

E. L. Godkin : The Nicaragua Canal. Nation, vol. 39, p. 516. December, 1884.

U. S. Grant: The Nicaragua Canal. North American Review, vol. 132, pp. 197–216. February, 1881.

Harper's Monthly Magazine, vol. 60, p. 935. (Easy Chair.) Lesseps and the Darien Canal.

The International Canal and the Monroe Doctrine. New York, 1880. Pp. 118.

L. M. Keasbey: The Nicaragua Canal and the Monroe Doctrine. New York, 1896. Pp. 622.

F. de Lesseps: The Interoceanic Canal. North American Review, vol. 130, pp. 1–15. January, 1880. Vol. 131, pp. 75–78. July, 1880.

A. Letellier: Les Travaux du Canal de Panama. Nouvelle Revue, 1 juil., 1882.

W. L. Merry: The Political Aspect of the Nicaragua Canal. Overland Monthly, n. s., vol. 23, p. 497, May, 1894.

The Monroe Doctrine and the Isthmian Canal. North American Review, vol. 130, p. 499.

The Nation, vol. 30, p. 90. February 5, 1880. The United States Government and the Panama Canal. — Vol. 33, p. 348. November 3, 1881. American Policy towards the Isthmus Canal. — Vol. 34, p. 92. February 2, 1882. Another chapter of Mr. Blaine's Diplomacy. — Vol. 34, p. 114. February 9, 1882. Mr. Blaine's Manifesto. — Vol. 34, p. 156–157. — Vol. 34, p. 200. March 7, 1882. "A Spirited Foreign Policy."

T. W. Osborn: The Darien Canal. International Review, vol. 7, pp. 481–497. November, 1879.

Popular Science Monthly. Vol. 16, pp. 842–849. April, 1880. Some Features of the Interoceanic Canal Question. Vol. 20, pp. 273–275. December, 1881. Our Policy respecting the Panama Canal.

J. R. Proctor: The Nicaragua Canal. American Journal of
Politics, vol. 2, p. 225, 1892.

Providence Public Library Monthly Reference Lists, vol. 1,
p. 45, 1881. The Panama Canal.

Revue Britannique, juil., 1879. Le Congrès du Canal Interocéanique.

J. C. Rodrigues : The Panama Canal : History, Political As-
pects, etc. London, 1885.

Dr. Rudolf Schleiden: Die rechtliche und politische Seite
der Panamá-Canal-Frage. Preussische Jahrbücher, Juni,
1882.

S. Webster: The Diplomacy and Law of Isthmian Canals.
Harper's Magazine, vol. 87, p. 602, 1896.

S. F. Weld : The Isthmus Canal and our Government. Atlantic Monthly, vol. 63, p. 341, March, 1889 ; The Isthmus
Canal and American Control. Atlantic Monthly, vol. 64,
p. 289, September, 1889.

H. White : The Nicaragua Canal. Nation, vol. 52, p. 44,
1890.

T. S. Woolsey : The Interoceanic Canal in the Light of Pre-
cedent. Yale Review, vol. 4, p. 246, 1896.

h. AMERICA NORTH OF THE UNITED STATES.

Nootka-Sound Convention between Spain and Great Britain.
October 28, 1790. Recueil des Traités, 2ᵉ éd., iv. 492–
499.

Treaty between the United States and Spain. February 22,
1819. Statutes at Large, viii. 252–267. Boston, 1867.

Ukase of the Emperor Alexander. September 4, (16,) 1821.
State Papers, Foreign Relations, V.

Message from the President of the United States . . . in relation to Claims set up by Foreign Governments, to Territory
of the United States upon the Pacific Ocean, 1822.

W. Sturgis : Examination of the Russian Claims to the Northwest Coast of America. North American Review, vol. 15,
pp. 370–401. October, 1822.

Robert Greenhow : History of Oregon and California and

other Territories on the Northwest Coast of North America. Boston, 1845. 8vo. (And treaties in appendix.)

Congressional Globe. 40th Congress, 1st (extra) Session. (Alaska purchase.) (Also Canada resolution.)

C. de Varigny : La doctrine Monroe et le Canada. Revue des Deux Mondes, 1879, vol. 32.

i. THE PAN-AMERICAN CONFERENCE.

United States : International American Conference. Reports, 4 vols. Washington, 1890.

W. P. Frye : The Pan-American Congress. Chautauquan, vol. 10, p. 703, 1887.

E. P. Powell : The Pan-American Congress. New England Magazine, n. s., vol. 5, p. 11, 1892.

M. Romero : The Pan-American Congress. North American Review, vol. 151, pp. 354 and 407, 1887. (Reviewed by R. Ogden. Nation, vol. 51, p. 182, 1890.)

J. Sheldon : Suggestions for the Pan-American Congress. New Englander, vol. 51, p. 469, 1889.

C. de Varigny : Un Homme d'Etat Américain : James G. Blaine et le Congrès des trois Amériques. Revue des Deux Mondes, vol. 97, p. 433, June 15, 1890.

j. THE VENEZUELA-GUIANA QUESTION.

C. K. Adams : The Monroe Doctrine and the Cleveland Doctrine. Independent, vol. 49, p. 205, February 18, 1897.

J. Bryce : British Feeling on the Venezuelan Question. North American Review, vol. 162, p. 145, February, 1896.

A. Carnegie : The Venezuelan Question. North American Review, vol. 162, p. 127, February, 1896.

Sir D. P. Chalmers : The Boundary Question [Venezuela]. Juridical Review, vol. 8, p. 1, 1896.

E. D. Cope : The Monroe Doctrine in 1895. Open Court, vol. 10, p. 4777, January 16, 1895.

E. Dicey : Common Sense and Venezuela. Nineteenth Century, vol. 39, p. 7, January, 1896.

E. L. Godkin : The Venezuelan Correspondence. Nation,

vol. 6, p. 458, December 26, 1896 ; The Venezuelan Settlement. Nation, vol. 63, p. 360, 1896.

G. H. D. Gossip: Venezuela before Europe and America. Fortnightly, vol. 65, p. 397, 1896.

H. C. Lodge : England, Venezuela, and the Monroe Doctrine. North American Review, vol. 160, p. 651, June, 1895.

D. Low : The Olney Doctrine and America's New Foreign Policy. Eclectic Magazine, vol. 128, pp. 161–169, 1897.

D. Mills : The New Monroe Doctrine of Messrs. Cleveland and Olney. Canadian Magazine, vol. 6, p. 365, February, 1896.

J. Morley : The Arbitration with America. Nineteenth Century, vol. 40, p. 320, 1896.

National Review, vol. 26, pp. 573 and 737, 1895. The Boundary Question (Venezuela).

M. Francis de Pressensé : La Doctrine de Monroe et le Conflit Anglo-Américain. Revue des Deux Mondes, vol. 133, p. 417, January 15, 1896.

J. L. Rice : The Duty of Congress [in Venezuelan Crisis]. Forum, vol. 20, p. 761, 1896.

W. L. Scruggs : The Venezuelan Question. Review of Reviews, vol. 12, p. 695, December, 1896.

E. J. Shriver : An American View of the Venezuelan Dispute. Westminster Magazine, vol. 1, p. 117, 1896.

H. S. Somerset : Great Britain, Venezuela, and the United States. Nineteenth Century, vol. 38, p. 758. November, 1895.

H. M. Stanley : The Issue between Great Britain and America [in Venezuela]. Nineteenth Century, vol. 39, p. 1, January, 1896.

United States : Report and Accompanying Papers of the Commission appointed by the President of the United States " to investigate and report upon the True Divisional Line between the Republic of Venezuela and British Guiana." Washington, 1897. 4 vols.

D. A. Wells, E. J. Phelps, and C. Schurz : America and Europe : Study of International Relations [Venezuela]. New York, 1896.

J. Wheeler and C. H. Grosvenor : Our Duty in the Crisis [Venezuelan]. North American Review, vol. 161, p. 628, November, 1895.

T. S. Woolsey: The President's Monroe Doctrine. Forum, vol. 20, p. 708, February, 1896.

INDEX

INDEX

ADAMS, JOHN, shocked at Monroe's levity in Paris, 71 ; not a friend of Monroe, 129 ; anticipates Monroe doctrine, 168.

Adams, John Quincy, on Monroe's retirement from army, 12 ; on his advocacy of Mississippi navigation, 27 ; on importance of Monroe's and Jay's foreign missions, 41, 48 ; receives one electoral vote in 1820, 128 ; secretary of state, 129 ; his career and character, 130, 131 ; contrast with Calhoun, 131-134 ; his appointment approved by Jackson, 137 ; vindicates Jackson's career in Florida, 144 ; secures annexation of Florida, 146 ; on Missouri excitement, 147 ; on reasons for favoring Missouri Compromise, 151 ; his candidacy for President in 1824, 157 ; describes Monroe's attitude toward Spanish colonies, 170 ; states Monroe doctrine to Russian ambassador, 172, 173 ; said to have drafted Monroe doctrine in Monroe's message, 174 ; held by Reddaway to be real author, 178 ; his opinion of Monroe, 240 ; anecdote of his toast to Monroe and Lafayette, 251.

Addington, Henry, succeeded by Pitt, 97.

Alexander, Emperor of Russia, arbitrates between England and United States, 202.

Ames, Fisher, on Monroe's career in France, 71.

Annapolis Convention, not favored by Monroe, 22 ; calls Federal Convention, 22, 23.

Armstrong, John, secretary of war under Madison, 111 ; criticised as inefficient by Monroe, 111-119 ; retained in office by Madison, 119 ; popular rage with, after capture of Washington, 126.

Auckland, Lord, on commission to treat with Monroe and Pinkney, 100.

BANCROFT, GEORGE, quoted, 24, 25.

Barlow, Joel, his instructions as minister to France, 110 ; fails to secure treaty of commerce, 110.

Barney, Captain Joshua, presents American flag to National Convention, 54.

Barras, Count, his policy influenced by Monroe, 74.

Benton, Thomas H., not in politics in 1817, 129 ; his elaborate estimate of Monroe, 241-244.

Bladensburg, battle of, part played by Monroe at, 119-126.

Blair, John, appointed delegate to Federal Convention, 28.

Bonaparte, Jerome, his marriage to Miss Patterson, described by Monroe, 90, 91.

Bonaparte, Napoleon, his power in 1803, 80, 81 ; discusses Louisiana question, tells Marbois to sell, 82 ; refuses offer of forty millions, 80, 84 ; announces war with England, 85 ; acquiesces in terms of sale of Louisiana, 85 ; receives Monroe, 86 ; his letter of acknowledgment, 87; takes leave of Monroe, 87, 88; notified of Jerome Bonaparte's marriage, 90; on future growth of America, 94; his arbitrary policy in the matter, 95, 96; promises to aid in acquisition of West Florida, 98; refuses to do so, 98.

Bowler, Jack, leader of slave plot, 36.

Breckenridge, John, defeated by Monroe for governor, 35.

Brock, R. C., his researches on Monroe pedigree, 249.

Burr, Aaron, candidate for French mission, 40.

CALHOUN, JOHN C., secretary of war under Monroe, 129; his career and character, 131-134; contrast with Adams, 131-134; urges appointment of Kent to Supreme Court, 138; has Seminole correspondence published in 1831, 145; doubtful as to proper reception of Lafayette, 154; candidate for presidency, 157; letter of Monroe to, on disunion, 239, 240; his opinion of Monroe, 241.

Cambacérès, French statesman, gives dinner to American envoys, 84; prevents Monroe from treating with Spain, 88.

Camden, Lord, efforts of Lee to secure portrait of, for Virginia, 6.

Campan, Madame, her friendship with Eliza Monroe, 211.

Canning, George, negotiations of Monroe and Pinkney with, 104; proposes American and English coöperation to prevent reconquest of Spanish colonies, 173; his connection with Monroe doctrine, 174, 175.

Carnot, French war minister, wishes war with United States, 74.

Carr, Dabney, forgotten celebrity of Virginia, moves appointment of committee of correspondence, 2.

Cary, Archibald, letter of Washington to, on Monroe, 11.

Castlereagh, Lord, on danger of war from Jackson's usurpations, 144; proposes joint mediation between Spain and colonies, 170.

Cevallos, Don Pedro, negotiations of Monroe and Pinkney with, 99.

Chateaubriand, Vicomte de, statement of Monroe doctrine to, by Gallatin, 172.

Chatham, Lord, portrait of, sent to Virginians of Westmoreland County, 7.

Church, Edward, approves Monroe's policy toward France, 72.

Clay, Henry, his position in 1817, 129; disappointed by not receiving State Department under Monroe, 135; hostile to Monroe's administration, 135; opposes Adams's Florida treaty, 146; candidate for presidency, 157.

Coit, Joshua, letters from, describing Congressional feeling in 1794, 42-47; on presentation of French flag, 66.

Committee of Public Safety, hesitates to receive Monroe, 48; demands information concerning Jay treaty, 61.

Confederation, Articles of, proposal of Monroe to amend, 20; the impost scheme, 20, 21; state of government under, 22, 23.

Congress, of the Confederation, services of Monroe in, 18-27; questions before it in 1783, 19; debates proposed amendments to Articles of Confederation, 20; debates impost scheme, 21, 22; receives Virginia's cession of Western territory, 23; appoints committee to consider division of Western territory, 25; debates Mississippi navigation, 26.

Congress, of the United States, feeling in, over foreign affairs, illustrated by Coit's letters, 42-47; appropriates money to secure Mis-

sissippi navigation, 79; forces
Madison into war with England,
107; prepares for war, 107; movement in, to attack conduct of
War Department, 118; sustains
Jackson in Seminole affair, 144;
debates admission of Missouri,
147; discusses Monroe doctrine
in Panama debate, 176, 177; application of Monroe to, for reimbursement, 232.

Constitution, Federal, formed, 28;
struggle over in Virginia, 28-33;
reasons for Monroe's opposition
to, 29, 30; in relation to power of
secretary of war to command in
field, 111-113; in relation to Missouri Compromise, 148-151; in relation to internal improvements,
152, 182, 191-202.

Convention, National, of France,
receives Monroe as American minister, 49-52; its decree in his
honor, 53; presented by Monroe
with an American flag, 54, 55;
Monroe's explanation of his dealings with, 55, 56.

Crawford, William H., secretary of
treasury under Monroe, 129; his
character and career, 133, 134;
nearly secures Republican nomination in 1816, 134; on evil results of Monroe's Northern tour,
141, 142; candidate for presidency, 157.

Croix, M. de la, summarizes French
complaints against Jay treaty, 64.

Crowninshield, Benjamin W., secretary of navy under Madison and
Monroe, 130.

Cullum, General G. W., on Monroe's
action at Bladensburg, 119.

Cumberland Road Bill, vetoed by
Monroe, 152, 191-202.

Dana, Francis, his mission to St.
Petersburg, 130.

Dane, Nathan, his share in slavery
restriction in Northwest Ordinance, 25, 26.

Dayton, Jonathan, a public dinner
to Monroe, 67.

Diplomatic history, services of Monroe in, 39; causes for Monroe's and
Jay's missions in 1794, 40, 41, 46;
Monroe's instructions, 48; his career in Paris, 48-65; slowness of
communications in, 59; dealings
of Monroe with Lafayette, 59,
60, 152, 153; efforts of Monroe
in behalf of imprisoned seamen,
60; anger of France over Jay
treaty, 61, 64; refusal of French
to receive C. C. Pinckney, 65, 66;
Thiers's view of Monroe's French
mission, 74; Monroe's second mission to France, 79-89; diplomates
involved in Louisiana negotiations, 80, 81; situation on arrival
of Monroe, 81, 82; dealings of
Talleyrand with Livingston, 82;
Marbois offers Louisiana to Livingston, 83; American counter
proposition, 84, 85; final agreement, 85; opinion of Bonaparte,
85, 86; conclusion of treaty, 86;
opinion of Monroe on, 89, 90;
question of share of Livingston
in, 91-93; Monroe's mission to
England, 96, 97; Monroe's mission to Spain, 98, 99; mission of
Monroe and Pinkney to England, 99-105; conclusion of treaty,
100; repudiation of treaty by Jefferson, 101; renewed negotiations
between United States and England, 104, 105; events preceding
war of 1812, 107, 108; negotiations
of Monroe with Foster, 108-110;
mission of Barlow to France, 110;
cession of Florida by Spain, 146;
mission of Rush to England, in
Monroe's administration, 146, 147;
origin of Monroe doctrine, 159-
179.

Directory, declares treaties between
France and the United States
abrogated by Jay treaty, 64; refuses to receive Pinckney, or allow him to remain in Paris, 65.

INDEX

cussion with Marbois and reports
to Madison, 83; suggests re-sale of
Louisiana, 83; agrees with Monroe
to offer forty million francs, 84;
congratulates Monroe on conclusion of treaty, 86; negotiates with
Spain without notifying Monroe,
89; chagrined at Monroe's share
in treaty, 91; explains to Madison
Monroe's minor part in negotiations, 92, 93.

Louisiana, ceded by Spain to France,
78; history of treaty ceding to
United States, 79-89; suggestion
of selling it to reimburse United
States, 83; question as to its relation to Florida, 88, 98; consequences of its acquisition, 93-96.

McHENRY, JAMES, letter to Washington on impost scheme of 1785,
20.

McKean, Thomas, at public dinner
to Monroe, 67.

McLane, Louis, opposes Panama
Congress, 176.

McLean, John T., postmaster-general under Monroe, 130; letter of
Monroe to, on his own career,
233-238; his opinion of Monroe's
impartiality, 241.

Madison, James, his opinion of
George Mason, 2; his birthplace
near that of Monroe, 5; correspondence of Monroe with, while
in Congress, 19-22, 24, 209; in
Federal Convention, 28; sus-
pected by Monroe of unfriendli-
ness, 28; in Virginia urges ratification, 28; attempt of Randolph
to use Monroe against, 37; de-
clines French mission, 40; connection with Louisiana treaty,
86, 89, 91; instructs Monroe to
treat with England, 96; connection with Monroe treaty, 99, 100;
instructs envoys to renew negotiations, 101; his candidacy for
Republican nomination, 105; re-

ceives indorsement of Virginia,
105; elected President, 107; his
cabinet, 107; favors peace, 107;
urged by Monroe to dismiss Armstrong as inefficient, 111-119; refuses to do so, 119; at battle of
Bladensburg, 120, 122-124; gives
Monroe charge of War Department, 124; continues friendly
with Monroe, 129; anticipates
Monroe doctrine, 167; Monroe's
affection for, in later years, 225,
226; correspondence with Monroe in 1831, 227-230; regent of
University of Virginia, 231; his
opinion of Monroe, 240.

Marbois, Barbé, his history of Louisiana purchase, 78; minister of
treasury under Napoleon, 81;
told by Napoleon to sell Louisiana, 82; discusses project with
Livingston and Monroe, 83; re-
jects offer of forty millions, 84;
warns Americans, 85; proposes a
treaty, 85; on Bonaparte's acquiescence, 85, 86; letter of Monroe
to, on conclusion of treaty, 89-
91.

Marshall, John, volunteers in 1776
with Monroe, 8, 9; original member of Phi Beta Kappa, 9; urges
ratification of Constitution, 28.

Mason, Gen. ——, at battle of Bladensburg, 123.

Mason, George, forgotten celebrity
of Virginia, 2; in Federal Convention, 28; opposes ratification of
Constitution, 29.

Mason, Thompson, forgotten celebrity of Virginia, 2.

Masson, ——, aide-de-camp, aids
Monroe to help Lafayette, 153.

Meade, Bishop, on Virginia's early
struggles for civil liberty, 7; compares Williamsburg to London, 8.

Meigs, R. J., postmaster-general
under Monroe, 130.

Mercer, Col. Hugh, services of
Monroe under, 9.

Merlin de Douai, receives Monroe

before National Convention, 53; demands a copy of Jay treaty, 61.

Messages, presidential, of Monroe, 180–207. See under Monroe, James.

Mississippi, navigation of, question of its maintenance under Confederation, 26, 27; hopes of United States to obtain through France from Spain, 48; blocked by Spain after cession of Louisiana to France, 78; secured by Louisiana purchase, 79.

Missouri, debate over its admission, 147; compromise concerning, 147, 148; Monroe's views on, 148–151; Adams's view of, 151.

Monroe, Andrew, supposed ancestor of James Monroe, 249.

Monroe, Andrew, brother of James, letter of Monroe concerning, 76.

Monroe, Eliza, daughter of James Monroe, her marriage, 211; her friendship with Hortense Beauharnais, 211; described by Mrs. Tuley, 216.

Monroe, Hector, ancestor of James Monroe, 4.

Monroe, James, annals of his life, xi.–xiii.; summary of his career, 1, 2, 3; ancestry, 4; birth, 4; college studies, 7, 8; volunteers at outbreak of Revolution, 8.

In Continental Army. Serves under Washington near New York, 9, 10; wounded at Trenton, 10; on Stirling's staff in battles near Philadelphia, 10, 11; loses place in line, 11; recommended by Washington and others for place in Virginia forces, 11, 12; acts as military commissioner, 12; chagrined at failure to obtain promotion, 12, 13; thinks of going to France, 13; studies law under Jefferson, 13; dissuaded by Judge Jones from abandoning Jefferson for Wythe, 13, 15; expresses gratitude to Jefferson, 15, 16; his career shaped by Jefferson's influ-

ence, 16; his life-long association with Jefferson, 16.

Political Leader in Virginia. Review of his services to Virginia, 17, 18; inconspicuous in Virginia House of Delegates, 18; his career in Congress, 18, 19; on problems of peace, 19; favors revision of Articles of Confederation, 20; favors collection of imposts by States, 20; thinks it best to postpone action, 21; describes opposition to plan, 21, 22; does not favor plan of Annapolis Convention, 22; later wishes to aid it, 22; describes secessionist feeling in New England, 23; thinks regulation of commerce by United States necessary to preserve Union, 23; delivers Virginia's cession of Northwest Territory to Congress, 23; his tour in Northwest, 23, 24; views on relations with English in Canada, 24; his second journey, 24; leads in consideration of organization of Western territory, 25; later in Virginia Assembly introduces bill ratifying Ordinance of 1787, 26; writes argument proving right to Mississippi navigation, 27; accepts position as arbitrator between New York and Massachusetts, 27; opposes Jay's proposed Spanish treaty, 27; hopes for success from Federal Convention, 28.

In Virginia Ratifying Convention. Opposes ratification of Constitution, 28, 29; his first speech against it, 29; sums up his objections, 30; finally agrees to conditional ratification, 30; later describes Federalists as monarchists, 30–32; tries at first to be noncommittal, 32; writes address to constituents, 32; writes pamphlet on Federal Government, 33.

United States Senator. Elected to succeed Grayson, 33; inconspicuous in debate, 33; opposes

INDEX

INDEX 305

Washington's administration, 33;
threatens Washington with exposure of Hamilton, 34; opposes
Hamilton's financial measures,
34; urges coercion of England, 34;
opposes appointments of Morris
and Jay, 34; surprised to receive
appointment to French mission,
34, 40.
Governor of Virginia. His two
terms, 35; bitter comments of
Federalists on his election, 35;
suppresses negro slave plot, 35,
36; efforts of Randolph to turn
him against Madison, 36, 37; later
charged by Randolph with time-
serving, 37; charged by Randolph
with having planned armed resistance to Union in 1800, 37, 38.
Envoy to France. Difficulties
of his diplomatic career, 39; reasons for his appointment, 40, 41;
his instructions, 48; directed to
work for opening of Mississippi,
48; reaches Paris after fall of
Robespierre, 48; much delay in
his reception, 49; writes letter
to president of convention, 49;
appears before convention, his
address, 49-51; carried away by
his enthusiasm, 51; French account of his reception, 52, 53;
presents through Barney a flag to
the convention, 54, 55; present
at interment of Rousseau, 55; tells
why he presented the flag, 55;
describes his perilous situation,
55; appeals from the Committee
of Public Safety to the convention,
55; justifies language of his address, 56; severely criticised by
Randolph, 57, 58; reports negotiations concerning Morris's passports, 59; negotiates in behalf
of Lafayette, 59; and of imprisoned Americans, 60; aids Thomas Paine, 60; condemns Jay
treaty as shameful, 62; accuses
Jay of misleading him, 62, 63;
dissuades Directory from sending

a special envoy to complain, 64;
censured by Pickering, 64, 65;
superseded by Pinckney, 65; said
to have prevented recognition
of Pinckney by Directorate, 65;
praised by Pinckney, 66; thinks
his recall delayed to prevent his
return before election, 67; welcomed by Republicans, 67; demands reasons for recall, 67; im-
polite to Washington, 67; pub-
lishes pamphlet attacking foreign
policy of Washington, 68; enu-
meration of his points of complaint, 68-70; comments of Washington upon, 70, 71; anger of
Federalists against, 71; accused
of incompetence and corruption,
71, 72; his honesty admitted by
Hildreth, 72; his policy praised
by Thiers, 74; controversy with
Hamilton in Callender affair, 74;
angry at publication of his dispatches concerning Jacobins, 75;
his letters home during his French
mission, 75, 76; advised by Jefferson to come into Congress, 77.
Louisiana Purchase. His opinion of Barbé Marbois's book, 78;
sent as special envoy to secure
outlet of Mississippi, 79; welcomed by Livingston, 81; learns
of readiness of French to sell
territory, 82; discusses matter
with Livingston, 83; not informed
by Livingston of progress of negotiations, 83; his presentation to
Bonaparte delayed by Talleyrand,
84; offers forty million francs,
84; later agrees to eighty, 85;
congratulates Livingston on success, 86; at same time complains
of Livingston's jealousy, 87; his
farewell interview with Bonaparte, 87, 88; determines to treat
with Spain for Florida, 88; prevented by Cambacérès, 88; discovers that Livingston has tried
to anticipate him, 89; letter to
Marbois on treaty and on Jerome

INDEX

Supreme Court as a Republican, 138.

Ticknor, George, on Monroe's treachery to Pinckney, 65.

Tompkins, Daniel D., vice-president during Monroe's administrations, 128.

Tucker, St. George, on numbers of forgotten yet eminent men in Virginia, 2.

Tuley, Mrs., describes Monroe's levee as President, 215, 216.

Tuyl, Baron, statement of Monroe doctrine to, by Adams, 172.

UNIVERSITY OF VIRGINIA, services of Monroe, Madison, and Jefferson as regents of, 16.

VIRGINIA, forgotten statesmen of, 2; history of, during war of Revolution, 11, 12; career of Monroe as leader in, 17; cedes Western territory to Congress, 23; confirms Northwest Ordinance, 26; insists on Mississippi navigation, 26; struggle in, over ratifying Federal Constitution, 28–33; ratifies conditionally, 30; elects senators, 33; twice chooses Monroe governor, 35, 77; negro plot in, 35, 36; prepares to resist Federalists in 1800, 37, 38; declares in favor of Madison for president over Monroe, 105; Monroe a member of Constitutional Convention of, 231.

WALKER, JOHN, named to succeed Grayson as senator, 33.

War of 1812, declared, 108; inefficiency of army in, 110, 111; conduct of, condemned by Monroe, 111–119; battle of Bladensburg, services of Monroe at, 119–126; Monroe's services in, as secretary of war, 126, 127.

Washburne, Elihu B., discovers French report of Monroe's appearance before the convention, 52; describes the *accolade*, 54.

Washington, Bushrod, neighbor of Monroe, 5; original member of Phi Beta Kappa Society, 9.

Washington, George, his birthplace near that of Monroe, 4; urges Virginia to give Monroe a military appointment, 11; letter on impost scheme of 1785, 20; letter of Randolph to, 22; in Constitutional Convention, 28; his administration opposed by Monroe, 33; threatened by Monroe with exposure of Hamilton, 34; appoints Monroe minister to France, 34; his reasons, 40; wishes to avoid war with France, 41; impoliteness of Monroe toward, 67; attacked by Monroe, 68; his comments on Monroe's attacks, 68, 70, 252–260; abused by Monroe's friends, 73; anticipates Monroe doctrine, 166, 167; Monroe's attitude toward, 234.

Washington, William, at battle of Trenton, 10.

Watson, E. R., describes Monroe's appearance, habits, and character, 218–226.

Webster, Daniel, not a leader in 1817, 129; defends Monroe doctrine in connection with Panama Congress, 177; on Monroe's impartiality, 241.

West, Benjamin, at Lee's suggestion makes vain attempt to paint Camden's portrait, 6.

West India trade, message of Monroe upon, 189, 190.

Westmoreland County, the Athens of Virginia, 4, 5; Revolutionary spirit in, 5–7.

Wilkinson, Gen. James, describes Monroe's gallantry at battle of Trenton, 10.

William and Mary College, studies of Monroe at, 7; its wealth and history, 7, 8; students and professors of, volunteer in 1776, 8.

Williams, Colonel J. S., on battle of Bladensburg, 120.

McCOOK COLLEGE